THEIR BACKS AGAINST THE SEA

THEIR BACKS AGAINST THE SEA

THE BATTLE *of* SAIPAN *and the* LARGEST BANZAI ATTACK *of* WORLD WAR II

BILL SLOAN

Da Capo Press

First Da Capo Press edition 2017
ISBN 978-0-306-82471-5 (hardcover)
ISBN 978-0-306-82472-2 (ebook)

Published by Da Capo Press, an imprint of Perseus Books, LLC,
a subsidiary of Hachette Book Group, Inc.
www.dacapopress.com

Library of Congress Cataloging-in-Publication Data is available for this book.

Editorial production by Christine Marra, *Marra*thon Production Services.
www.marrathoneditorial.org

DESIGN BY JANE RAESE
Set in 13-point Adobe Jensen

LSC-C
10 9 8 7 6 5 4 3 2 1

TO MY LATE, DEAR FRIEND, FLOYD WOOD,

who suggested Wake Island as the subject
of my first military history.
That was fourteen years and five books ago.
Thanks, Floyd.

Contents

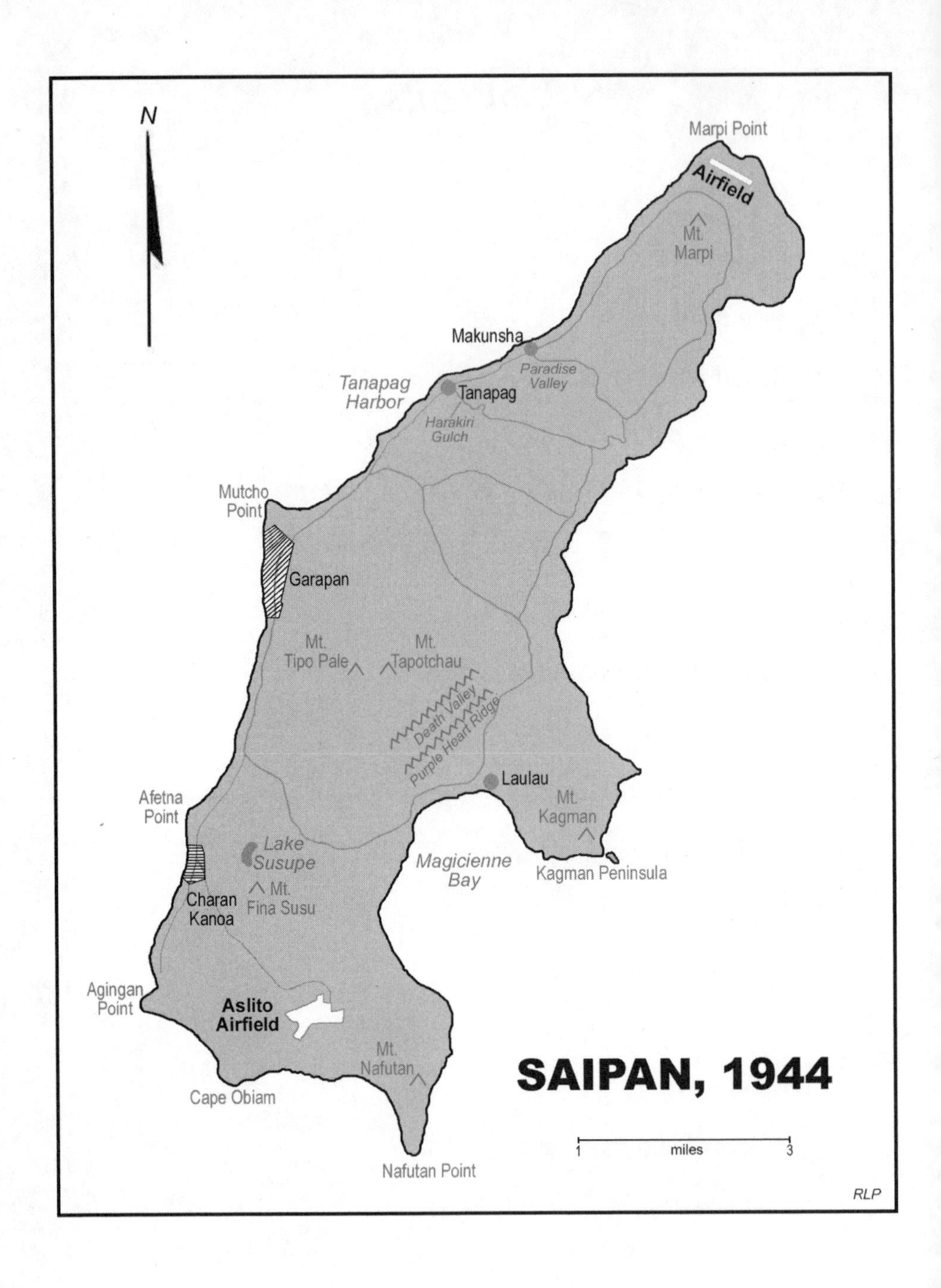
N
Marpi Point
Airfield
Mt.
Marpi
Makunsha
Paradise
Valley
Tanapag
Harbor
Tanapag
Harakiri
Gulch
Mutcho
Point
Garapan
Mt.
Tipo Pale
Mt.
Tapotchau
Death Valley
Purple Heart Ridge
Laulau
Mt.
Kagman
Afetna
Point
Lake
Susupe
Magicienne
Bay
Kagman Peninsula
Mt.
Fina Susu
Charan
Kanoa
Agingan
Point
Aslito
Airfield
Mt.
Nafutan
Cape Obiam
Nafutan Point
SAIPAN, 1944
1
miles
3
RLP

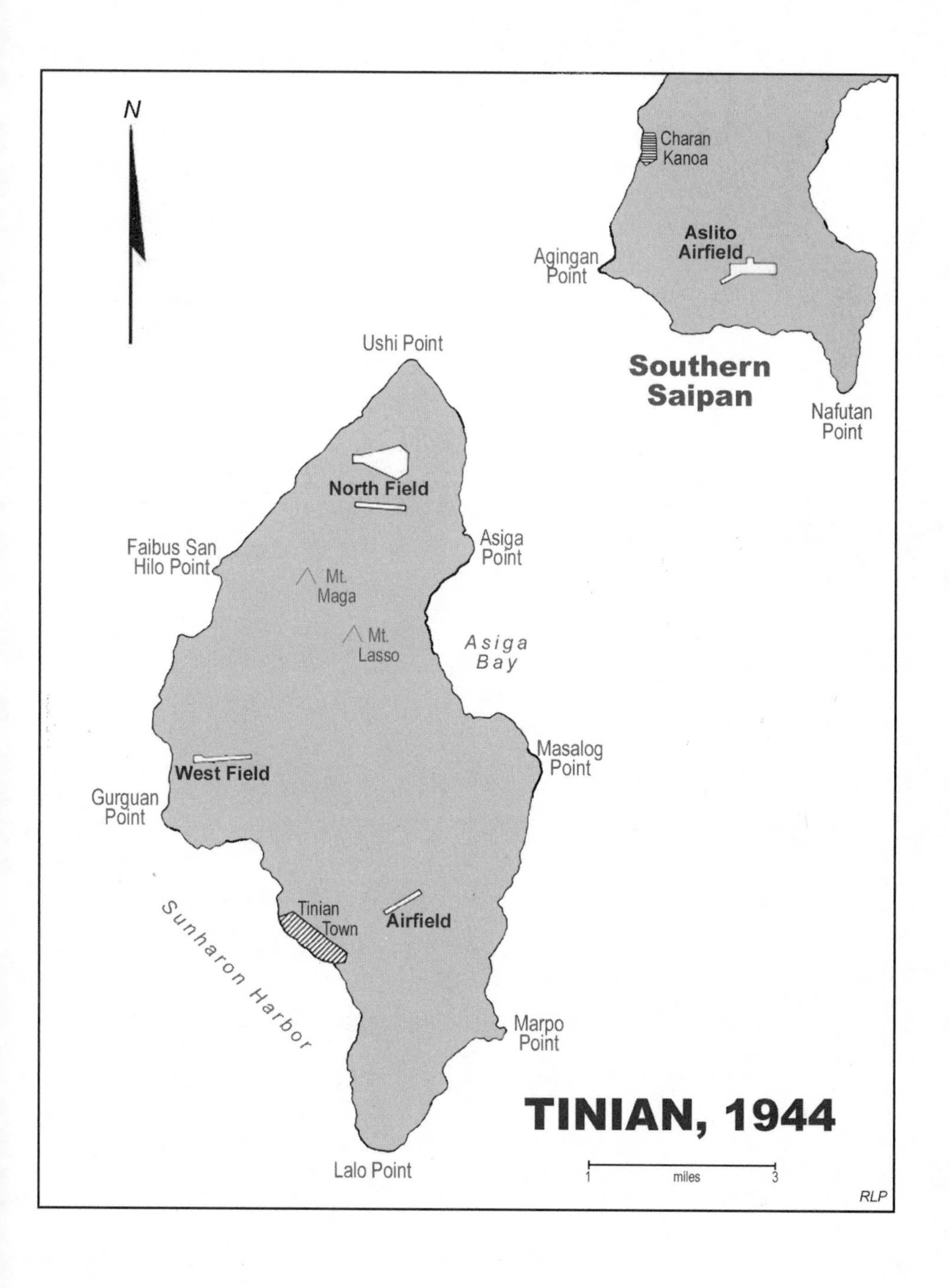
N
Charan
Kanoa
Aslito
Airfield
Agingan
Point
Southern
Saipan
Nafutan
Point
Ushi Point
North Field
Asiga
Point
Faibus San
Hilo Point
Mt.
Maga
Mt.
Lasso
Asiga
Bay
Masalog
Point
West Field
Gurguan
Point
Sunharon Harbor
Tinian
Town
Airfield
Marpo
Point
TINIAN, 1944
Lalo Point
1
miles
3
RLP

★ ★ ★

Prologue

ONE DAY in early June 1944 the heavily laden troop transports lifted anchor and began moving slowly out of Pearl Harbor. Sergeant Tom Tinsley watched as they slipped past the submarine nets toward a destination that only God—and a few high brass—knew.

Somewhere on an obscure island that nobody even knew the name of yet, Tinsley and the rest of the 8th Marines, 2nd Marine Division, were among tens of thousands of young men—many of them still in their teens—sailing into hostile, unknown waters for the first time that day.

He wasn't sure why the thought of past Christmases suddenly crossed his mind, but it did. He thought of his mother and father and his younger sister, Helen, getting up at the crack of dawn to open their presents. He remembered the Christmas when he got the baseball glove. And the year he got the roller skates—that was a surprise. It almost made up for the time when he got a set of Tinkertoys that he had to share with Helen.

The thoughts of Christmastime brought to mind an old-salt Marine named Russell McCurdy, whom Tinsley had gotten to know. McCurdy had been aboard the battleship USS *Arizona* when she was torpedoed and sunk on 7 December 1941. He was one of the lucky ones—he got off alive, while hundreds of his fellow crewmen died.

The recollection of Christmases past caused Tinsley to think of food. Chow lines were long, and eating was almost a continuous process on board the ship. But eating, as far as he was concerned, was not nearly as important as finding a place where he could have some time to himself. He searched for a spot to just stretch out, read a book, or sit quietly and dream of home, back in the small town of Paris, Arkansas, not far from Pine Bluff. He found a place that wasn't too crowded. The one he liked best was behind a 40-millimeter gun turret where there was always a cool breeze blowing across the bow.

The hardest thing about being aboard the troop transport was what lay ahead. In spite of more than a year spent on guard duty at Pearl, he had never been in combat before, and he knew that shortly he would be storming ashore on some unknown beach on some unknown island. Sometimes he wondered whether he would end up dying alone there.

Those thoughts would come creeping into his mind, and he tried hard not to dwell on them, but some of his friends did. Just a few days before, one buddy had been joking and kidding around, the life of the party. Now he wouldn't talk at all, not even when Tinsley brought him something to eat. He'd just sit there and stare at the deck. Tinsley tried to ignore him by keeping busy, reading, playing cards, and cleaning his weapon.

Now it was the early morning of 15 June 1944, and the ship had stopped. For Tinsley, everything seemed to have stopped. Conversation among the men was in a low tone, almost a whisper.

Men standing in line could see a dark, almost shapeless form far across the water. It danced before their eyes in a reflection of bright explosions a few miles away—the artillery bombardment had already begun. Most of the men had never heard of Saipan until a few short days ago, but that was their destination. It was going to be a tough row to hoe, everyone said.

Although many guys didn't sleep well the night before, they climbed aboard their landing crafts (known officially as LVTs, for landing vehicle, tracked, and unofficially as Amtracks, for amphibious tractors) and headed for shore. Most of the 2nd and 4th Marines had been up and reasonably alert by 0200 that morning, and soon after, they sat down to the kind of breakfast that, under normal circumstances, would've been fit for a king—sizzling steaks, eggs, bacon, ham, fresh milk, and an endless supply of juice and coffee. Tinsley ate his fill. This was a sure sign that this was it.

At the stroke of 0700 all hell broke loose. Navy and Marine planes started bombing runs. Battleships opened fire with their sixteen-inch guns. Cruisers and destroyers kicked in with their five-inch and 40-millimeter weapons. If a ship had a gun, it was firing at the beach. Tinsley couldn't see how anyone could possibly live through that kind of bombardment.

It wasn't all that it was cracked up to be, however. As the Amtracks moved forward and approached the beach, Japanese shells started hitting the water and exploding. It had all sounded so easy on paper: the 6th Marines would take Beaches Red 2 and Red 3, the 8th Marines would take Beaches Green 1 and Green 2, the 23rd Marine regiment would land on beaches designated as Blue 1 and Blue 2, and so on . . .

The Amtrack Tinsley was in got about a hundred yards from the beach, then it high-centered on a large part of the wide coral reef that lined the shoreline and started spinning around and around like a windmill. It whirled crazily but refused to move forward.

To Tinsley's right, another Amtrack was suddenly struck in the middle by Japanese artillery. At first it was there—then it wasn't.

Tinsley's captain gave the order to abandon ship. The front ramp was dropped, and most of the men made a run for the front of the Amtrack and jumped into the water, which was somewhere between their neck and shoulders deep, until everyone but Tinsley and three other Marines were left.

Two men froze in their seats and refused to move. They were Sergeant Major Solace and Private First Class Berberick, guys Tinsley knew well—or thought he knew—and no one could drag them out of the Amtrack. Meanwhile the Japanese artillery had the Amtrack bracketed. The next shot they fired was almost certain to be a direct hit.

"There's nothing more we can do," the captain said. "We better get the hell out before we get killed."

The captain and Tinsley jumped into the water and were about halfway to the beach when the Amtrack was hit and exploded into a million pieces, killing Solace and Berberick instantly.

Tinsley hit the beach running and threw himself into a slight incline behind an embankment landing beside another Marine. He yelled a half-dozen words to him before he realized the man was dead.

Tinsley had lost sight of the captain, and he had no desire to hunker down with the dead Marine, so he got up and ran. Dozens of Marines—all of them dead—lay in his path.

My God, he thought, is everyone here but me dead?

chapter 1

★ ★ ★

Islands of Mystery

THE ISLAND of Saipan was approximately four miles wide and fourteen miles long, giving it the second largest landmass, after Guam, in the Marianas archipelago, a group of fifteen islands that runs in a shallow, curving line for 425 miles in the mid-Pacific. Traces of human settlement found by archeologists on Saipan covered approximately four thousand years. The islands were officially discovered in 1521 by Spanish explorer Ferdinand Magellan in the course of his first voyage around the world.

Magellan was struck by the magnificent sailing power of the native boats and by the similarity of their rigging to those of the small sailing craft he had encountered in his own Mediterranean, and he labeled his discovery "Islas de las Velas Latinas" (Islands of the Lateen Sails). Some of his crewmen, however, preferred to call them the "Islands of Thieves" because of the larcenous habits of the natives, and the name remained popular well into the twentieth century.

Late in the 1600s Maria Anna of Austria, wife of Philip IV and queen of Spain, dispatched a group of missionaries and soldiers to the islands, and the official name from that time on became the Marianas Islands.

The Chamorros were the original native population of the Marianas, and as time wore on, they became agitated toward the rigid rule of the Catholic priesthood, and armed revolution broke out in the islands in the 1690s. Many of the Chamorros fled to other islands further north, where they were largely pursued and persecuted. When the US invasion of the island occurred on 15 June 1944, about 3,900 Chamorros were still living on Saipan and the neighboring island of Tinian. Many of them worked as slave laborers for the Japanese.

Imperial Germany challenged Spanish control, which had become progressively weaker during the nineteenth century. This led to the eventual 1899 cessation of all Spanish possessions in the Caroline Islands, the Marshall Islands, and the Marianas. Germany paid Spain about $4 million to acquire the islands.

In 1914, shortly after the beginning of World War I, Japan seized all but one of the islands in the chain. The League of Nations officially recognized the seizure, and in 1920 it mandated the rest of the Marianas—less Guam—to Japan with the stipulation that none of the islands would be fortified, a stipulation that Japan made a point of overlooking. Guam, the largest island in the Marianas, was owned by the United States and used as a vital coaling station and a small naval base.

IN THE YEARS between the two World Wars Saipan became known as one of Japan's "Islands of Mystery" because so little was known about what was taking place there. Japan withdrew from the League of Nations in 1935 and let it be known that she would not tolerate any challenge to her sovereignty in this part of the Pacific. She began to settle and develop the island vigorously, immigrating thousands of Japanese, Koreans, and other Asians in the process; they soon outnumbered the natives as they built sugar plantations, refineries, and other infrastructure. By 1943 approximately 33,000 civilians lived on Saipan, including the 3,900 Chamorros. The islands were very jealously guarded against visits by anyone from the West, mainly because Japan was hurrying to build a series of naval installations and airbases there. These included two airfields and a seaplane base at Saipan along with two airfields on the island of Tinian, located just three and a half nautical miles to the southwest.

By the early 1940s the Japanese regular army was composed of seventeen divisions with 464,000 men. Every Japanese division was self-sustaining with its own artillery, cavalry, engineers, tanks, and quartermaster troops, and each division contained exactly 22,000 men.

But that was only the beginning. In a crisis situation there were 738,000 members of the army reserve, all of whom had undergone the same rigorous training and could be activated at a moment's notice. This meant that the Japanese army actually totaled more than 1.2 million men. The Japanese generals had vowed to create the finest army in the world, and there were strong indications that they had done exactly that.

The typical Japanese soldier was tough and well trained to do whatever was necessary to win a battle. American reporter John Goette, who spent more than four years covering the exploits of the Japanese soldiers in China, including the killing of an estimated 200,000 civilians in the Rape of Nanking, observed, "There are no volunteers in the Japanese army, only conscripts . . . every Japanese male is a potential fighting unit who remains subject to call for the rest of his life. Bodily comfort, non-essential equipment, food, transport, promotion, rest and glory are purposely subordinated to achieve the high results of team play."

It was an exciting time when a Japanese boy was inducted into the army. As the train carrying the boy pulled away to conscript training, friends and family waved flags and shouted, "Banzai! Banzai!"—the traditional Japanese war cry that literally meant "[May you live] ten thousand years." The flamboyant departure let the boy know that in his people's eyes he was already considered a hero and a representative of the emperor and his country.

EVEN AS THE Japanese were fortifying the island, Saipan was also being developed as a rich agricultural center, especially for sugar. Cane fields covered hundreds of acres in lower-lying areas of Saipan, and narrow-gauge railroads were built to carry the syrup to a long pier for loading directly onto Japanese cargo ships. The railroad almost completely encircled the island along the coast, save for a few places on the more rugged eastern side.

Saipan's major peacetime industry was sugar production, with the crops from large plantations and a giant sugar mill turning out huge quantities of alcohol for producing synthetic Scotch whisky, port wine, saki, and beer. These products would come in handy for Japanese troops in the days to come. Widespread usage of alcohol would become a common tool for motivating Japanese soldiers when World War II broke out.

Because of its strategic location in the Marianas, Saipan served as a major stepping stone connecting the Japanese Empire to its Pacific island fortresses. The Japanese understood the importance of the Marianas in defending their homeland and recognized that an American invasion could result in a struggle that would decide the war's outcome.

Saipan was located 1,260 miles from Tokyo. That put it out of reach from the newest US land-based bombers in the early 1940s, but when the United States developed the huge B-29 Superfortress in the mid-1940s, the entire context changed. Suddenly Tokyo and the rest of Japan would be within striking distance if US forces could secure Saipan.

Saipan was the most heavily fortified island in the Marianas. If the United States could capture it, it would have secure airbases for its B-29s. Saipan's Aslito Airfield, with a 3,600-foot runway located near the south end of the island, and another airfield, Marpi Point, under construction at the extreme north end of the island, made it even more attractive. The airfields on Tinian, slightly smaller and just three and a half miles south of Saipan, also had promise, but US forces were less familiar with them.

American proponents such as Admiral Ernest J. King, commander-in-chief of the US Fleet, advocated for capturing the island to provide a base of operations from which protected lines of Japanese communication could be severed and from which long-range aircraft could be used to bomb Tokyo and the Japanese home islands. Not everyone shared Admiral King's conviction, however. General Douglas MacArthur opposed invading the Marianas because it would be "time consuming and expensive"; he argued that an approach along the northern coast of New Guinea "offered much better chances for success."

King held his ground against MacArthur and others, however, and Saipan was chosen.

SAIPAN WOULD NOT be an easy target for an invasion at any time, but even more so in the month of June. Although the Japanese used it extensively as a rest area and training center, the island lacked the natural facilities of a major naval base. A treacherous coral barrier reef fringed much of the island, with a submerged arm curving out from the upper west coast to enclose Tanapag Harbor. Invading troops would be forced to go in over a reef seven hundred yards across in some places. Still, it was the only possible landing site, as steep hills characterized the other side of the island.

Rainfall totaled about 125 inches per year, with an average of 275 rainy days annually—and June and July were far and away the wettest months. Although the temperature ordinarily hovered between 76 and 80 degrees, June was a bad month for heat waves. The high temperatures sometimes topped out at around 95 degrees.

Almost in the center of Saipan the huge bulk of Mount Tapotchau humped its back against the sky, rising to a height of 1,554 feet, and its steep, almost perpendicular sides made it seem even higher. This mountain was a key terrain feature that gave the Japanese an excellent place to observe—and shell—the US beachhead.

THE US PLAN of attack was straightforward. The lower western coast of Saipan was divided into eight landing beaches that stretched for six thousand yards. Each beach was code-named Red Beach 1, Red Beach 2, Red Beach 3, and so on for the remaining eight areas designated by Green, Blue, and Yellow. The 2nd Marine Division would land on the northern Red and Green beaches. The 4th Marine Division would land on the Blue and Yellow beaches. Landing sites on the eastern sides of the island had been weighed and ruled out because of a variety of problems, including the rough and rocky cliffs that would give the Americans a mass of trouble in the days to come.

The west coast was the only place that would allow the two divisions to land side by side. The attack plan called for the 2nd Marine Division to anchor itself on the coast and turn left (north), while the 4th Marines would turn eastward and then north. Then both divisions would sweep to the northern end of the island, destroying the defending Japanese in their path.

In charge of the US ground troops in the invasion was Marine Lieutenant General Holland M. Smith. To many outward appearances Smith was a perfect choice to lead an amphibious landing on Saipan. He had been instrumental in making the LCVP (landing craft, vehicles, personnel) adopted by the Navy to land troops and materials on an invasion beachhead. But Smith's devotion to Marine tactics also made him an unfortunate choice to head up the Saipan assault. He considered the Army and the Navy deeply resistant to cutting-edge battle tactics, and he lost no time in saying so. Holland Smith's animosity earned him the nickname "Howlin' Mad" Smith.

The "floating reserve," consisting of the Army's 27th Infantry Division, which could be committed to battle whenever needed, was headed by Army Major General Ralph Smith (unrelated to "Howlin' Mad"). Ralph Smith was a highly decorated officer who spoke French and specialized in military intelligence and tactics. He also had, said one of his contemporaries, "extreme consideration for all other mortals."

These two general officers were destined to clash during one of the bloodiest battles in history. At the time few realized that a disagreement between two American generals would become one of the most controversial stories to come out of that struggle.

On 15 June 1944, US military forces launched the Battle of Saipan in a place totally unknown to most Americans. The invasion represented the first attempted breakthrough in an inner line of islands the Japanese had built over the past twenty-five years to protect their far-reaching—and ill-gotten—Pacific empire. When the battle ended on 9 July, Saipan would go down in history as one of the key operations of the Pacific war, one that unlocked America's air power and opened the way for US aerial attacks on the home islands of Japan.

The US military had planned that the entire process of taking Saipan would take three days. It would be among the longest three days any fighting man who was there could remember.

chapter 2

★ ★ ★

The Infernal Beach

FOR FULLY two and a half years after the Japanese attack on Pearl Harbor, the war between Japan and the United States remained far away from the shores of Saipan and her sister islands in the Marianas, except for Japan's quick and easy takeover of Guam. During this time the Marianas served the Japanese primarily as the supply and staging bases for troops, ships, and planes in battles fought far to the east and south. In May 1943, just over a year before the US attack, the Japanese had slightly more than nine hundred military troops stationed on the island—not nearly enough to repel any type of incursion.

Admiral Marc A. Mitscher and his Task Force 58, after administering a two-day shellacking of Truk in February 1944, turned toward the Marianas and gave Saipan its first baptism of fire. Suddenly what had always been considered a rear area of the war had now become front and center. And Japan got cracking—or tried to. But so did the US submarines.

On the afternoon of 29 February a Japanese transport, the *Sakito Maru*, was torpedoed and sunk with 3,080 troops aboard. Only 1,688 were rescued, but according to Japanese reports, all their weapons were lost except for seven rifles, one grenade thrower, two light machine guns, and 150 bayonets. American submarines played havoc with Japanese shipping for the next three months.

The last major Japanese troop movement to Saipan was the transfer of the 43rd Division, and the first shipment of troops managed to avoid the US submarines. It arrived only a few weeks before the American invasion and would play a leading role in defending the island. Its commander, Lieutenant General Yoshitsugu Saito, would assume control of the Saipan defenses. But a second shipment set sail on 30 May when a convoy of seven transports carrying more than seven thousand troops of the 43rd Division headed south. It was subjected to almost constant submarine attack, and within three days five of the seven transports were lost.

A group of three US attack submarines, known as "Blair's Blasters"—the USS *Shark*, *Pilotfish*, and *Pintado*—commanded by Captain Leon Nelson Blair, was instrumental in all five of these sinkings, losses that undermined Japan's ability to defend the island.

About 80 percent of the troops from the convoy were saved, but when the survivors landed on Saipan, they arrived without weapons or equipment. Altogether, from January to early June 1944, the Japanese dispatched about 45,000 Army troops to the Marianas. Of these, 40,000 were designated for Saipan, though only about 30,000 reached their destination. Although many of the survivors were reorganized and re-equipped, many others—up to 5,000 soldiers—became stragglers on Saipan, armed only with their resolution to die for their emperor.

All told, US submarines accounted for the loss of more than mere manpower. In many cases, essential building materials went to the bottom of the ocean along with the men. Captain Blair's wolf pack alone completed twenty-two successful war patrols in enemy waters, sinking thirty-four enemy ships, including two 4,700-ton freighters. Blair sent ships transporting 7,200 Japanese soldiers—and twenty-two tanks—to a watery grave.

A report from the chief of staff of Japan's 31st Army—equivalent to a US Army Corps, with 25,000 to 50,000 men—gave a clear picture of the difficulties they faced in their efforts to construct adequate fortifications on Saipan. "We cannot strengthen the fortifications appreciably now unless we get material suitable for permanent construction," read the report. "Specifically, unless the units are supplied with cement, steel reinforcements for cement, barbed wire, lumber, etc., which cannot be obtained in these islands, no matter how many soldiers there are, they can do nothing in regard to fortifications but sit around with their arms folded, and the situation is unbearable."

Captain Blair was awarded the Navy Cross and a presidential Legion of Merit for his contributions to the Saipan campaign—even before it officially started. For his conduct as commander of Submarine Division 44, he was later promoted to rear admiral.

AN ENEMY DOCUMENT published on 20 May 1944—less than a month before the US landings—called for "the immediate construction of defensive positions that when they are fully developed, they can destroy the enemy landing force on the beach. We will transform these islands into a fortress so that we can expect, absolutely, to hold our airfields."

No mention was made of constructing permanent defensive positions inland. The entire Japanese scheme of defense was committed to destroying the enemy landing force "on the beach." Through counterattacks, launched during the night from specified points, the Japanese hoped to demolish the American landing units at the water's edge—if not before.

The conclusion was inescapable: despite all their efforts, the Japanese were not fully prepared for the American landings on Saipan when they came. If they had had several more months, it might have been a different story. The Japanese found it physically impossible with the means at hand to build their defenses to a point where they might successfully resist a landing by US forces. But prepared or not, the Japanese forces on Saipan were neither weak nor feeble—far from it.

Despite the shortcomings of the defensive installations, one vital characteristic of a good defensive plan was present: the individual Japanese soldier was determined to hold the island at any cost and to give his life to realize this end. It was this characteristic that would present the greatest challenge to American forces throughout the struggle for Saipan.

IN THE BREAKING dawn of 14 June—the morning before the US landings—Rear Admiral Jesse B. Oldendorf arrived off the coast of Saipan with two bombardment groups. His force included seven old battleships, eleven cruisers, twenty-six destroyers, and a small number of destroyer transports and minesweepers. Four of the old "tin cans," the USS *Tennessee, Pennsylvania, California,* and *Maryland,* were survivors of the attack on Pearl Harbor two and a half years earlier.

The bombardment was especially effective against prepared gun positions used by antiaircraft units. A Japanese naval officer noted in his diary that "practically all our antiaircraft guns and machine gun positions were destroyed." Otherwise, the American preliminary bombardment was far less than perfect, leaving intact observation posts and gun emplacements protected by splinter-proof shelters that were capable of withstanding the shelling.

On the night of 14 June most of the support ships retired, with only a handful remaining to continue harassing fire along the coastline. In the early hours of 15 June, the Western Landing Group, consisting mostly of transports and LSTs (landing ship, tank) carrying the 2nd and 4th Marine Divisions was slowly approaching the island from the east.

As the landing crafts moved toward shore, US carrier planes came in at treetop level to make one last assault, and the shell casings from their machine guns fell red-hot into many of the boats. Some of the troops thought they were under attack by their own planes.

The Amtracks were loaded with Marine troops. And they were the first to come under attack.

Private First Class Carl Matthews heard the sound of an incoming shell, and suddenly one of the Amtracks to his left received a direct hit and vanished into a cloud of flaming smoke. He realized that the shells were coming closer and closer, and at that moment he averted his eyes and quit looking. Instead, he started some serious praying.

He closed his eyes and thought about his home and family back in Hubbard, Texas. He thought of his mother and father and his two little sisters. They seemed so far away—almost like they were in another world.

Matthews looked at Lieutenant James Stanley Leary Jr., the leader of Matthews's 2nd Platoon of C Company, 2nd Marines.

He had the most serious expression on his face that Matthews could ever remember seeing. He was probably thinking about home, Matthews thought, and realizing that some of the men in his command would likely be dead a few minutes from now.

When the Marines reached the three-hundred-yard mark from shore, the Japanese shells were coming thick and fast, just as the Japanese had planned. Every twenty-five yards or so, about once every fifteen seconds, another shell would burst. Marines who had been at Tarawa or Kwajalein knew what to expect, but the greenest troops—those with no combat experience—smoked or kept their heads down and prayed. Some of them vomited as the Amtracks heaved up and down in the choppy sea.

The Marines hit the beaches at 0843. In the landing the 6th and 8th Marine Regiments got hopelessly mixed up, and the troops ended up concentrated on Red Beach 2, Red Beach 3, and Green Beach 1, which gave the Japanese a huge target to shoot at, and the casualties in these first few minutes were tremendous. Further down the beach the 4th Marines landed in a more orderly manner.

They were supposed to advance and take Afetna Point, a small protuberance jutting into the sea, and the town of Charan Kanoa and the ridge above it. But intensive Japanese shelling caused the attack to bog down, and some of the Marines were trapped on the beaches under withering fire.

Marshall E. Harris of the 2nd Armored Amphibious Battalion was crawling slowly through the water in his tank toward Green Beach 1 and talking to a close friend, Robert Lewis, in another amphibious tank nearby when Lewis's voice was drowned out by the sudden sound of an explosion. Harris felt a hard concussion. Then there was another explosion, and he saw dark smoke and fire on the water.

"Flames boiled up out of a blackened piece of metal that I realized was Robert's tank," Harris remembered, "but my platoon commander motioned for me to keep going. I never saw Lewis again. Our armored tanks just weren't up to slugging it out with an enemy land tank because of our lack of protective armor."

The 6th Marines hit a stone wall about a hundred yards inland. The driver of Private First Class R. J. Lee's amphibious tank tried to push inland away from the beach, but a deep trench stood in its way. The driver quickly threw the tank into reverse and backed out to the water's edge. As he fired his 75-millimeter cannon, he drew an instant reply from the Japanese, and the open turret of the tank took a direct, ruinous hit.

Lee saw his platoon leader and two sergeants shot dead. He watched one of his crew take a bullet in the face and go down. Lee was reaching out to him when two bullets hit him simultaneously. "I heard my four-year-old son calling, 'Get up, Daddy, get up,' and by the grace of God—and my son—I made it back to the beach," Lee said later. "Then it was lights out for me."

The American shells and bombs had torn huge craters in the sand, and smashed and burned-out Amtracks and amphibious tanks covered the beach. Behind many of them wounded men lay in every kind of agony, awaiting evacuation.

Robert Sherrod, a correspondent for both *Life* and *Time* magazines who had been at Tarawa, scribbled in his notebook: "I fear all this smoke and noise doesn't mean many Japs killed."

LIEUTENANT COLONEL WARREN ADAMS entered the Marine Corps as a well-educated New Yorker with several degrees, including a PhD from Princeton. "They put me to training new Marines," he recalled, "but after about six classes I couldn't stand it anymore, so I went to the commandant and said I wanted to quit this teaching business and get where the action was.

"I was an officer, and the only protection I had was a .45-caliber revolver." Adams said. "It was my 'war equipment,' but when you've got a mob of people coming at you, what good is a revolver? With a revolver you got in one or two shots before you were killed, but with a machine gun, you could keep the bad guys away.

"I knew a fellow in the armory department, and I gave him a bottle of whiskey and told him I wanted a submachine gun. He gave it to me, and I used it." A couple of Adams's superior officers told him he wasn't supposed to be carrying the tommy gun, but he refused to give it up, and no one insisted.

As his boat approached the beach he realized he was scared. But then he got angry at himself for being scared—the Marines had trained him well, even in hand-to-hand combat. By the time he hit the beach he wasn't scared anymore.

Adams had fought on Kwajalein and Tarawa, but for him Saipan would be the bitterest business of the lot. He had trained with five other officers, and they had become good friends. Adams would be the only one to survive: "I was the only one with a submachine gun."

PRIVATE OLIAN THOMAS PERRY was nineteen years old when he heard that the Japanese had bombed Pearl Harbor. He lived in sparsely settled Leon County, Texas, and grew up in a household with eleven brothers and sisters. He had dropped out of school and was earning a living driving a concrete truck in Houston. On the Sunday when the Japanese attacked Pearl Harbor, he was visiting his older brother, who was working on a rock crusher at Lamesa, Texas. He didn't even know what Pearl Harbor was when he first heard the news; he thought they were talking about some woman. But everything in the world changed forever that afternoon.

The next day he drove over to Waco along with two other young men, intent on joining something, even if it was the Coast Guard. As it turned out, the Navy and Coast Guard were out to lunch. But there was an old Marine there who said, "We never close, and we'll sign you up," so the three boys did just that. He told them to be in Waco early the next morning and they'd be put on a train and sent to Dallas. That's where they would be mustered in. They spent that night in a hotel and really thought they were living it up. The next morning they shipped out for San Diego—twenty-six of them on a train—and the old Marine got kind of tough on them. He said, "You're all Marines now, and from now on, by God, I want you to act like one."

The recruits were told that they would have ten weeks of training, then get a leave to go home, but it never happened. They were only in San Diego for seven weeks before they were shipped overseas. Perry didn't get his first leave for three years.

Private Perry was bound for New Zealand, although nobody knew it at the time. The only thing he knew was that it was a long trip—six or seven weeks in all—and the ship he was on was the former ocean liner *Macedonia,* which had been converted to wartime use and was traveling alone. He never got seasick, but a lot of the other boys did. At first he made fun of them, but he soon found out that it wasn't the thing to do because he had to clean up after them.

He was now a member of the 2nd Marine Division, Company C, 1st Battalion, 18th Marines. And because he had some experience as a rock crusher, he was designated as a "dynamite man." "We blew out trees for the artillery," Perry remembered, and he became a booby trap specialist. At first he didn't know what a booby trap was, but it didn't take him long to find out.

New Zealand was in a state of flux when they arrived, but the civilians there were glad to see them because they were worried that the Japanese were ready to land. On the coast the civilians had stood up old, wooden guns to look like real ones and scare off the Japanese. After a few weeks the Americans were loaded onto four troop ships, and they went straight to Guadalcanal. There the men could hardly get any sleep at night because "Washing Machine Charlie," an old Japanese plane, would come flying over. "Charlie" would leave and come back, leave and come back, and wouldn't drop its bomb until a little before daylight. The plane kept everyone up all night—that was all it was intended to do.

Then it would rain, and they would have to get in the foxhole with the water, and the land crabs would come sliding into the foxhole and pinch the men. Some crabs were nearly as big as a dinner plate.

From Guadalcanal Perry went to Tarawa, where 3,700 American troops were wounded or killed and the Japanese lost 4,690 men—all in three days.

And then Saipan. It was the worst case of all for Perry. He got on a half-track with a lot of dynamite and convinced the driver to take him up to the front because they desperately needed the dynamite. The driver told Perry to get in the back between the water cans because they were going through areas with lots of land mines. Perry held his breath all the way, sure the dynamite would explode at any second. It didn't.

PRIVATE FIRST CLASS SAM SMODDY of the 8th Marines never had a chance to use the machine gun he'd been taught to handle during a three-month crash course. Something big and ugly like a mortar shell hit the tractor Smoddy was on just as he was stepping ashore on Saipan. It threw up masses of shrapnel, and pieces of it struck the eighteen-year-old farm boy high and low.

He saw that one of his best friends was killed, and he didn't know where the rest of the guys went. All Smoddy knew was he was hit in the knees and shoulder. An explosion behind him knocked him forward, and then somebody gave Smoddy a stiff shot of morphine—enough to knock him out cold. When he woke up someone was trying to get him aboard a merchant ship. He got close to the side, and they threw over a cargo ladder for him to climb. Later he couldn't remember how he did it, but he found out that if you were scared enough, you could climb almost anything.

As he reached the top of the ladder he got shot again. They laid him on the deck. Soon they had most of his clothes off. He had no money except for the silver dollar his grandfather had given him as a good-luck piece.

He wondered if his grandfather's gift could be the reason he was still alive.

IT TOOK SERGEANT TOM TINSLEY more than six hours to find his way to the place where he was assigned. He didn't know it at the time, but about 10 percent of the twenty thousand men who landed on the beach had been wounded or killed—and he thought he had seen most of them by now. He had picked his way through their scattered forms along the way to his assignment at the Regimental Message Center, where he was supposed to be in charge.

Because of the heavy fire, the 8th Marines—Tinsley's regiment—had landed several hundred yards north of their assigned landing area. They had fought a flanking action down the beach to the south to hook up with the unit. A lot of the beaches were under fire, and the ones he crossed were filled with the blood of Marines and Japanese.

It was almost dark when Tinsley finally met the regimental executive officer, Colonel Jack Juhan. He wanted Tinsley to take him to the command post (CP) Tinsley had just left.

Tinsley explained to Juhan that the Japanese were laying artillery barrages up and down the beaches. They would fire one barrage, then move fifty or a hundred yards, and lay down another barrage. He had seen their barrages hit many wounded men again.

"What I'm telling you, sir," he told the colonel, "is we'd better get moving!"

Tinsley and the colonel hadn't gone far when they heard the whine of approaching shells. "I yelled at the colonel to take cover, and I made a dive for a hole," Tinsley remembered. "I felt a sting in my right shoulder, but I never thought too much about it. I took the colonel to the CP, and both of us saw that I'd been hit, and the colonel shouted for a corpsman."

The corpsman cleaned up Tinsley's wound, but he had unwelcome news: the corpsman couldn't remove the shrapnel, and one of the larger pieces was stuck in the bone. Tinsley was told he had to go to a hospital ship

But the hospital ship was full. Tinsley was assigned a bunk in a large room that must have contained at least fifty bunks. A doctor removed the shrapnel and told him he would be all right in a few days. The problem was that he would need to stay aboard the hospital ship on its cruise to Kwajalein Island and endure several days of moaning, crying, and dying of Marines. Burials at sea constantly interrupted his stay on deck: "There must have been hundreds of them, and my nerves were at a breaking point when the ship dropped anchor at Kwajalein." As far as Tinsley was concerned, it was more than any sane person could take. Or so he thought.

They had told Tinsley that he would be sent back to Pearl Harbor for reassignment to another unit. But he desperately wanted to stay with his assigned unit. He had been aboard the hospital ship for about a week when an LST (landing ship, tank) anchored nearby and started loading smudge pots to take to Saipan. Tinsley boarded the LST that night and was headed for Saipan within the hour.

"It was peaceful just lying on deck, breathing fresh air without the sound of moaning, groaning, and dying," Tinsley said. "I hoped to God I never witnessed another burial at sea."

THE MARINES HAD been digging in on the beaches when the Japanese mounted a counterattack, aimed at where Colonel James Riseley, newly appointed commander of the 6th

Marines, was trying to establish a command post on Red Beach 2. But the Marines were well prepared and cut the attackers down with machine guns and M-1 rifles.

Around noon two Japanese tanks came down from the foothills, but the commander of the tanks became confused and paused for a look-around. Marine rocket launchers and riflemen made short work of the tanks. A few minutes later three more tanks approached, again headed for Riseley's command post. Two of the tanks were stopped well short of their target, but the third reached a point no more than fifteen yards from the CP before it was hit and disabled.

By 1300 Riseley estimated that 35 percent of the 6th Marines had become casualties, but the beachhead had been expanded to about four hundred yards. He sent an assault against the ridgeline ahead, which was heavily infested with Japanese mortars. It was thrown back with even heavier losses.

IN ADDITION TO being a radio operator, Private First Class Wayne "Twig" Terwilliger of the 2nd Tank Battalion held a gunner's position with a .30-caliber machine gun armed with a periscope, and he thought he was in pretty good shape. As his tank rolled across the beach he spotted several Japanese. He squeezed the trigger and started to fire. Then the seven-passenger tank twisted and jerked to a stop, and he lost his aim.

"Hey, what the hell's the matter?" he yelled.

Somebody said, "We're stuck in a damn mud hole. We gotta get out of here!"

Twig abandoned the gun and climbed out of the tank. The island of Saipan stretched out before his eyes, and a Japanese tank was heading toward him. He saw dead Marines on the ground and some that maybe weren't quite dead. He squeezed his eyes shut, and a scene from the past flashed before him.

It was a day game at Briggs Stadium in Detroit, and the New York Yankees were in town to play the Tigers, when the immortal Lou Gehrig came to bat. Twelve-year-old Terwilliger, a skinny, curly-haired kid, was watching the game with his father.

"We were in the right-field bleachers," Terwilliger remembered, "when Gehrig took a big swing at the second or third pitch and busted the ball right at us. My dad said, 'Here it comes! Here it comes!'"

The ball was headed straight at Twig. The only thing he could think to do was get the hell out of the way. At the last second he ducked, and somebody else caught the home-run ball. Twig would never forget how mad his father was when he didn't catch it. Ivan Terwilliger played on a semipro baseball team when he wasn't serving up drinks at a place he owned in Charlotte, Michigan, called the Dearborn Bar, and his son figured Ivan would've caught the ball if it killed him.

Now, six years later Terwilliger hit the shore at Saipan, manning a machine gun with a periscope he could no longer see through—so he ran. The Japanese tank was heading straight for him. An American tank fired at it, and the impact blew Twig's helmet off.

The only thing he knew to do was duck under his own tank and try to hide: "It was what I'd done when that ball was headed straight toward me—and that's what I did."

At the last possible second the American tank knocked out the Japanese tank.

UNFORTUNATELY MANY OF the crewmen of amphibian tractors and tanks were having much the same problem. For the most part the scheme of employing amphibian tanks as land tanks and LVTs as overland troop-carrying vehicles was rapidly becoming a failure. They had neither the armor nor the armament to withstand the terrible pounding from Japanese artillery that could be expected in this phase of the assault. Most of the amphibians were underpowered and stopped by sand, trenches, holes, trees, and other minor obstacles, most of which a land tank could have negotiated with ease.

And once Amtracks and amphibious tanks were out of the water, their hulls were exposed, making them easy targets for enemy fire, which their armor was too light to resist. On shore they were clumsy and slow. It was much healthier for troops to extricate themselves from these vehicles as rapidly as possible and find protection in whatever the terrain and vegetation offered.

On the 2nd Marine Division's beaches the situation rapidly became impossible. Trees, shell holes, and even muddy patches of ground stopped some of the 2nd Armored Amphibian Battalion before they could even cross the beach. Between the beach and the tractor control line, twenty-eight of the vehicles—more than one-third the total number—were disabled and abandoned.

"We started out with fifteen tanks in our squad," recalled Corporal Canara Caruth, the commander of Terwilliger's tank, "but after the first day all we had left was five tanks that were still in running condition." Caruth, who had grown up on a farm outside of Pampa, Texas, one of the driest spots in the Western Hemisphere, was amazed to see how wet the island was. "Saipan had had a lot of rain recently," he said, "and it was literally covered with swamps."

MARINE PRIVATE FIRST CLASS CHARLES PASE came from a small town in West Virginia called Thomas. It was about as "big as a minute" and way up in the Hill Country next to the Maryland border in Tucker County. When he got to high school he moved to Georgetown in Sussex County, Delaware, just a few miles from the Atlantic Ocean.

He came by his trade honestly. One of his older brothers had been a Marine in Peking, China, before World War II. Joseph Pase served with the Legation Guard and came back to the States in 1938. When they started drafting people a couple of years later, he decided to join the Army. They made him a first sergeant and sent him overseas to serve with the Philippine Scouts. The Japanese captured him at Corregidor, and nobody knew for several years whether he was alive or dead.

That brother was really the reason Pase joined the Marines. When Joe was finally released from the prisoner-of-war camp at war's end, his overall health was so bad that he only survived for a couple more years.

Charles Pase had dropped out of high school at the start of his senior year with the avowed intention of joining the Marines. He was a little young for it, only sixteen, and he was working on a cattle ranch in southern Montana. On his seventeenth birthday in January 1943 he drove into Billings, Montana, to join up. Their quota of seventeen-year-olds had already been taken, so they told him that his best chance was to catch a bus down to Denver and sign up there, which is what he did.

Pase was sworn in on 16 February 1943 and went to Camp Elliott for special weapons training—the .50- and .35-caliber air-cooled machine guns, anti-aircraft guns, 75-millimeter antitank rifles, and various types of small hand weapons. In June 1943 he had been in the Marines for about five months when they bundled him up with fifteen hundred other new troops and said they were sending them to Guadalcanal on an old Dutch tramp steamer that had been converted to a troop ship.

"There was a five-inch gun on the fantail of this ship—and that was our armament," he recalled. "The bunks were five high, and it was a very bare-bones kind of a troop ship. There were two latrines for the entire ship, and they were big, long, open latrines in the belly of the ship."

They were fed twice a day. The morning meal was almost always either beans or SOS ("shit on a shingle"—the military nickname for creamed chipped beef on toast), and for the evening meal they sometimes had genuine meat of some kind. "I'm not sure what it was," he said, "and I don't want to guess."

The Marine recruits did a lot of complaining about it, and they had another name for it too that was less complimentary. "But remember, this was right after the Depression," Pase said, "and we had to admit that it was better than we ate before we joined the service."

The troop ship never made it to Guadalcanal. It stopped at Noumea, New Caledonia, then moved on to New Zealand. Early one morning, when they had been out of Tonga about five or six days, they saw a smudge on the southwest horizon. The captain sounded general quarters, and the ship made a right about-face and headed back for Tonga as fast as it could go, about fifteen knots.

As the ship got closer, they were pretty sure it was the USS *Tennessee*. "As soon as the watchers found out she was on our side," Pase said, "we turned around and headed to New Caledonia again. There were loud sighs of relief because the little five-inch gun that was the only weapon on board wouldn't have reached very far if the ship had been Japanese."

After narrowly avoiding a trip with Carlson's Raiders, an elite special-ops team within the Marines, Pase traveled from New Caledonia down to Wellington, New Zealand, where he joined the 2nd Marine Division and put in some long, hard training from July to October 1943, when he once again set sail for . . . somewhere.

Pase and his shipmates had no idea where they were going, although they were sure the officers knew. All they were aware of was that they took off aboard a small troop transport called the USS *Frederick Funston*. Once they boarded ship and pulled out, they were told their destination would be an atoll in the Gilbert Islands. It was fortified but not expected to be any problem because the Navy promised they would have all the Japs killed by the time they got there.

The name of the atoll was Tarawa—and the Navy was dead wrong.

"Of course, the story is well known," Pase said later, "that the Marines were unable to cross the reef with most of the boats, and the men had to walk from the outer reef four or five hundred yards, completely unprotected from Japanese machine gunfire all the way to the beach. We were still close enough that with our field glasses we could see what was going on, and it was a very awful thing."

They watched the lines of Marines climb out of the Higgins boats as they worked up onto the reef and then try to walk ashore. Then the men started to disappear. Hundreds of them were dropping into the water. Pase and the others couldn't see the blood, of course, but they knew what was happening. The men were being picked off by machine guns. The watchers could see the bullets hitting the water like raindrops.

"It made us feel sick because all of a sudden it became abundantly clear that the Navy had not been able to do all the things they talked about," Pase said. "We were going to go against a contested beach with absolutely no cover whatsoever."

As luck would have it, on the afternoon of the second day Pase and the others got the word that they were to go ashore, but not where the other Marines had been gunned down. They landed on a small atoll facing the main island of Tarawa and set up their machine guns to stop the Japanese from retreating.

A lot of Japanese had already escaped, but once Pase and the others got there and set up their lines, they pretty well closed the beach to any more Japs. "A lot of them tried it, but we stopped all of them," Pase said. "That was my initiation into fire. I was seventeen years and ten months old. And on top of everything else, I had tonsillitis so bad, I could hardly walk. When I went ashore at Tarawa I could barely stand up, but oddly enough, after I got ashore I don't remember the tonsillitis at all. There were other things happening that wiped that out completely."

Pase's group, having been spared the casualties of the other units that landed on the main island, were given the job of burying the dead.

On that three-hundred-acre island there were some six thousand dead bodies that had been laying out in the sun for close to a week. "I can't remember a lot of it," Pase said, "except these sturdy Gilbert Islanders working with my platoon, collecting pieces of humans and moving them off." If somebody found a leg, they tried to tell if it was an American leg or a Japanese leg, he noted. If it was an American leg, they put it on one pile. If it was a Japanese leg, they threw it in a trench and covered it up. For a kid of seventeen it was a rude awakening as to what war was really like. By the time Pase boarded ship for that quick run to Hawaii, nearly all the glamour of war against the Empire of Japan had pretty well worn off.

His next assignment was Saipan. "But this time the Japanese tried to outsmart us. They let the first wave or two get in," Pase said, "and then they started shelling anything that moved in to reinforce them. The beach master—who was in charge of everything on the beach—saw what was happening and, after losing a bunch of Amtracks, said, 'That's enough of that. We're closing the beach down. There will be no more reinforcements going in this afternoon. We know the Marines that are in place will hang on. We'll get to them first thing in the morning.'

"They closed the beach down solid," Pase said, "and they refused to let us—and our guns—get in there. So we lay there all night, bobbing up and down in those Amtracks, seasick as dogs." Everyone in the group was fairly seaworthy and had been at sea for a long time, so nobody was supposed to get sick. "But believe me," said Pase, "after you've been smelling those diesel fumes and vomit and carbon dioxide gas, *everybody* got sick!"

The next morning a troop ship happened along, and they paused long enough to feed the guys huddled in the Amtrack breakfast. Those who could eat did so, and they topped it off with ice cream. Everybody got at least one scoop before they got back in the Amtrack and headed for the beach.

This time they made it. "We lost a lot of men on the beach at Saipan," said Pase. "But thank God, it was nothing like Tarawa."

Sometimes the amphibians—"amphibs," the guys called them—that made up the 773rd Amphibious Tractor Battalion seemed to have a mind of their own. Such was the case of the *Texas Tornado* and the three young Army men from Texas who made up its crew. At age nineteen Private James Fulbright had put aside a college career at Abilene Christian College to become captain of the *Tornado*. Privates Paul Stauffer and Dale Brown were the crew.

The trio had dodged bullets while helping to unload about eight thousand Marines on the shores of Saipan as a firefight between American and Japanese forces raged around them. Now the melee was over as Fulbright drove back into the water and headed for the ship. Each amphib could carry up to twenty-five fully armed Marines plus the crew of three with no problem.

"We had our sidearms and four mounted machine guns," Fulbright remembered. "The sides of the tractor were of heavy metal to ward off shells when possible. We would haul food, ammunition, men, or whatever was needed. We just did whatever job they had for us."

Bodies of dead and wounded Marines were floating around them, and several of the amphibs had been sunk. Among the corpses Fulbright could see Marines fighting desperately to stay alive.

They had gone only a short distance when something strange happened to the *Tornado*. The amphib started spinning around and around. It wouldn't go straight no matter what they did. The three crewmen soon realized they had a real problem. They might have picked up metal from a shell and stripped a track, but they absolutely could not go straight. Soon they started drifting out to sea.

They floated helplessly on out through the armada of ships. They were waving frantically, but no one saw them. "We had a distress flag up, but there was so much going on that nobody noticed," Fulbright said. "Everyone was concentrating on the job of securing the beachhead."

They knew their situation was desperate. Soon the ships were almost out of their sight. The roar of the guns grew fainter and fainter.

"We had some food and water," Fulbright recalled, "but that wasn't our biggest worry. We were afraid the Japs would get us. We knew what would happen if the enemy captured us."

That night Brown fell overboard. He'd gone to the front of the *Tornado* to relieve himself, and the waves bounced him into the sea. Fulbright grabbed a long pole called a fishhook and hauled him back onboard. "It was pitch dark, and the waves were high," said Fulbright, "but he managed to catch hold of the pole. It was a miracle."

About 1000 the next morning they were about twenty miles out to sea when the three men looked up to see a small fighter plane fly over. After a while an LCM (landing craft/mobile), capable of carrying up to fifty men, came alongside.

When the LCM crew said they could take the men but not the amphib, the crew took the bolts out of the machine guns and threw them into the ocean. "We didn't want the Japs to get them," said Brown. "We didn't want them to be able to use any part of our *Texas Tornado*."

When the three boys from Texas got back to where they were supposed to be, they were told that one amphib in their group had lost every member of its crew, though the vehicle was still seaworthy.

"We replaced them," said Dale, "and this tractor became the *Texas Tornado Number Two*."

THE 4TH MARINES' landing at the Blue and Yellow Beaches went a little smoother than the landing of the 2nd Division. On Blue Beach 2 and Yellow Beach 1 many of the LVTs were able to reach shore and drop Marines at hundred-yard intervals.

Not so lucky were the Marines on Yellow Beach 2, where heavy Japanese fire forced many of the men to jump into shallow water and run for cover. Of all the 4th Marines beaches, Yellow 2 was the most difficult, with heavy resistance that lasted all morning. As the LVTs moved inland, enemy artillery zeroed in on them, and counterattacks developed along their right flank.

On Blue 2 and Yellow 1 most of the LVTs made it to shore and were able to deposit Marines beginning at about a hundred yards and extending to about seven hundred yards inland. On Yellow 2 heavy Japanese fire forced some Marines out of their vehicles in shallow water, where they had to run for their lives to find cover.

The 4th Division's plans called for the LVTs driving all the way to the objective, known as the O-1 line, about twelve hundred yards inland. That would put them on the slopes of Mount Fina Susu, which towered approximately three hundred feet high, but not many of the vehicles made it that far. In some spots a heavy undergrowth of vegetation stopped the Amtracks, and their inability to cover the ground set an unfortunate pattern—with the Marines falling short of their objectives as the battle wore on.

After a full hour's fighting, the 1st Battalion, 25th Marines, had succeeded in pushing just twelve yards in from the beach, and the 2nd Battalion's progress was only slightly better. Despite all the would-be amphibious help, the infantry was still pretty much on its own. Marines tried to find cover as artillery shells exploded around them, and Japanese snipers picked them off before they could get away from the tractors.

"There were dead Marines all around us," remembered Corporal Joe Ojeda of the 4th Marines. "There were bodies and body parts all over, with everyone yelling for a corpsman." Many Marines who survived a first wound were struck again by enemy artillery and mortar fire as they lay helpless behind wrecked vehicles awaiting transportation back to safety.

THE "O-1 LINE" was the exact spot—twelve hundred yards into Saipan—that each unit of Marines was supposed to hold secure at the close of the first day. It was also where the driver of each Amtrack was supposed to pause long enough to let the Marines he was carrying get off and take up their positions. The first wave that day was supposed to be a squadron of Army amphibious tanks, and the second wave was the Marines. It didn't happen that way.

"They showed us the map, and we started getting information on how we would set up, where we were supposed to go, and so on and so forth," said Private Arthur Liberty, who dropped out of Richmond High School in Vermont to join the Marines. "Our Amtracks were supposed to travel all the way to the O-1 line, but as soon as we hit the beach, the driver said, 'Get Out!'"

"What the hell do you mean?" a bunch of guys started to yell. "You're supposed to take us to the O-1 line."

"Those goddamn tanks refuse to move because they're drawing artillery fire from the Japs," the driver said. "They stopped right on the beach instead of going where they were supposed to go. So goddamnit, get out!"

They got out and started moving inland, but the next thing they knew, a Japanese soldier came charging at them. One Marine emptied all fifteen rounds from his carbine, but he kept coming. The bugler carried a shotgun with double-ought buck, and somebody yelled, "Shoot him, shoot him!" He hit the soldier twice before he dropped him.

The unit moved in about five hundred yards, and Liberty and the others started attracting artillery shells. "They told us to move back, but as soon as we started, we could hear the artillery shells coming, so we hit the deck," Liberty said. The shells landed right behind the Marines, and they jumped up and ran until they were chased all the way back to where they'd come from.

That was as close as anyone got to the O-1 line. The whole unit ended up hugging the beach that night.

EARLY IN 1942 two brothers had set aside attractive law practices in the South Louisiana town of Houma to join the Marines, and now, as luck would have it, Lieutenants Claude and Stanwood Duval were both huddled in the same landing craft headed for shore on Saipan.

"I will never forget my first sight of Saipan—this huge, black island rising out of the mist, with battleships, cruisers, and destroyers everywhere," recalled Claude, who was twenty-eight at the time. "Artillery shells were exploding in the water around us, and .50-caliber machine gun bullets were whizzing over us, and to make matters worse, the tractor was hitting the coral reef, and we were bouncing straight up in the air, not knowing whether the bouncing was caused by an artillery shell or the coral reef. Nevertheless, we got ashore and went inland with the tractor pretty close to a little narrow-gauge railroad that carried sugar cane. This reminded me of home in South Louisiana."

The men were under heavy artillery and mortar fire, and there was considerable light arms fire from the pier jutting out from the little village called Charan Kanoa. "We made it ashore, and the heavy fire continued," said Claude. "The plan was that we would ride in the tractors up to the O-1 line. There was just no way this could be done, as tanks started down this one road, and they were immediately knocked out."

When the men got closer to the narrow-gauge railroad, the artillery fire and mortar fire were intense, and the Japanese seemed to be zeroing in on the Marines' tractors. "So out of the tractors we piled and ran along the railroad tracks," Claude said. He tried to dig his first foxhole but could never really get started. He ended up digging about five quick, small foxholes as he moved from spot to spot.

There were Japs in the trees and in holes in the ground who were using small arms to give the Marines a lot of problems. But worse yet, there was Japanese heavy artillery fire that chewed up masses of Americans. Carrier-based US planes firing rockets, dropping bombs, and strafing provided some quick relief, but as soon as the planes were gone, the artillery would open up again.

"There was great difficulty in locating where the enemy was," Stanwood said. "The artillery fire was coming from over the ridge on the other side of Mount Fina Susu, a hill that jutted up several hundred feet. At least that's where I think it was coming from. To make a long story short, we didn't ride to the O-1 line. In fact, we didn't get there at all—not for two or three days."

AT SAIPAN THEY had a reef that seemed like it was about a mile wide, and those Japs zeroed in on that reef," remembered Private First Class Robert Groves, a member of the 2nd Marine Division and a native of Fort Towson in Choctaw County, Oklahoma. He was sixteen when he arrived at Guadalcanal and had turned seventeen while he was there. He served as a machine gunner on an LVT.

The LVT his outfit was in got hit hard. They were just about halfway across the reef when a Japanese shell hit them. Groves was exposed from the waist up, and he got hit by shrapnel in the shoulder going in, but it wasn't enough to get evacuated. A corpsman put a Band-Aid on it, and Groves just went on about his business.

Some of the other men in the boat were not so lucky. "When we made it to shore, we attacked across this little narrow-gauge railroad," Groves remembered, "and one of the mortar shells hit right behind us and just decapitated our flamethrower man. Blew him all to pieces."

The Marines got about five hundred yards off the beach with a cane field out in front of them. "All of a sudden here come these Japs with these three little light tanks," Groves said. "We pelted them with hand grenades, and they just bounced off the tanks, but when they got within about ten feet of us our bazooka man opened up on them and knocked all three of them out. A Jap pulled one of the hatches open, and about a half-dozen guys shot him when he stuck his head out.

"As it turned out, that was the last Jap I ever saw," said Groves. "I tried to get up, and I couldn't walk." Groves looked down. His right leg was covered in blood. His shoe was full of blood too, and he realized he had no feeling in his right leg at all. "I didn't even know I'd been wounded," he said.

A corpsman threw Groves down to the ground and cut his right britches leg off. "You've got a bad wound," the corpsman said, "but you're not going to lose your leg." Blood from the wound sprayed a foot or two high until he got it under control.

"He gave me a shot of morphine, and that ended the war for me," Groves said. "I could see these tracers going back and forth while I was lying on that stretcher, and I didn't really care. Morphine does that to you."

PRIVATE FIRST CLASS RAYMOND RENFRO was born in Atoka, Oklahoma, and when he was a small boy his parents moved to Denison, Texas. He finished high school in Denison, and one day in November 1942 he drove to the recruiting office in Wichita Falls and did what many other eighteen-year-old American boys were doing—he signed up to join the Marines.

"I was mad as hell at the Japanese," he remembered, "and I wanted to do everything I could possibly do to rectify what they'd done to my country!"

But Ray Renfro also had another axe to grind. His brother, Robert Leon Renfro, who was four years older, had joined the Army Air Corps in 1938 and been sent to the Philippines. He was stationed at Clark Field, where he had been told that there might be a flying job open. But the Japanese attacked and burned to the ground General Douglas MacArthur's flock of B-17s on Monday, 8 December 1941, so that idea was out the window.

Robert was originally scheduled to go to Australia with MacArthur, but he got left behind—along with a lot of others. "My mother and my aunt were crying and listening to the radio for all the news that was available," said Ray, "and they probably would have been horrified if they'd heard the real news." His parents eventually learned that with no room for these troops in MacArthur's plans, Robert had joined a group that had somehow managed to get an inner-island boat and had planned to sail from the Philippines to Australia on it.

The group started out, and they would hide in the daytime and only sail at night. According to Ray, Robert and his comrades had either anchored or abandoned the boat for a while when the Japanese sank it. They formed a guerrilla squad, and Robert did his fighting in the backwoods of the Philippines until he was spotted by a Japanese patrol boat and captured around the first part of April 1942.

Ray didn't know at the time he joined the Marines what had happened to Robert—not even whether he was dead or alive. "I watched my mother turn from a beautiful, brunette woman into a gray-headed lady," he said. "I went to the Marine Corps in November, and that's when I joined up. I went to Dallas, where we were given physicals and sworn in, and then we headed to California by train, but I had to admit that those first few weeks in boot camp I got to wondering if I'd made the right choice."

Boot camp was rough, but he'd known it would be. Renfro was a country kid who'd never been to the dentist. They found three or four cavities in his jaw teeth and sent him to a Navy dentist. "They enjoyed pleasure drilling in my mouth without any deadening," he remembers, "and my mouth got so hot, it started to smoke!"

When he got off the train at San Diego everyone made fun of the new recruits, saying, "You'll be sorr-rry!"

With his teeth all fixed, he was assigned to the 4th Marines, which was just forming up. "I made 'Expert' on the rifle range, and that was five dollars more in my paycheck every month," Ray said. "I got the feeling I was doing all right."

Now, at Saipan, he was in a rifle platoon with the 4th Marine Division, carrying a Browning automatic rifle (BAR) and riding in an LVT. When the order came to go in they started to move, with a battleship belching those sixteen-inch guns all around them and smoke and fire everywhere. The Japanese were shelling the beach, and they hit a few of the LVTs.

"Some of my friends didn't ever make it ashore," Ray said. "Some of them turned over. Hit that reef and just flipped over. But the one I was on made it in okay." Marines jumped over the side to get out while the Japanese shelled all around them. It was about a hundred yards to the beach, so all of them jumped up and started running.

Ray got knocked down by a mortar shell hitting the ground close to him, but it didn't really hurt him at all. He just jumped up and ran on. There wasn't anything else to do. They got up to the railroad track, and somebody said, "Dig you a foxhole." So he did. All during the night he could hear the Japanese on the other side of the railroad hollering at the Marines: "You want to give up, Ma-lines? You want to give up?"

Renfro wasn't saying anything. He tried not to make any noise at all because he'd give away his position. But during the night a Japanese snuck over and jumped in the foxhole with a friend who was maybe a hundred feet to his left, and he tried his best to cut the soldier's legs off with a machete. In the scramble that followed, another Marine tried to shoot the Jap, but he missed and hit his friend in the leg. They finally killed the Jap, but the soldier lay there all night with his legs bleeding. He somehow managed to live through it.

ONE OF THE most terrifying mistakes during the invasion of Saipan happened when a landing craft loaded with Marines came within a hundred yards of invading the island of Tinian. The two islands are only a little over three miles apart, and in the wee hours of the morning they looked just alike—but the real "invasion" was almost a month too early.

"We were told to circle, not to go in yet," remembered Corporal Frank M. "Tommy" Thompson, a native of Indianapolis and member of the Marines' V Amphibious Corps. "We circled for almost eight hours, and some of the guys were getting seasick from all that circling."

Other Marines had taken off their boots and were dangling their feet in the water just to have something to do. The rest of them were packed in like sardines. They kept circling until the coxswains started worrying about running out of fuel. It was the third night of the Saipan invasion, after more than a dozen previous landing waves.

"It was about two o'clock, I guess," Thompson said, "and pitch-black, mind you, and everybody by now was falling asleep from sheer inertia. You'd just get to the point where you'd just fall asleep on one another. The officers were even asleep. And all at once a guy woke up and saw that we were close enough to see the silhouette of the trees on shore, but there were no fireworks going on." All the fireworks were behind them.

"Captain," Thompson said uneasily, "things don't look right here!"

"What the hell do you mean?" the captain said.

"Look, here's where all the fireworks are going off," he said, pointing to the rear. "But over here there's nothing!"

"Jesus Christ," somebody said, "we're about to land on the wrong island."

The captain got out his maps and turned his light on real low. "Oh my God," he said, "Turn around! Turn around!"

"I never heard four engines gunning up so fast to get the hell out of there," Thompson said. "We were within a hundred yards of Tinian."

No one was ready to invade Tinian. That would come later. Right now the Marines had all they could handle on the beach at Saipan.

chapter 3

★ ★ ★

The Eternal Beach

"I REALLY DON'T have any idea how many Japs I killed between June 15 and 16, but it was one helluva lot," remembered Sergeant Harold Haberman, an ammunitions runner for the 2nd Marines special weapons company. "They told everybody to dig in," Haberman said, "and let the Japs come to us, and that's what we did." Haberman had a bazooka, and he started firing at the Japanese. He didn't stop until he'd killed everything in sight.

At night Haberman and a buddy lay on their backs in their foxhole, holding Ka-Bar knives at their chests. They heard Japanese soldiers running everywhere. A few of them jumped over their foxhole, and they could hear the sound of other Marines fighting Japanese troops. "I was primed and ready," said Haberman. "No Japs fell on me, but I can't describe the fear I felt." He and his buddy spent two nights there, without food or sleep, while shells and mortars exploded all around them.

On the second or third day Haberman and a companion stumbled across two unmarked graves. During a short break in the fighting they ran into a group of native Chamorros.

"We were curious, so we asked them about the two graves we'd seen," Haberman said. "They told us that several years before Pearl Harbor a plane crashed off the coast of Saipan and the Japs went to the crash site and picked up a man and a woman pilot. They took them to the town of Garapan, where they were jailed and tried as spies from the United States. They were later executed and buried in the graves we'd discovered."

Both Haberman and his friend were intrigued by the story. They assumed that the bodies buried there might be the graves of the famous female flier Amelia Earhart and her navigator, Fred Noonan, who disappeared on a round-the-world flight in 1937.

But then the Marines were quickly caught up in a Japanese counterattack, and Haberman was soon fighting for his life. Every day he saw more of his buddies killed and wounded, but from time to time he still wondered about those graves.

"I WAS IN THE first wave on Saipan," remembered Sergeant Joe Brown of the 2nd Marines, a Texan from Wichita Falls. "We ran into a little resistance there, but at first it wasn't real bad. We moved in maybe three hundred yards, and then our platoon got isolated from our outfit, and there was hell to pay."

During that night on Saipan Brown and his comrades were stuck by themselves at the edge of a sugar cane field. There were about twenty or thirty cane marshes out there, and the Japs evidently slipped back from the beach to take cover in them.

That night the Marines lost their platoon leader and his runner. In addition, another platoon sergeant was wounded and so was a platoon guide, and that left Brown with three squads. Ordinarily he was the squad leader of the second squad, but now he had two other squads to deal with. He moved back near the edge of the water and regrouped with the battalion. They spent that second night on the beach.

Brown and his men caught quite a bit of artillery fire that night, and the next day they started their move up the island. By nightfall, after they had moved up quite a ways, Brown was wounded by shrapnel from a hand grenade. Some fragments penetrated his left side and left eye, but his injuries weren't bad enough to get him shipped out. He would end up commanding that platoon all the way through the campaign.

A short time later the Marines were pinned down by machine gunfire, and several of the men were hit. The captain came through and told Brown to take the stretcher cases back to company headquarters. As they started back across some rice paddies with the wounded, the Japs opened fire on them from the adjacent woods.

They had to drop all the stretcher cases, and the Japanese killed every last one of them. Out of the whole group, Brown was the only one who had a rifle that would fire, so he'd crawl a little ways and then raise up and shoot. One of the walking wounded, Private First Class T. T. Moore, a platoon guide from Dallas, managed to get back to the company and tell them what was happening. "Old Joe's in trouble," he said. "Who wants to volunteer with me and help him out?"

When nobody volunteered, Moore returned. For a while he and Brown traded shots with the Japanese until they somehow managed to get back with what was left of the walking wounded.

"Boy, that was a close one!" said Moore, squatted down on his knees and sighing. As he spoke, a Japanese machine gun opened fire from somewhere and hit him squarely in the back.

Brown turned in time to see one of the bullets come out of Moore's chest. He was dead before he hit the ground.

THE YOUNG LIEUTENANT was soft spoken, hardworking, and proud of his southern heritage. Four of his great-uncles had fought in the Civil War. Two of them had been killed in battle, and a third had lost a leg at Chickamauga. His father was a lieutenant in the Army field artillery in World War I, and his mother was a native of South Carolina.

He grew up in Fort Worth and went to public schools there, and somewhere along the way he started thinking of becoming a writer. But suddenly there was a war on, and there were more important things to do. When Japan attacked Pearl Harbor, he was attending a small, scholarly college in Houston named Rice Institute, and he was six months away from finishing a reserve officer class that gave him a commission in the Marine Corps.

"What I wanted was to see the fighting," remembered Lieutenant John Graves. "If you'd grown up on tales of Rebel great-uncles and the Marines at Belleau Wood, you tended to feel that way."

After graduation Graves put in thirty weeks at Quantico. Then he was sent to Camp Pendleton, where the 4th Marine Division was about to be formed. His first big job was when he and a friend were given the task of turning about sixty or seventy college kids into artillerymen.

"We knew quite a bit about artillery," Graves said, "but we didn't know that much about being officers. We kind of spoiled them, and we gave them a farewell beer bust when they graduated. They all got tipsy, and they were slapping us on the back and saying 'Good old Ed, good old John,' and so on. When we got out of that we sat down and smoked a cigarette and said, 'Shit, we learned something.'"

Graves became battery executive officer. That was a fancy-sounding name for the guy who gives fire commands to an artillery battery. In January 1944 the whole 4th Division moved out.

"We trained like hell until that time," Graves said, "and it was intense training, on those California hills out there, and practice landings at San Clemente." After that they spent about forty days on an LST. They landed at Kwajalein. Graves's battery had 75-millimeter pack howitzers, small cannons that broke down into pieces that could be loaded into amphibian tractors for getting over coral reefs that would stop regular landing boats.

At one point, far out to sea, they hit such a bad storm that one of the tractors broke the chains holding it down, and it started slamming into other tractors, a couple of which were knocked loose. The officer in charge of the tractors was Lieutenant William Wilson, and he had guts enough to climb up to the overhead, dangling with his hands from cables and pipes, and shouted instructions to his people below, who finally got the mess tied down. After that they called Wilson "Willie the Ape" for the way he'd looked up there. "But it was admiration, more than anything else," Graves said, "because we were really plenty grateful to him."

After Kwajalein Graves and the rest of the company returned to Hawaii for three or four months. Then they went to Saipan.

"A whole bunch of the LVTs got smashed right away," said Graves. "There were Japanese guns in the hills that were zeroed in on those things—so there was a shortage of them real quick." Graves ran around trying to find some way to get in over the coral reef, but it was all along the landing beaches, so he couldn't find anyplace. He finally found a channel going into a town called Charan Kanoa. It was a sugar refinery town that had been smashed by naval gunfire and planes by then, but a stone pier jutted out from it, so he got the coxswain to start in there.

About that time a Jap gun started firing on them, and the first shot hit right behind them. Then the Japanese fired again, and this time it hit right in front of them. They had a good idea where the next one would hit. Graves turned and told the coxswain to turn around and get the hell out of there.

The group finally found a place to land, but it was well north of the primary landing area. Graves knew he was going to have to go down south, where the main shooting was, to try to find his battalion, but he also knew that he couldn't take all those people with him. Marching down that beach under fire was a tough job for anybody, so he looked around to find someone who might be able to do it on his own. The first soldier he saw was a kid from the Midwest named Hallstein, who saw Graves looking at him and frowned.

He said, "Aw shit, Lieutenant, not me!"

Graves nodded. "Yes, you!"

Hallstein and Graves took off, and the further south they got, they saw a lot more wrecked-out LVTs and bodies of dead Marines. They came suddenly to a clearing where there were four huge 105-millimeter batteries. "I don't know how they managed to get those damned things across the reef," Graves said. "But anyhow, they had them there, and the executive officer was in a foxhole giving fire commands."

Leaving Hallstein on the beach, Graves struggled up to the foxhole and was surprised to find himself face-to-face with Lieutenant Jack Armstrong, who had originally been in Graves's battalion but was now serving as the 105th Battery's executive officer.

"Get down, man," Armstrong said. "We're still getting some pretty good shell fire."

Armstrong didn't know where their outfit was, and he was very busy. Graves just slapped him on the shoulder, said, "Good luck," and moved on.

It couldn't have been more than thirty minutes after Graves saw him that the Japanese hit Armstrong's ammo dump. He put everyone undercover, then went in and started carrying out the shells until one of them blew up on him. He got a Navy Cross—posthumously.

"As soon as you land, plans don't mean a thing," remembered Private First Class Bob Verna of G Company, 4th Marines. "You have to react, and the adrenaline keeps you going." Instead of being dropped at the O-1 line, Verna and other members of his company jumped out of the landing vehicle and tried to make it on their own. En route three-fourths of the company was wounded or killed.

By the time darkness descended that first night the Marines were ashore, but they were far short of their goal. The Japanese still held half the territory that the Marines had expected to control by the end of the day, and their presence on the ridges above the beaches constituted a severe threat.

Private First Class Jack Vigliatura of the 2nd Marines carried a BAR, which weighed more than twenty pounds when loaded. He would never forget the sheer terror of nonstop gunfire in battle. "You don't know where they're coming from or how many there are," remembered the Worcester, Massachusetts, native. He admitted he was "scared shitless" but that he joined the Marines "to fight, not sit on my butt."

Private First Class Bob Talbot, from the East Texas town of Corsicana, felt the same way—up to a point. "I talked to the Army, Navy, and Marines before I joined up," he recalled. "I liked what the Marines promised. They said, 'You'll be in combat in six months.' The others said, 'We can't promise you that.' But now, after Guadalcanal and Tarawa, I wasn't so sure that was such a good idea anymore."

At Tarawa Talbot had saved four brutally wounded men by holding their heads above the water for six excruciating hours. "A Marine directly in front of me was hit in the face with a bullet," he remembered. As the unconscious man began to sink, Bob grabbed him and pulled the belt-like life preserver up under the wounded man's armpits, inflating the belt. The Marine was able to float with his head above water.

Talbot started for the beach about four hundred yards away. Then he saw another Marine wounded nearby. He swam over to him, pulling the first Marine along. He removed the second Marine's backpack, inflated the life belt, and slipped it under his arms. Once again he started for the beach.

He had gone only a short distance when he saw a third Marine hit, and then a fourth. The men were falling like flies, but when Talbot turned toward the shore with the four Marines, a sense of helplessness rose in his chest. Trying to keep the four wounded Marines together in the current was like trying to push marbles up a hill.

Talbot removed his belt and the belt of one of the Marines and managed to tie the men together in pairs. Then he saw a group of Higgins boats plucking wounded Marines out of the water. They came over and one by one picked up the four wounded men.

Finally Bob turned again toward the beach. "I remember explosions, stumbling into underwater shell holes, and crawling over barbed wire," he said, "but somehow I managed to reach the shore. Believe me, I talked to God a whole lot that night."

He also suffered an injured leg that gave him trouble later at Saipan and for years afterward. After he got ashore and found his outfit, he saw that his leg was covered with blood. He never found out what was wrong, and he stayed awake most of the night. He put morphine patches on the leg for three or four days, and a doctor finally X-rayed it, but there was no sign of any shrapnel or gunshot wound.

Years later Talbot happened across a story about the young lieutenant who organized the rescue with the Higgins boats and how he had been awarded a Bronze Star for his actions that day. Bob wrote him a letter and soon received a reply from Lieutenant Eddie Heimberger, who by this time was an actor known by his stage name Eddie Albert.

MANY TIMES THE Japanese aggressors came singly or in pairs, stepping silently and with one thing in mind—killing Marines. Private First Class Jim Monroe of Brownwood, Texas, who'd turned eighteen on the eve of the Saipan invasion, and another Marine shared a deep ditch, and they took turns keeping watch.

"My buddy and I were doing this all night," recalled Monroe, "and here is one of the things about the war that I'll think about forever. We were less than three feet apart, and he took a bullet right through the head. I'll always wonder, 'Why him and not me?'"

Despite the chaos, Lieutenant General Thomas E. Watson, commander of the 2nd Marines, came ashore and set up a command post in a captured ammunition dump. Not to be outdone, Lieutenant General Harry Schmidt, head of the 4th Division, also established a command post ashore, despite the fact that the division had given up part of the ridgeline in its area and fallen back to safer quarters to prevent a possible counterattack in the dark.

Sure enough, at about 0330 a tank-led major attack hit the 6th Marines, overrunning a 60-millimeter mortar position. But as the tanks passed, they were struck in the rear by mortars, bazookas, machine guns, and grenades. A pair of young Marines, Privates First Class Charles D. Merritt and Herbert J. Hodges, fired repeatedly with bazookas at seven tanks, disabling them all.

When the tank and infantry attacks started, the Marines called for help from the Navy. The battleship USS *California* fired at the base of the ridgeline to stop Japanese tanks from coming down, and a squadron of US medium tanks also rumbled onto the scene. The fighting was intense, but when the tank battle was over, the Japanese withdrew with heavy casualties.

"His name was Cunningham, and he was the leader of our group when we landed on Red Beach 1," remembered Corporal Roy William Roush of F Company, 2nd Marines, a native of Alva, Oklahoma, who joined the service when he was seventeen years old. "I've forgotten his first name," he said, "but

I'll never forget what he did that day when three tanks charged our lines."

Each of the group leaders, including Cunningham, was equipped with what they called an antitank grenade. It was about the size of a thick fountain pen that you could bolt onto the end of your rifle and then fire at a tank; it would become an antitank missile for maybe fifty feet or so.

When one of the tanks got so close you could almost spit on it, Cunningham hit it in the tread. The tank was crippled. The Japanese quickly realized that there was no way they were going to get out of there. They tried to back out, but the tank just started to spin.

Cunningham calmly fired another antitank grenade and hit the tank again, this time right below the turret. "Japanese tanks were what we considered just plain junk," Roush said. "They were nowhere near the type of tank our Shermans were or even the light tanks we had before that." Their protective metal wasn't very thick at all, and Cunningham's shot easily penetrated the tank and exploded. Several Japanese tried to exit the tank through the turret, but Cunningham leaped up on top of the tank and threw another grenade inside, destroying it and the whole crew. The remaining two Japanese tanks retreated as fast as possible toward the town of Garapan.

About that time a large mortar barrage struck the area, lasting maybe fifteen or twenty minutes. No one could see anything for all the dust going up. For a minute Roush thought everyone had been killed. When the barrage lifted, he moved forward. The first person he saw was Cunningham. For knocking out that tank and the crew, Cunningham received a medal.

Roush didn't get much sleep that night because the Japanese kept moving down toward the Marines. All through the night they heard the sound of the Japanese trucks coming. Roush could hear where they stopped and turned their motors off. Then, about 0100, they decided to stage a banzai charge.

"I wasn't sure how many there were—probably at least two hundred—and they came right down the road toward our position," Roush said. "Our machine guns were plenty busy for a while. We had a lot of machine guns along the road because we knew that's where they would be coming from.

"The second attack was about the same number, and right in the middle of that second charge a Navy ship fired a star shell and lit up the whole area for miles around. Every Jap was slaughtered," said Roush. "Not a one of them got through. They later reported sixteen hundred Japanese bodies right out there in front of the Marines' little platoon after it was over."

Roush walked on up to his foxhole position. There was Cunningham, lying next to where his foxhole had been. The one-man killer of tanks was lying on his back. He was covered with blood and looked like he was dead.

Roush asked a sergeant sitting there, "Is that Cunningham?"

The sergeant nodded.

"Is he alive?" Roush asked, and the sergeant shook his head.

Roush walked over and touched Cunningham and whispered his name. "Cunningham opened his eyes and looked at me," remembered Roush, "and it scared the hell out of me. I thought a dead man had come back to life."

Cunningham had been shot through the right side. He had also been shot on the cheekbone below his eye, and that bullet had exited through his ear. A third bullet had struck him in his lower neck; that round had lodged in his body. He also had another bullet wound near his heart.

When Roush opened his canteen, Cunningham grabbed it with both hands and started chugging water. Roush knew that so much water could make a thirsty man sick, so after he drank about half of it, Roush pulled it away.

There weren't any stretchers in the area, but a small Japanese shack stood maybe a hundred yards away. Roush got one of the other guys to go with him, and they tore off a door and then used it to carry Cunningham to an aid station. Roush didn't see how he could possibly live with all those wounds, but at least he could say he tried.

Roush found out later how Cunningham had been shot up so severely. Earlier that morning a group of engineers had pulled a light 37-millimeter cannon off the road and taken it down onto the sandy beach where they could get a better field of fire. Within minutes the men attempting to fire the gun were either killed or wounded.

"But here came Cunningham again," said Roush. "He manned the gun by himself and got off a series of shots with it until a Japanese machine gun finally found him and riddled him with bullets." When Cunningham was left at the aid station, everyone who saw him was certain he would soon die.

About six months later Roush got rotated back to the States. While in the chow line at the Marine Corps depot in San Diego he saw Cunningham in uniform standing in line. He thought for a minute he was seeing a ghost, but he slowly walked up to him.

"How're you doing?" Roush said.

"Well, I still can't hear anything out of this ear," Cunningham said. "But other than that, I'm okay."

By the morning of 16 June everything about Saipan had changed. On 15 June, when the landings began, Admiral Richmond Kelly Turner had been jauntily predicting that Saipan would collapse within a week. Now Turner and Lieutenant General Holland Smith faced the disturbing news that none of their Marine units had managed to get more than halfway to their objectives on the opening day of battle. It was clear that the initial plans had underestimated the size of the Japanese forces on Saipan.

It was also clear that the Army's 27th Infantry Division, which had been originally slated as the reserve force for Saipan—and that Holland Smith didn't trust in the slightest—would have to be committed to the battle. After his experience with the 27th at Makin and Eniwetok, Smith was reluctant to use them again in the Marianas. But they were the only troops available in Hawaii, so he had to take them.

The 6th Marines were busy mopping up pockets of Japanese resistance behind the US lines, left there after the counterattack of the previous evening. Their work proceeded at a slow pace—finding the Japs in their holes and using grenades and flamethrowers to flush them out.

Meanwhile the 8th and 23rd Marines linked up at Charan Kanoa, closing a dangerous gap in the lines by moving up to the edge of Lake Susupe, a shallow body of water, and pausing there. Early on the morning of 16 June about two hundred Japanese moved through another gap in the lines between divisions. Fortunately troops from the 23rd Marines were able to hold onto their position and kill many of the advancing Japanese.

That night Holland Smith had ordered the 27th Division to begin landing its troops, and it was obvious by now that the Marines would need these reserves if they were to move ahead. Upon landing, the 27th pushed forward to Aslito Airfield where they were about to surprise the unsuspecting Japanese.

BY THE TIME darkness fell on 16 June, twenty thousand Marines—if the dead and injured were included—had come ashore on Saipan. The troops had established a beachhead about ten thousand yards long and over a thousand yards deep in most places. Two divisions were in place with most of their reserves. Seven battalions of artillery had landed, and so had most of two tank battalions.

The troops began to dig in. Both division command posts were set up, although the 6th Marines' regimental commander, Colonel James Riseley, established his CP practically at the water's edge. The 4th Division commander, General Harry Schmidt, established a command post that was actually a series of foxholes about fifty yards from the beach. It was poorly protected from enemy light artillery, which was firing from the high ground some fifteen hundred yards away.

Meanwhile, south of Afetna Point, the 4th Marine Division was having its own share of problems. Opposition in the rubble of the town of Charan Kanoa was comparatively light, but Japanese riflemen still sniped away at Marines as they moved through.

As for the Japanese, their artillery had taken a heavy toll. The US landings had been made against what the enemy considered his strongest points, and at a time when the defending garrison was four battalions above strength, massing at least sixteen 105-millimeter howitzers and 75-millimeter field pieces on the nearest high ground. Directly east of the island's airstrip they emplaced a 150-millimeter, four-weapon howitzer battery with a similar battery south of it. All of these weapons were well situated, and they poured a tremendous amount of fire on the landing beaches.

MANY MARINES BELIEVED that if you heard the artillery shell, it most likely had already passed you by, and you wouldn't hear the one with your name on it because the shell arrived before the sound did. But Private First Class Richard Hertensteiner, who joined the Marines at seventeen in his hometown of Sheboygan, Wisconsin, and was experiencing his first battle at Saipan, learned that it didn't always work that way.

Hertensteiner, a member of an artillery battery, was talking to a couple of other Marines when they heard incoming sounds and dove into a shell crater. When the first round hit, he was the first person to fall into the hole. After the shelling he got up and began talking to the other Marines again. But they were both dead. Hertensteiner never received so much as a small scratch.

WHEN SERGEANT HANK MICHALAK was twelve years old he was pretty sure that when he got old enough he would join the Navy. That was an unhappy time for him because his mother died that year and his father decided to leave Louisiana and move back to Texas, where Hank had been born. They settled in the town of Marlin. Hank went part of the way through high school there, but deep inside he still heard the Navy calling him.

He was working a summer job, putting a new roof on the high school, when he and a friend decided to go to Waco and volunteer for the Navy. The friend chickened out, but on the way to the Navy recruiting office Hank happened to run into an old Marine who started telling him tales about China, and one thing led to another.

When he left Waco he was in the Marine Corps, 3rd Battalion, 2nd Marines. His father signed for him, and he wound up in San Diego going to boot camp.

One weekend in December Michalak was on liberty in Los Angeles when he heard about the Japanese attack on Pearl Harbor. He caught a ride back to Camp Elliott immediately. He found everybody talking about the bombing, fearful that the Japs were going to hit the West Coast.

His first assignment was Guadalcanal, a campaign he thought would never end. Then there was terrible Tarawa, where the Marines sustained more than 4,500 casualties in three days' time. The next operation turned out to be Saipan. Everyone was worried that it would become another Tarawa.

"When we pulled up there and I saw the size of that island, my first thought was 'Man, that's going to be a good deal,'" Michalak remembered. "That was a big island compared to what Tarawa was. Saipan had mountains on it, big mountains. And we got ashore okay. The Japs had it pretty well fortified, but we were able to land without the same kind of catastrophe that we had at Tarawa, and that was a relief."

During the second day on Saipan some of the 2nd Marines had advanced to the edge of the foothills of Mount Tapotchau. "The Japs were on the high ground, and we knew or suspected that something was going on up there," Michalak said. "But the problem was, we didn't know what."

On the third night, at about 0200 in the morning, the Japanese blew their bugles and came down that mountain like thunder, with artillery and tanks and antitank guns and anything else that would shoot. They completely overran the Marines, and that was the end of Hank's operations on Saipan. He caught a bullet in the right elbow and some shrapnel in the hand.

"That was the last thing I remembered," Michalak said. "The next thing I knew, I was out on a ship, and they were wheeling me in to operate on my arm or do whatever they were going to do to it. And right there beside the door was a trash can with arms and legs sticking out of it that the doctors had just thrown in. I wasn't fully conscious, but I thought to myself, 'Okay, that's where your arm is going, right there in that trash can.'"

Michalak woke up with a cast on his arm and a separate cast on two of his knuckles that had been ripped off by the shrapnel. Eventually all the wounds healed up.

IT WOULD BE six days before the beachhead was considered totally secure, but it was the first day's action that was most important. After that day the most critical stage of "the most critical stage" in the invasion was behind the Marines. They, at least, were ashore.

Nightfall came, but it brought no peace. The Marines dug in on their narrow strip of beachhead with the Philippine Sea at their backs and a vengeful enemy lurking in the darkness. Every

Marine knew that a night counterattack lay ahead, and it wasn't long in coming.

The Japanese high command had already issued orders to drive the Americans back into the sea before daylight the next day: "The Army this evening will make a night attack with all its forces," the 31st Army radioed Tokyo, "and expects to annihilate the enemy at one swoop!"

To Japanese troops, the order was plain and simple: "Each unit will consolidate strategically important points and will carry out counterattacks with reserve forces and tanks against the enemy landing units and will demolish the enemy during the night at the water's edge."

The 6th Marines, 2nd Division, which held the left flank of the beachhead, was the first to feel the effects of these measures. A large force of Japanese infantry, supported by tanks, charged the American lines from the north along the coastal road.

With swords waving, flags flying, and a bugle sounding, the Japanese descended on the Marine lines. The regiment under attack had only one battalion of 75-millimeter pack howitzers at its disposal because they had been unable to land any of their 105-millimeter howitzer battalions the previous day. Naval star shells fired from US destroyers silhouetted the attackers as they approached, and the withering fire of machine guns, rifles, and naval five-inch guns stopped the attack.

"THE BATTLE EVOLVED into a madhouse of noise, tracers, and flashing lights as the tank attack came at us out of Garapan and hit our battalion on the left," remembered Major James Donovan of the 1st Battalion, 6th Marines, who had fought his way through Guadalcanal and Tarawa. The Marines had been warned that an enemy tank formation would be coming down in their direction, so they were well prepared for it. They were all dug in about eight or nine hundred yards from the beach, and at about 0330 they heard the Japanese tanks coming.

In addition to the Navy's star shells, the Marines had their own star shells with their 60-millimeter mortars, so the area was well lit up.

"It was an eerie scene out there," Donovan said. "The flashing shells, the smoke drifting around, and as soon as we heard the tanks out in front, we called in our supporting artillery fire, and all our own supporting weapons—mortars, antitank grenades, bazookas, and demolition charges."

As enemy tanks were hit and set afire, they illuminated other tanks coming out of the flickering shadows toward the front. In the dense darkness Marines saw only a few tanks at a time. Moving out of their holes, they attacked them with antitank grenades, bazookas, and hand grenades.

Then Marine machine guns opened up, and the Japanese foot soldiers following the tanks were badly cut up. Before that battle was over, they had destroyed twenty-seven to thirty tanks, and the supporting infantry men were all dead. That tank battle went into the record books as the largest of the Pacific War up to that time. When the confrontation ended after about forty-five minutes, the 6th Marines had polished off twenty-four of the tanks in hand-to-hand fighting.

"The Marine bazookas had proved amazingly effective against those thin-skinned Japanese tanks of that period," said Donovan. "There were no prisoners among the foot soldiers. We killed them all."

Among the men who became heroes that day was twenty-year-old Sergeant Jim Evans of the 6th Marines. He'd been a Marine for four years and had seen action at Pearl Harbor, Guadalcanal, and Tarawa. When a Japanese tank stopped near him and the hatch opened to allow the driver to peer through the smoke, Evans shot the driver and hurled a phosphorous grenade into the tank.

Not far away Corporal William Jefferies and his buddy, Private First Class Bob Reed, both of the 6th Marines, fired their bazooka shells and knocked out four enemy tanks. Reed received a Navy Cross for jumping on top of a fifth tank and disabling it with an incendiary grenade in the turret. Jefferies received a Silver Star.

THE 8TH MARINES, meanwhile, were pushing east in the seemingly endless swampland around Lake Susupe. Men found themselves standing waist-deep in muck that stretched a thousand yards north and south of the lake. The area was covered with nests of snipers, with Japanese soldiers holding positions both in the swamp and to the east and south of the lake.

Simultaneously, the 2nd Marines moved up the coast toward Garapan, and the 6th Marines moved northeast toward the densely defended hills. Navy battleships and cruisers—those that hadn't accompanied Admirals Raymond Spruance and Marc Mitscher on their "Turkey Shoot" in the Philippine Sea—began a heavy bombardment of Garapan, a town already pounded and flattened by naval gunfire.

"The city was gone by the time we occupied it," remembered medical Corpsman Chester Szech, who carried a .45-caliber pistol and a carbine and whose Marine uniform was similar to an infantryman. The entire population had moved into the hills and nearby caves. Small clusters of Japanese troops hidden among the ruins of the town seemed at first to be the only opposition, but that afternoon seven tanks showed up. The Marines responded with bazookas and grenades until six of the tanks were destroyed.

I WAS CRITICIZED FOR being too much of a Marine and not enough of a pharmacist's mate," recalled H. L. Obermiller, who had somehow managed to join the Navy and in some peculiar fashion had ended up in the Marine Corps as a pharmacist's mate.

The youngster from Milam County, Texas, took a troop train to San Diego, where he was sworn in, went through boot camp, and then had a chance to leave the Navy and join the Marines. "So I grabbed it," he said.

From the beginning Pharmacist's Mate Obermiller enjoyed carrying a rifle—and he was pretty good with it. He liked to go out with the Marines, and he could shoot as well as they could. He could also out-walk them, as he'd been raised on a farm and had to walk three or four miles to school every day. He didn't wear the Red Cross emblem on his sleeve as they did at Guadalcanal, where the Japs used the red cross for target practice, but he knew that if the Japanese on Saipan could pick out a pharmacist's mate or an officer, they would shoot the pharmacist's mate first.

When Obermiller's Higgins boat landed on Saipan, the sky was lit up with shells and flares. As they made their way through the town of Garapan an officer called out to him.

"There are some Navy frogmen who came ashore on the wrong side of town," he said. "Now they're behind Japanese lines, and they've gotten ambushed. You think you can get them out?"

Obermiller said he would try. "So I go down there and get to the Jap lines, and there was a fence I crawled under. I found the guys, and there were six or seven of them, but I never heard any of them speak a word, I guess because they were too scared. I got them out of there by crawling on our bellies back to our lines. I told them to line up behind me one by one and walk up the main street.

"As I walked, I shouted, 'Marines coming through! Marines coming through!' so the US sentries wouldn't shoot us," he said. "So I got them all the way to sick bay and then went back to my bunk."

From that point on, it was rough going. "The Japs decided that they would come down and hit us, and they were well trained and potent," he said. "They didn't seem to have any scruples at all. They didn't care if they got killed or not.

"I don't know how I did it. I knew I was walking into sudden death, but somehow that was just the way it was. With the Marines, you're trained to just accept things as they come. You don't question orders. When the officer has one more stripe than you do, when he says jump, you jump."

Even with the help of a pharmacist's mate, it would take the 2nd Marines until 3 July to root out the last of the Japanese from their underground caves and pillboxes amid the carnage of Garapan.

Sergeant Arwin Bowden, who was born in Wichita Falls, Texas, was a radio and telephone man, and that first night he set up his radio in a concrete building in Garapan that originally had been a Japanese burial crypt. Shelves ran all the way around the crypt, and urns were everywhere.

"About two o'clock in the morning the Japs made their final run at us," Bowden recalled, "and they lost five of their 10th Marines' 105-millimeter artillery pieces in that blast.

"By daylight we were back in the lines, and it was kill or be killed. That was all there was to it," Bowden said. "In an area about half a mile square there were about three thousand Japanese bodies. They sent in bulldozers to cut trenches. Then the same bulldozers just pushed the bodies into the trenches and covered them up. Some of the Japs surrendered, but some of them wouldn't. Those that wouldn't should have."

Privates First Class Samuel "Red" Spencer and Jack Wren were both from Michigan, and they joined the 2nd Marine Division at the same time. "We saw a movie about the Marines wearing their dress blues and thought we'd really look sharp in those blues when we joined up in September 1942," remembered Spencer.

Their first action was at Tarawa. "It was pretty rough," remembered Wren. "I carried a wounded guy down to the beach, but he'd been shot in the head and was dead by the time I got there. Our colonel was a very good guy, but he died trying to get off the water." In the space of a few hours there weren't any officers left, and a sergeant was running everything.

They ended up on separate boats at Saipan. "We were all over hell, trying to find each other, but at the end of the battle neither one of us could find the other one," said Spencer. Both thought the other was dead.

When Jack was located, he was in Garapan in street-to-street, house-to-house fighting. "You had to go one house at a time, room to room," said Spencer. "You never knew where the Japs were. They were everywhere."

During the day Marines could move up close behind the tanks and walk, and the Japs stayed away because of the tanks. Instead, they waited until night and came in. "If they came during the day, we would stand still and knock them off," Spencer said. "A guy in my outfit had a BAR, but he got hit and had to leave, and I took over the BAR. I knocked off a bunch of Japs. I told the other guys that I would shoot high and they would shoot low to make sure we got all of them. That was the only time I had a BAR, and I'm really glad I did."

A few days later Spencer was on the lower levels of Mount Tapotchau, the biggest mountain on Saipan, and it was a bad place to be. When Spencer and a group of Marines came out of the jungle into a clearing, he got hit in the back with shrapnel and was knocked out cold.

When he woke he looked up to see the blue sky. It was strangely quiet, and the Marines around him were all dead, and he thought he was dead too. *This must be what Heaven looks like,* he thought. Then a big sergeant came through and kicked him with his boot. When Spencer turned to look at him, he heard him yell, "Hey, Red's alive! Get over here!"

Several men appeared and gave him morphine, and others carried him down to where he could be put on a Jeep. Next thing he knew he was on a ship. *Boy,* he thought, *isn't this nice!*

Wren didn't find Spencer until he was back in Hawaii. "He came running over to where I was, and I heard him yelling, 'Where's Spencer? Where's Spencer?' I thought for all the world Jack was dead. Seeing him was quite a shock," said Spencer.

PRIVATE FIRST CLASS Wayne Terwilliger was remembering the day he joined the Marines. It seemed ages ago, but it had been less than a year. After high school he'd enrolled at Western Michigan University—it was a big baseball school, and he knew if he did okay there, it could mean a contract for him with a professional ball club.

He played shortstop and was pretty good for a kid who only weighed 130 pounds. But that first semester was tough. He ended up with an A, a B, and a C. But there was an F in there too, and he went to talk to Dr. Russell Siebert, his history professor, about his grades, hoping against hope that there was a way to sidestep the F and keep playing baseball.

"I'll have to give it up," he said. "Unless I can do something about this grade, they won't let me play baseball anymore."

"I'm sorry, son," Dr. Siebert said, "but that's just the way things are. There's nothing I can do."

Terwilliger was crestfallen, but he tried not to show it. "Hell, I'm going down to the Marine Corps," he said. "I think those blue and white Marine uniforms are real pretty. I'll see if they'll let me join up."

"Well," said Dr. Siebert, shrugging, "good luck in the Marines."

In lots of ways the Marines had been good luck. The train was crowded as they headed west for San Diego, and it was the first time he'd ever been out of the state of Michigan. He'd even enjoyed boot camp. He'd never shot a gun before, but he made "expert" as easy as pie. The DI was kind of an easygoing guy, and they got along fine. He was good at Morse code, so they assigned him to an amphibious tank. He still wasn't sure why.

Now the whole crew of the tank was huddled outside, with the tank itself a few yards away. Private First Class Billy

Schrader spotted something moving on top of the tank. "Hey, listen," he whispered. "A Jap's out there, messing around the tank." He raised his gun and fired. "I think I got him."

Several members of the crew crept out to check. The Jap was dead, with a bullet through the side of his head. He had a lot of ammo with him. He could've easily blown the tank to hell and back if Schrader hadn't seen him.

"THE SECOND LIEUTENANT that was in charge of us said we'd ended up on the wrong beach, and we had to move down," remembered Private First Class Bill L. Steel, a kid from Nashville with the 2nd Marines. "So he started moving us down this railroad track, with us hollering at him, 'Get us off! Get us off! It's too wide open out here!'

"The lieutenant said, 'Shut up! I know what I'm doing!' and just about then the shells started falling, and I got hit." A shell hit between his feet, and he went flying through the air. When he landed he was a little dazed, but he was still pretty mobile. He'd been wounded in the left ankle, left leg, and left hand, and he had sand and gravel in his nose, ears, and mouth. He got out of there and took cover under a tree, where he grabbed somebody's machine gun and started firing.

"When it was over there were forty-two of us in the platoon, and only nineteen of us were able to walk out," Steel said. "The second day on Saipan I was evacuated out to a Merchant Marine ship, where they dug the shrapnel out of me and put me back ashore. On the fifth day I was back in the front lines on the side of Mount Tapotchau."

ONE OF THE most intriguing stories about the early days of the invasion involved the tall, brick smokestack of a sugarcane refinery in Charan Kanoa. Although the American naval barrage had gutted the town, many Marines believed the smokestack had been purposely spared as a visual guide for the incoming Amtracks. The smokestack looked like it had been pierced a thousand times, but it still stood.

After a few days the Marines discovered that a Japanese hiding in the smokestack was directing artillery fire on US forces. As a forward observer, he had been looking down on them the whole time.

Marines in the vicinity experienced destructive damage from Japanese mortars for about two and a half days until someone discovered the spotter. The smokestack and the spotter were quickly destroyed.

FOR PRIVATES FIRST CLASS JACK GILBREATH and James V. Reed, both 4th Division Marines, the terrors of Saipan were almost a letdown, in a manner of speaking.

Gilbreath, from tiny Mercury, Texas, and Reed, from Pine River, Minnesota, had already experienced a heart-stopping tragedy before even leaving Pearl Harbor—a raging, runaway fire in which 163 sailors and Marines had died and 396 were injured.

By jumping into the water as flames and explosions rocked his LST (landing ship, tank), Gilbreath escaped with only a few minor burns, while dozens of others died a tragic death in one of the strangest and most bizarre disasters of the war. It happened in the West Loch area of Pearl Harbor, where twenty-nine LSTs were tied up, beam to beam, at six different piers.

It happened on a Sunday. Half of their rifle companies had liberty, while the other half stayed aboard the LST. Gilbreath was up on deck, reading a book, when he heard an explosion down below. He wondered what it was. When a second explosion occurred, he knew he had to get off the ship—something was terribly wrong. He threw down the book, ran to the side of the LST, and jumped off. Soon a Higgins boat picked him up.

"When the third explosion hit, the fire hadn't gotten back to the main wheelhouse, where it was stocked with anti-aircraft ammunition. But when it blew, the ship just folded up like a big horseshoe and sank," Gilbreath recalled. All the other LSTs were locked in at the same pier, and it was impossible for them to get away from the fire, which covered everything in a matter of minutes, so they burned up too, along with all the Marines' sea bags, rifles, and just about everything else.

Gilbreath was taken to a hospital and checked all over, but he had only a few superficial burns. "The Navy did everything they could," he said. "They pulled a lot of men out of the water, but many others drowned or were killed. Those who were rescued remained at Pearl Harbor for about a week, waiting for new LSTs from the States."

When Reed awakened in the early light of Sunday morning, it looked as though "the whole bloody world" was on fire aboard LST 143.

"I'd taken my shower and crawled into bed because I'd had liberty the night before," he recalled. "I hadn't been asleep very long, not more than about twenty minutes, and when I opened my eyes all I could see was flames in every direction."

Reed was sleeping in an upper berth, and he jumped onto the floor, which was about eight feet down, hitting his leg as he did. "I don't know what I hit, but my leg was so sore I could hardly move on it," he said, "but I jumped in the water and started swimming." He hadn't gone far when a large sailor pulled him out. Sometime later Reed could hear the sound of explosions, and an ambulance came and outfitted him with some clothes—all he had on was shorts—and took him down to the docks. His leg was black and blue by then, and he was all torn up. But at least he was alive.

A press blackout was enforced, and Navy personnel were ordered not to talk about the incident. The disaster was classified information until 1960. Even today it is still not well known.

As it turned out, the Japanese on Saipan had some surprises up their sleeves—surprises that even took Gilbreath's breath away.

Reed was still hobbling around from his LST injury when he got to Saipan, so his CO told him he didn't have to go in with the rest of the troops. In a few days, though, he went in anyway.

"One of the most miserable things I saw on Saipan was one night when the Japanese had some civilians out in front of them, and they drove the women and children right into our front lines," he said. "Naturally the Marines didn't know anything about this, and they started firing and—oh, my God—they killed most of those women and children. One of the poor guys, he had a Browning automatic rifle, and he was the one who'd done a lot of the killing. When he could see what had happened, he committed suicide.

"Then there was this little girl about four or five years old hiding in a cave," Reed said. The Saipan children were dying of dehydration, but they wouldn't touch the water unless one of the Marines tasted it first—the Japanese had told them that the Americans were going to kill them. "We had a big can that we poured the water out of, and this kid was reaching out with a cup she had when her mother came along. Just as the girl was holding out her cup, her mother jerked her away. I can still see the expression on that kid's face. It was a little thing, I guess, but it made me feel kind of sick. I knew how thirsty she was."

A Japanese officer was also found hiding inside the cave, and an interpreter started talking to him, trying to get him to come out. Instead, the officer started shooting, and one of the bullets hit Reed in the back of the neck. He was transported to the hospital ship, the USS *Solstice*, and survived.

IT WAS THE fourth or fifth day—Private First Class Ray Renfro wasn't sure. He couldn't remember the last time he had slept. "All I knew was that we went day and night with no sleep, and I lost count of the days," Renfro remembered. "We ran out of water too."

None of the Marines knew where the Japanese were, but the Japanese seemed to know exactly where they were. They were constantly shooting at the Marines from holes in the ground.

"We heard a shot, and the wind went right by my ear, and of course we all hit the dirt," he said. "The longer I lay there, the madder I got. I took the safety off that old BAR and jumped up and ran right up to that hole in the ground, firing that thing as I went, spraying bullets everywhere when I got up there. But damn, I'd run completely out of ammunition, and I had to move fast and get out of the way."

Renfro got behind a tree to reload his BAR with twenty fresh rounds. Meanwhile a close friend of his, Private First Class Gerald Vandemere, ran up beside him.

"If you'll get a grenade ready," Renfro said, "I'll jump out and fire, and you pitch the grenade at 'em."

But something went wrong. As Vandemere jumped out and threw the grenade, the Japanese shot him right in the gut.

"He was my foxhole buddy, and he didn't make it," Renfro said. "I sat there and listened to him groan for a long time before he died." That wasn't the end of it. Two more Marines ran up to where Renfro was standing behind the tree, and the Japs shot them both in the head. They hit the ground and didn't move. Renfro never knew how the Japs missed him, but they did.

"Finally, they got a half-track up there with a 75-millimeter cannon," he said, "and he pulled up close and fired straight-on into that hole. That was the last we ever heard from those Japs."

WHEN PLATOON SERGEANT GEORGE GRAY began feeling homesick, sometimes he'd close his eyes and remember the time when he and his whole 4th Marine Division company were making a name for themselves on the silver screen. They'd been training at Oceanside, California, when a movie crew descended upon them and started filming *Guadalcanal Diary*, based on the best-selling book by Richard Tregaskis. Gray's whole company was invited to participate.

"We spent the better part of six weeks surrounded by movie stars," remembered Gray, a young man from Arkansas who was an Amtrack driver. The actors were playing the roles of Marines carrying out the landing at Guadalcanal, but it got scary when they started using live ammunition in some of the scenes.

"Part of the time they were using sharpshooters," said Gray. "If they wanted to really emphasize a scene, those sharpshooters would fire from up above. They'd start kicking up the sand pretty close to you. They were really good at what they did. We had a lot of fun, and nobody got hurt."

William Bendix, Preston Foster, Lloyd Nolan, and Anthony Quinn were among the stars. But the six weeks passed all too quickly. Then it was back to the real-life 4th Amphibian Tractor Battalion, and Gray and the other Marines went straight into action.

"There was one driver—that was me—and two crewmen," Gray said. "The LST had three machine guns, one .50-caliber and two .30s, and they got a real workout. Our first stop was Roi-Namur in the Marshall Islands, then we went to Kwajalein Atoll. We landed with the assault troops, and this time the bullets were for real. I carried a .45 and one of those small M-1 carbines. Our standard payload was twenty fully equipped Marines. If the Marines needed ammunition, we brought it in, and it was the real stuff.

"We took a platoon of Marines down about forty miles and checked out all the islands there," Gray recalled. "We'd move from island to island, checking to see if there were any Japanese on it. If there were, we'd let 'em have it. We were in and around Kwajalein for about fifteen days. Then we went back to Maui, Hawaii, and got new supplies, and then we were off again."

This time the target was Saipan. "My God, it was terrible," Gray remembered. "There were lots of casualties, lots of losses, and the beach got so cluttered with tractors and boats in just a little while that there was hardly anyplace to land. We captured a Japanese major who said they never expected us to even get ashore. And if it hadn't been for the tractors, he would've been right."

He made four landings that day, and every time it was just artillery and mortars—"just like rain coming in," Gray remembered. "And when we got enough people ashore, we started hauling supplies in and taking wounded Marines out to the hospital ships.

"When the beach was cleared, we buried close to twelve thousand bodies ourselves, and those caves they were sealing up, there's no telling how many bodies they held."

The landing on Saipan had been a costly one on both sides. But there would be many more dead bodies to come.

chapter 4

★ ★ ★

Enter the 27th Division

TO CAPTAIN EDMUND G. LOVE, who would go on to spend a large portion of his life writing about the exploits of his unit, the Army's 27th Infantry Division became his life and the center of his universe. His comrades in arms took the places of his family. He talked with hundreds of infantrymen. In many cases he watched them suffer and die. And when he asked them what it all meant, most of them talked of one vast overwhelming desire—not to let their comrades down.

"There seemed to me to be no more compelling force than this one thing," Love wrote. "Comradeship."

THE 27TH INFANTRY DIVISION was a National Guard unit from the "Apple Knocker" country of upstate New York when it was called into federal service by President Franklin Roosevelt in October 1940. A lot of the men were soldiers with Italian, Irish, Jewish, Polish, and Russian names. Many were the sons of European immigrants. They came from Troy, Amsterdam, Saratoga Springs, Cohoes, Cobleskill, Cooperstown, New Baltimore, and Lake George. But they all got along just fine.

"It was like a family gathering. Everyone was congenial—we had a lot of fun," said Sergeant Nicholas Grinaldo of C Company, 105th Infantry Regiment. "We drilled about once a month, then we went to camp. We did maneuvers in the field. The night before we left, one of the guys went to a 'house of ill repute' in Troy. He picked up a dose of crabs, and he spread it through the whole First Battalion because we shared latrines. But they were all good guys."

By the end of its wartime tour of duty almost five years later, it had lost much of its local character. Men from every state in the union ended up serving in its ranks.

On 15 October 1940, the entire division was put on a train to Fort McClellan in the Deep South state of Alabama. There were high points along the way, like the time General George C. Marshall, chief of staff of the US Army, put in an appearance at Fort McClellan to conduct an inspection tour of the 27th Division. But there were plenty of "downers" sandwiched in between.

"We marched through the streets of Aniston, Alabama, to go to Fort McClellan, and they were up on the rooftops and out of the windows throwing bricks at us," Grinaldo remembered. "They yelled, 'Yankee, go home!' When we first got there we slept in pup tents. They had no quarters for us. We were killing rattlesnakes and copperheads, and a bunch of the guys got bitten by them."

AFTER QUITTING SCHOOL in the eighth grade and finding little work to do, Private First Class Frank Pusatere joined the 27th Division and became a member of D Company of the 105th Regiment. "When I heard someone say what a beautiful place Alabama was, I was all for it," he remembered. "But when I was done with it, one word more or less described it for me: lousy!

"It started out by wallowing through Tennessee's red clay," he said, "and ended up in the loblolly of Louisiana, which was infinitely worse."

The southerners were awfully stiff with the boys from up north in the beginning, but the men from the 27th would've taken anything their southern counterparts could give and been happy about it if they'd known what the Japs had in store for them.

WE WENT TO ALABAMA, and they were still fighting the Civil War there," recalled Lieutenant Joseph Meighan, who was in charge of a mortar platoon of M Company, 3rd Battalion, 105th Infantry Regiment. "There was a 'Mister B' on the radio. He had a drawl as thick as syrup, and he did not like these 'Damnyankees' from up north. When we had leave there was a little city in Georgia called Mineral Wells, and all the fellows who were looking for action got it, but then they gave it a nickname: 'Venereal Wells.'

"Maneuvers were like going hunting for two or three days. That's all it was," said Meighan. "You had a blue team and a red team, and you're trying to eliminate the other guys. We weren't allowed to go into the cities. You were told not to make friends with the families. The funny thing is, every time we'd go on a drill or a twenty-mile hike, there was a farmhouse and a beautiful girl, built like Venus, and every time a group would march by, she had a well and was pumping water and showing her ass, and we called her Venus at the Pump. And we were told by our leaders to 'Look straight ahead! Eyes left!'"

SAMUEL DINOVA DROPPED out of school in Troy after the eighth grade, and when he was unable to find a job he joined a Civilian Conservation Corps camp to keep body and soul together.

"I just didn't think there was going to be any war," Dinova recalled, "but a lot of my friends were joining the Army for a year, and I decided I'd give it a try, so I enlisted. It paid $18 a month, which was a good bit of money, so I joined up and went with the National Guard guys down to Alabama. We were the Blue Army, and we fought the Red Army, which was made up of guys in the 36th Infantry Division from Texas.

"We'd fight all week and then get a pass to go into Greenville, Mississippi, or someplace like that. The maneuvers lasted till the end of September of '41, and then we went back to New York. My enlistment was up at that time, and I still didn't think there was gonna be any war.

"It was a Sunday afternoon, and I was coming out of the Lincoln Theatre in Troy when I heard that the Japs had bombed Pearl Harbor," Dinova said. "It wasn't long before I got a notice to report back to active duty. That's how I ended up with a Purple Heart and a Bronze Star."

"I only had one more week to go, and then I'd be a free man because my year in the 27th Division's 105th Regiment would officially be up," recalled Private First Class Robert Covell of Saratoga Springs. "I was just back from Fort McClellan, and oh, how I was looking forward to getting out of uniform and relaxing."

Then his sergeant came rushing in and told everybody that the Japs had just bombed Pearl Harbor. Covell shook his head and shrugged, "Well, I guess I won't be going home any time soon."

"I was right," Covell remembered. "We stayed for about a week in New York. Then we loaded up and shipped out to Hawaii—and the next time we moved you could hear the bullets hitting."

MOST MANEUVERS INVOLVED one factor—walking. "When we were the Blue Army against the Red Army, it seemed like all we did was walk," Nick Grinaldo recalled. "As far as tactics were concerned, I guess the upper brass knew what the hell they were doing, but to me it was nothing but walking all the time."

After Fort McClellan—and the bombing of Pearl Harbor—the 27th moved to northern Alabama to guard the Wilson Dam. They were there about two weeks, then they moved back to Fort McClellan. "We stayed there for three or four days," said Grinaldo, "then we boarded trains for Fort Ord, California, filled up with more replacements and got all new equipment. Then the next thing we knew, we were on board the HMS *Aquitania*, sister ship of the *Lusitania* [whose sinking by a German submarine pushed the US closer to war in 1915] and bound for Hawaii." The 27th became the first division to be declared "combat ready" and to leave the continental United

States for overseas. Before it returned, its soldiers would fight at Makin, Eniwetok, Saipan, Tinian, and Okinawa.

"You're not told a thing except to get aboard ship," Meigan recalled. "Then after few days at sea you were told your destination. They break out the maps, and you try to familiarize yourself with where you're going. While you're on the ship it seems like you'll never get there. The ships are zig-zagging, there is naval protection in the form of submarines, but for entertainment there's nothing to do but read. Like a fool, I got on the bow of the ship and watched the little flying fish playing in the bow wake, jumping out of the water. At night you could sleep on deck for the fresh air—most everyone did. I lost my foot locker at sea when the rope line between ships broke—all my stuff went to the bottom. I think later on I got a check for fifty bucks."

Along the way Grinaldo was promoted from corporal to buck sergeant, then from buck sergeant to staff sergeant. "Finally I made platoon guide," he said. "I was second in command of the platoon if something happened to the platoon leader."

Grinaldo was temporarily assigned to the 165th Regimental Combat Team that hit Makin and Eniwetok, and he learned a lot: "Rule number one: don't touch anything you don't have to because of booby traps, and don't get foolish and try to win the war by yourself because you can't do it. It's got to be a group effort."

After that, they returned to Hawaii, but there was no time to rest. "Get ready to move out," they were told when the time came. A few days later they were headed to Saipan.

PRIVATE JOHN EARLY of the 27th Division's 165th Infantry Regiment remembers listening to the ship's public address system off the coast of Saipan in the early morning of 16 June to stay informed about the Marines' progress. Everything looked good at first.

"They kept telling us that all was well, and nobody expected us to land," Early recalled. "Then all hell broke loose, horns blasting, and the soldiers were ordered to their landing stations. The result was mass confusion."

A rumor spread like wildfire as Early climbed down to his assault boat. It said that the Marines were being pushed back and might lose the beachhead, that they were being hit hard from the rear. But instead of heading toward the beaches, the boats started circling and circling again and again—and it went on for hours. "I don't believe any of us thought we could survive this night," Early said. "Everyone was exhausted long before we hit the beach."

The arrival of the 27th Division on Saipan was definitely not a study in close-order drill. By the time most of the men were loaded onto boats, it was already totally dark. The first troops to reach the beach were from the 2nd Battalion of the 165th Infantry Regiment. They arrived in a hopelessly separated and uncoordinated mass of boats that landed all the way from the Green Beaches on the north to the Yellow Beaches on the south—instead of the Blue Beaches where they should have been.

In most cases the coxswains, finally tired of circling aimlessly, drove their boats up to the reef and ordered the troops into the water—even though it was neck deep in some places.

Scores of dead Marines lay on the beach in the half-light of the flares and exploding shells. Early and a close friend, Private Arthur Conlon, jumped into a large shell hole, and both fell asleep from exhaustion. They woke up shortly after daylight to find that two dead Marines were occupying the hole with them.

PRIVATE CLIFFORD HOWE of Havre, Montana, expected to move toward Saipan immediately. But he and the rest of C Company, 1st Battalion of the 165th Infantry Regiment ended up circling endlessly for several hours. Their Amtrack finally headed for the beach at about 0400 on 17 June. As he neared the battle zone Howe was struck by a grim realization: he was at the very front on the boat. He was afraid he'd be the first casualty when the ramp dropped.

But Howe was fortunate. He moved through the shallow surf until he could fall into the wet sand, then he advanced on his stomach. Howe served as a radio operator for Captain Paul Ryan, who was not so lucky. That afternoon he was killed by a mortar that struck a rock next to him.

SERGEANT EDWIN LUCK lucked out on the first assignment he was given as a leader of the 1st Squad, 1st Platoon of G Company of the 105th Infantry Regiment. "There was no opposition to our landing," he remembers, "but we got all hung up on the reefs, and we couldn't go anyplace. We had to transfer into amphibious tractors. We landed at Charan Kanoa. Then it got really bad. We suffered a lot of casualties. One of our own cruisers moved in and mistakenly wiped out one of our battalion headquarters."

That was their first taste of combat.

The "mortars" Luck and the men of the 27th used in training weren't actual mortars—they were pieces of wood painted olive green, so they had to pretend a little. "I think there was one actual mortar in the whole regiment," he said. The mortar squads were familiar with the sight mechanism and all the gears that went with a mortar, but they had zero experience with the actual weapon.

The Japanese foes that Luck and the other members of the 27th Division fought were superb fighters. They were very skilled soldiers and were first-rate at fighting you to a standstill. "We found this out in the middle of a sugar cane field," Luck said, "with Japs lying in there hidden under the sugar cane. None of us could see them, but they had no trouble at all seeing us."

CAPTAIN WILLIAM CORCORAN joined the 27th Division when he was barely fifteen years old, quite possibly becoming its youngest-ever member. It was in the depths of the Depression in 1933, and he was fairly tall, so they let him in.

What followed for young Corcoran was probably the quickest round of promotions that any fifteen-year-old has ever seen—first to private first class, then to corporal, then to first sergeant—and he was still only sixteen years old. They had him train all the recruits that came in—maybe because he was nearer their age.

By the time the war started Corcoran was a lieutenant. When Pearl Harbor was bombed they sent him off to artillery school, and he emerged as a twenty-six-year-old captain. And before going to Makin Island as his first assignment they gave him a job as operations officer for the 24th Corps.

"We cleaned up Makin in three days, and they wrote me up for a Bronze Star for devising a plan for landing my men," he recalled. "The funny thing about it was, I wasn't even mentioned in the admiral's statement. They sent the medal over, and I didn't even know about it in advance. But I'll tell you this: when we landed on Makin not a single shot was fired at us." Now he hoped they could do the same at Saipan.

THE FIRST APPLE KNOCKERS to reach the beach were from the 2nd Battalion of the 165th Infantry Regiment. These men waded onto dry land two full hours after they had left the rendezvous area. Lieutenant Colonel Joseph Hart immediately ordered a system of patrols out to find and assemble the various units of the regiment on Blue Beach. This was a task that took well over an hour, and even then the entire regiment was not found.

Company commanders searched until the wee hours of the morning, scrambling around in the darkness and gathering as many of their own men as they could find. At one point Captain Lawrence O'Brien of A Company of the 165th was challenged by a sentry who told him that a probable enemy counterlanding was expected on the beach, and no one had told him that the 165th was coming ashore. The fact that the sentry verbally challenged O'Brien before he opened fire prevented what would have amounted to an all-American slaughter.

Units of the 165th were ordered to move to the far right side—the southern side of the Marine lines—and prepare to attack in the direction of the Aslito Airfield on the morning of 17 June. The scattered soldiers of the regiment made their way down the beach, hugging the waterline to avoid both enemy artillery and Marine patrols that might mistake them for Japanese.

Once they found the Blue Beaches—it took about five hours in the darkness, with the only light coming from artillery flashes—the movement of the 165th Infantry Regiment south from there was an unbelievably slow and tedious process. Colonel Hart was forced to halt his men every few yards, answer challenges, and identify his command. The men were confined to a narrow strip of sand along the water's edge to avoid contact with the units of Marines they continued to encounter. They were sometimes in the water, sometimes not.

The men later dubbed Colonel Hart "Jumping Joe" for the number of times he led them to sprawl flat on the ground and get back up again. The name would stick with him for the rest of his Pacific career.

One more serious challenge awaited the 165th Infantry Regiment. The troops, faced with crossing a thousand yards of open ground just as dawn was breaking, operated at double-time just as Japanese shelling began. The last soldier in the column, a man from B Company, was the only casualty. He was struck by fragments of the first shell to land in the area. It was almost full light of another day, 17 June.

WE WENT IN with the Marines to support them, and there was an awful lot of small arms fire," recalled Private First Class Donald Elliot, assistant driver of a tank in the Army's 708th Amphibious Tank Battalion and also the operator of a .30-caliber machine gun on the front of the tank. After spending a year at Camp Chaffee in the constant company of the 27th Division, Elliot had assumed it would be troops of the 27th he would be ushering ashore. As it turned out, it was the Marines who marched close behind the tanks, and the 27th followed in their wake when they came ashore. The men of the 27th soon found out that the amphibious tanks were definitely not up to par. One .30-caliber bullet in the right place would knock one out. The armor in the tank was next to no armor at all.

There were twenty-five tanks in the 708th Battalion, divided into five platoons with five member tanks each. But the Japanese had a wide variety of weapons to cope with them, including a 37-millimeter gun that no one in the battalion could locate. The Japanese were continuously moving it from place to place and putting new camouflage on it. They also had an old Swiss gun that knocked out four US tanks in quick succession—until a gunner finally spotted it and put a shot right into it.

The 27th Division was realigned by morning, and their first attack was scheduled for 1130 on the Aslito Airfield, near the southern end of the island. The American brass wanted very urgently to capture the airfield, which in coming months would allow them to have direct access by the new B-29 Superfortresses to the home islands of Japan.

A large part of the job was given to the 1st and 2nd Battalions of the 165th Regiment, and they pressed the attack that morning. Their goals were the airfield and nearby Nafutan Point, located just southeast of the airfield. The Japanese had about fifteen hundred troops infesting the ridges behind the airfield and another five hundred supporting them at Nafutan Point.

The first attack on the airfield was a complete washout. The Japanese artillery defending the airfield was not where it was supposed to be according to sketchy American intelligence. Instead of on a high ridge to the south, the heaviest weaponry was concentrated on Nafutan Point, an appendage of land jutting into the ocean near the airfield and separated from it by heavy undergrowth and coral outcroppings.

The generally accepted theory that the Japanese could see infantry movements in the island's vast sugarcane fields was seriously flawed, the 27th quickly learned. The Japanese troops were high enough on the upper ridges to look down and trace every movement in the cane fields, then lay down deadly, accurate fire on the 27th Infantry.

When the first assault failed, a second attack was to kick off at 1230 on 17 June after a brief round of US artillery fire. But it bogged down within a few minutes in the face of intense enemy fire. For two hours the US artillery bombarded the ridge from a distance, but the barrage did little damage to the Japanese defensive line.

The airfield itself was undefended, but on the reverse slope of a ridge above it the Japanese had built some pillboxes and other fortifications, and these fortifications were the key to the airfield. As long as the slope remained in Japanese hands, the airfield could not be safely captured or supplied—much less have US planes taking off from it.

The two unsuccessful attempts to take the high ground had been due largely to the failure of American artillery to damage the enemy holding it and also to the failure of US support fire to keep the Japanese underground long enough for infantry to reach them and destroy them. The solution was to call in the 249th Field Artillery to add to the amount of fire placed on the hill. The second was to move the cruiser USS *Louisville* up the Saipan Channel to the east, to a point where she could bring her guns to bear on the reverse slopes of the ridge. The use of a couple of tanks also helped.

The tide didn't turn until the morning of 18 June. With twice as many troops in line as on the previous day and with tanks laying down supporting fire in front of the troops, the enemy-held ridge was captured with very little actual fighting. The Japanese had pulled back to Nafutan Point, which would give the 27th Division pure hell for close to a week. The airfield itself, though, was a lost cause for the Japanese.

Shortly before 0900 large numbers of enemy soldiers were reported withdrawing from the battle area. The ridge that had caused so much trouble the day before was basically abandoned, opening the way for a remarkably easy capture of Aslito Airfield.

In addition to planting artillery on Nafutan Point, many of the Japanese troops leaving the airfield were withdrawing toward Mount Tapotchau, the highest point on the island, in the highly defensible mountainous terrain of central Saipan. With no hope of being relieved or resupplied, winning the battle had basically turned hopeless for the defenders. But the Japanese were determined to fight to the last man. Their leader, General Saito, organized his troops along a ridge where heavily armed soldiers could fire directly down on the Americans.

The nicknames given to various places in the area—Hell's Pocket, Purple Heart Ridge, and Death Valley—told of the brutal difficulties facing the Marines and the 27th Division in the tortuous terrain. The Americans gradually developed tactics for clearing the many caves in the volcanic landscape—using flamethrower teams supported by artillery and machine guns—but it was slow, grueling, dangerous work.

For the record, Colonel Gerard Kelley, commanding the 165th Infantry Regiment, attacked ahead of schedule on 18 June and captured Aslito Airfield almost without firing a shot, when two previous attacks by the 27th Division had gained nothing.

"We walked right across that field in a skirmish line, and not a damned shot was fired at us," said Sergeant Grinaldo. "We got to the other side, and we were told to dig in again because they figured a counterattack was coming, but it never developed."

Staff Sergeant Jack Lent of the 2nd Marines from Dallas was pretty sure that a bullet that grazed his head and left him unconscious was as close as he'd ever come to dying in battle. But he was wrong.

"I was sort of feeling sorry for the Japanese. I thought, 'God, they're going to wipe them out, the poor things!'" The Marines found out later that they probably didn't even kill one Jap with all that shelling.

Lent got ashore underneath a pier that reached out into the ocean. About half of the men got out of the boat and went under the pier, and about half of them stayed in the boat. Then the boat took a direct artillery hit and got blown apart. Everyone in the boat was killed.

It seemed to Lent that he spent eight or ten hours under that pier, all the while trying to get ashore but hopelessly pinned down by the constant machine gunfire. When he finally made it to the beach it was pitch-dark.

The next day he found his commanding officer, Colonel David Shoup, who told Lent, "We're getting awfully bad sniper fire coming at us. Get up on that pillbox and see if you can tell where that fire is coming from."

Lent and another man climbed up on the pillbox, where they spotted a Jap hiding in a coconut tree. They both fired at him, and he came down head first and hit the ground. Lent was elated and had begun looking around to see if he could spot another Japanese when a bullet ripped right through his helmet and knocked him out cold.

He woke up with Shoup pouring brandy down his throat. "That brought me around real quick," he said, "and I felt my head to see what was left up there, but all I could feel was a little cut on the top of my skull." A little blood was running out of the cut, so they took Lent over to sick bay and patched him up. When they were finished they handed him his helmet. He took a peek at the massive hole in it. The round would have torn his head off.

After he recovered, Lent was assigned to take over duties as an air observer at Aslito Airfield. When the plane he was aboard started to come in for a landing he looked out the window and yelled to the pilot. "Hey, you can't land down there!" he said, looking out. "My God, they're still fighting for the airstrip. You'll get us all killed!"

"But I've got to land," the pilot said. "I don't have enough fuel to fly around all day. We've got no choice. I've got to land."

The plane touched down, and when it did it was literally riddled with bullets that went through the wings and fuselage. Everybody inside jumped out on the tarmac and ran like hell. By some quirk of fate, a Marine in a Jeep appeared from somewhere and screeched to a halt. "You crazy people!" he said. "Why are you landing? Can't you see we haven't taken the airport yet?" Somehow the man driving the Jeep got out to the Marine Corps line without anybody getting shot. The next day Lent had to take up his duties as an air observer. He had to watch everybody, even if they were going up in a PBY (a light cargo plane with no armor). That was his duty—just flying over to spot where the enemy was and relaying it to the commanding officer.

But a funny thing happened as Lent was flying over the mountains: he spotted his old group, huddled up in an observation post. He recognized who they were and dropped a message down to them.

"I'll see you guys pretty soon," it read.

A couple of days later he found an old Japanese bicycle, got on it, and rode up the mountain to visit his buddies he hadn't seen in six or eight months. They had a good reunion, and as he was preparing to leave, somebody asked, "How in the world did you get up here?"

He said, "Well, I rode right up that main road on this bicycle."

"Holy shit," the soldier said. "But we haven't captured that road yet."

Lent had ridden through the Japanese lines on that bicycle, and now he had to go back that same way. "I think I went back about ninety miles an hour on that bike," he remembered.

When Lent got back to Hawaii, he put his helmet in a box and mailed it to his mother. In the meantime the War Department had sent her a telegram stating that Lent had been wounded in action, but she hadn't yet received it.

"She got that helmet first and thought I was dead," Lent said. "The *Dallas Morning News* came over and took pictures of the helmet with my mother holding it and crying. It was the saddest picture you ever saw. I called her as soon as I was able and told her I was fine. The first thing she wanted to know was how my head was."

ASLITO AIRFIELD WAS under the full control of American forces on 18 June, and within four days flights of seventy-four P-47 Thunderbolt fighters were providing support for US ground troops. The field was found to be in relatively good condition, and it contained the largest cache of airplane parts and damaged aircraft captured from the Japanese up to that time.

By the next day Seabees with bulldozers were working on the field to clear it. Also discovered and put to good use were an oxygen tank, a power plant, a million-gallon reservoir, and a number of shelters and warehouses with steel-reinforced concrete walls. Japanese troops had moved out in such haste that no demolition or destruction had been carried out.

Thanks to the Battle of the Philippine Sea and the downing of hundreds of Japanese planes (see Chapter 5), the P-47s had almost no enemy planes in the area to interfere with them. Meanwhile the 165th and elements of the 4th Marine Division had arrived at Magicienne Bay on the east coast of Saipan, isolating the southern part of the island.

Earlier, while two battalions of the 165th Infantry Regiment were contesting Japanese forces at Aslito Airfield and Nafutan Point, the 105th Regiment and the rest of the 165th, temporarily stranded by a shortage of Amtracks, reached land without incident. Many, however, had to wade ashore in chest-deep water to reach the town of Charan Kanoa—or what was left of it. There was nothing but twisted wreckage everywhere—and plenty of dead Japanese.

Nevertheless, General Holland Smith and his chief of staff, Brigadier General Graves B. "Bobby" Erskine, the youngest brigadier general in the Marine Corps, came ashore and established a headquarters at Charan Kanoa. For reasons best known to him, Holland Smith never visited the front lines; instead, he received his information from Erskine—though for a period of approximately two weeks Erskine also avoided the front lines.

As Holland Smith put it, "He was a brilliant staff officer. His office buzzed with activity and his only regret was that he could not get away more frequently to visit the front. For nearly two weeks, his personal knowledge of Saipan was limited to the area immediately adjacent to our quarters. Duty tied him to his desk."

Erskine did supposedly remain in constant contact with officers in the 2nd and 4th Marines, and he met with Holland Smith two or three times a day to discuss the current situation and make plans for the following day.

Just how much—if any—of Erskine's long-distance communications problem affected Holland Smith's advanced planning is still unknown today.

EARLY IN THE afternoon of 18 June the 1st Battalion of the 105th Regiment, commanded by Lieutenant Colonel William O'Brien, got its first taste of action in the fight for Saipan. O'Brien, forty-five, had joined the 27th Division in 1918 during World War I, and he'd been with the division ever since. Before the Battle of Saipan was over, O'Brien and two other members of the regiment would be caught up in some of the fiercest fighting of the war, and all three of them would receive the Medal of Honor.

"O'Brien was like a banty rooster," remembered Lieutenant Joe Meighan. "He was the kind of guy who would go out and do it himself before he'd tell you to do it."

On 18 June O'Brien's inexperienced troops were given the job of fighting their way eastward across the island. At first they made rapid progress, but the next day they ran into serious problems. Concentrated in an area known as Ridge 300, the Japanese had dug several strong points and pillboxes into the hilly, rocky terrain. Several 1st Battalion soldiers, faced with constant fire, volunteered to infiltrate enemy lines to destroy those positions, but machine gunfire and grenades pushed them back.

Late in the afternoon Sergeant Thomas Baker borrowed a bazooka from a comrade. He walked out under heavy fire, knelt down, and fired his weapon into a dual-purpose gun position, knocking it out with his second round. Then he stood up and ran back to his company with machine gun bullets dancing around him all the way. His action ultimately enabled his company to take the ridge.

STAFF SERGEANT FLOYD MUMME was one of the few Texans—if not, in fact, the only one—to become a member of the 27th Infantry Division in the early days of World War II. Mumme graduated from high school in 1936 in Alfred, Texas, and he was happily driving a truck for a local lumber yard and working in the oil business when he learned that the Japanese had attacked Pearl Harbor.

He was out hunting that morning when he heard it on the car radio. At twenty-three he was single and knew there was little doubt he'd be called up quickly, but it happened the very next day—on 8 December—and he was sworn in on 9 December. Mumme could scarcely believe he was in the US Army Medical Corps.

"We didn't have any choice in those days. We were just numbers," he remembered. "They didn't pay any attention to your qualifications or anything. Later on I think they did, but we got up there that day and everything was so messed up. They came down and rounded us up like a bunch of billy goats!"

The recruits were sent to Camp Barkeley, a training camp about thirty miles south of Abilene, Texas. The training started with 3,100 men, and after six weeks they had a first shipment of 360 men ready to go. Mumme was the seventeenth man called. They were put on a train that had priority all the way to the West Coast. They were still planning to try to get a division of troops in to save the Philippines, but by the time he got there they'd changed their minds. That was supposed to be the role of the 27th Army Division, but they had backed off because the Japs had taken over too much of the Philippines by then.

When the recruits got to Hawaii they were trained briefly with rifles. "They claimed we were the only Medical Corps group that ever got that training," Mumme said. "Otherwise, we did stuff on bandages—how to splint things and how to clean a wound out, how to give shots and give first aid. And marching, oh yeah, there was a lot of marching."

A total of twenty-eight medics were attached to the Marine Corps for the trip to Saipan, each one from the 27th Division. When Saipan was over, they would return to the 27th—if any of them were still around.

In addition to the medics there were also six doctors. Mumme and the other medics were loaded down with medical equipment. Mumme had no rifle, but he had medical pouches hanging around his waist on both sides. He carried sterile bandages and plenty of an antibacterial they used for infection in those days.

Conditions on the beach had been considerably worse a few minutes before the medical team landed, but now the 2nd Marines had the Japanese backed up far enough that when the medics landed, they had to go around the 2nd Marines to get to the 4th Marines, which was where they were supposed to be.

Mumme found himself surrounded by wrecked boats, debris of all kinds, and casualties. "Far too many," he said. "We had an awful job of getting this one guy to stop bleeding. We did everything we could, and we thought we had saved him, and then he was hit by a damned stray bullet that finished him off just when we thought we had him stabilized."

Mumme was on hand when the first hospital ship sailed away. It was loaded to the brim, carrying more than six hundred patients. Shortly after that he and the other members of the medical team joined the engineers in constructing a new evacuation hospital on the island.

The toughest thing he ever did was help on an amputation in which both legs had to come off above the knees. "The doctors used us medics like nurses," he recalled. "I was there with forceps to pinch back the blood veins. Then they pulled all the way up your leg muscles and cut it where they could still pull something back over the bone."

Years later, when Mumme saw a man with two legs missing, he thought it might be the same guy: "They said he was a Marine and a World War II veteran, but I couldn't quite bring myself to go up to him and ask him about it."

MYRON BAZAR CAME to America from the Ukraine when he was barely five years old. His mother and father were divorced, and his father had custody of the boy. They settled in Amsterdam, New York, where Bazar graduated from high school in the spring of 1941.

At the time many male high school graduates, including some of Myron's best friends, were joining the Army National Guard, but Bazar was in love with the Navy. "I always wanted to join the Navy," he remembered. "I don't know exactly why. When President Roosevelt announced he was spending a billion dollars on the Navy, I was really enthused. I was only two blocks from the post office, where the Navy recruiting officer was stationed, when the announcement was made that the Navy would be under the draft system. I heard about it on my car radio. I went straight there and told him I wanted to join up."

Bazar and other recruits went to Albany and boarded a train going to Newport, Rhode Island, where they spent the next three months in training. But when it was completed he was told he would be going to Boston for more training.

"You're going to the Wentworth Institute, which is a technical school that's been taken over by the Navy to train engineers," an officer told him. "The best part is that you're going to stay at the Somerset Hotel, the best lodging in the Back Bay section of Boston."

The young Navy recruit found the Wentworth Institute amazing. "They took me to Boston, and this hotel was unbelievable," Bazar said. "They kept the same staff, used the same kitchen, the same chef, the same waiters, the same food they served the civilians. The program was four months long, and I was relieved of all duties except studying. I had weekends off, and I brought my car—a 1941 Plymouth—up from Amsterdam and spent the evenings cruising around Boston."

Along with all this, he found time to study the engineering of pumps, turbines, steering mechanisms, refrigeration, and other technical aspects aboard ships. When it came time to graduate with a rank of petty officer, his commanding officer called him in and said, "You're a lucky guy. Washington's decided to send you to Syracuse for additional training."

"In what?" Bazar asked.

"The Carrier Corporation has a small school there where they teach refrigeration and air conditioning, and you've been selected to go there." Bazar laughed as he remembered it. "You'll get an allowance, and you can live anyplace you want. You'll have to be at work at eight o'clock in the morning, and you're out at four or five o'clock in the afternoon. You're on your own."

Bazar studied at Carrier with ten other Navy students, all of them learning air conditioning and refrigeration. After about five weeks he took a train to San Francisco, where a new fleet oil tanker was under construction. He was assigned to handle all the air conditioning for officers' quarters.

Before leaving, Petty Officer Bazar sold his two-year-old 1941 Plymouth for $1,100—he'd only paid $700 for it brand new. During the train ride along the way he discovered another America.

"The train would stop in these small towns out in the Midwest, wherever a water tower was located," he said, "and the women from these towns would come down to the train with food and clothing and everything they could possibly give you that you might need. They'd give you sweaters and socks and sandwiches. They were too remote from the big cities to do anything in the factories, but what they could do is give whatever they could to the troops."

In San Francisco the ship was being built in a new Kaiser shipbuilding plant, and Bazar was told it would take four months to complete. "There's only seven Navy men aboard," he was told. "You're one of the seven. All the rest are civilian workers. Your job is going to be to walk around and make sure everybody's working and nobody's sleeping. You'll be given a sizable allowance for food and clothing. Good luck."

By this time Bazar was getting used to being spoiled. "They gave me an armband that said SP for 'shore patrol.' For four months I couldn't find a person who was sloughing off or sleeping or doing anything wrong. Everybody was so patriotic. It was unbelievable.

"At that time Americans' feelings weren't so much against Hitler as they were against Tojo because of what he'd done at Pearl Harbor," he said. "Americans had the feeling that, 'We're gonna get those Japs if it's the last thing we do!' Even when we got involved in the war in Europe, it was never Hitler. It was, 'Let the Europeans take care of Hitler. We'll take care of Tojo!'"

After four months the ship was ready to go. "There were two fleets, the Third Fleet and the Seventh Fleet. We were with the Third Fleet—all the new stuff, battleships like the *New Jersey* and *Wisconsin,* and all the new carriers. We stayed with the fleet. We went everywhere with them, slightly in back. Our first trip was to the Aleutians," Bazar said. "They needed the fuel for airplanes and oil for the ships. So we went up to the Aleutians in the month of January. That was a disaster. We spent a month there. When all the ice froze on that ship, everything was frozen. We had to chip the ice off the walkways. We put ropes in walking areas, something to hang onto so you didn't slip."

He was gone for about two months, sometimes as much as three. He accumulated six separate battle stars for the invasions he was in. Hawaii was his next stop. He saw a bunch of old buddies from the 27th Division, guys from Troy and Albany. Then he found out what was coming up next:

The invasion of Saipan.

chapter 5

★ ★ ★

The Marianas Turkey Shoot

FEW IF any of the Marines and soldiers who captured Aslito Airfield had any idea that something happening several hundred miles across the ocean would have a resounding effect—not only on the outcome of the Battle of Saipan but on the entire Pacific War.

It was one of the greatest naval air battles of all time. It went into the history books as the Battle of the Philippine Sea, but it came to be known to those who fought it as the "Great Marianas Turkey Shoot."

There was a strong feeling among Japanese naval commanders that if they could force a meeting between Japan's First Mobile Fleet and the US Fifth Fleet's Task Force 58, they could not only save Saipan—at least for the time being—but also inflict heavy damage on the US Navy. They called the plan Operation A-Go.

The plan had some serious flaws. Vice-Admiral Jisaburo Ozawa, head of the First Mobile Fleet and considered by

Americans to be one of Japan's top naval commanders, thought he had more than 480 land-based planes in the southern Marianas. But many of these planes were only myths. They had been destroyed before Operation A-Go could be put into effect, although Japanese officers on the islands continued to insist they existed. Not only that, but these nonexistent planes were supposedly inflicting heavy damage on the Americans.

More experienced pilots and speedier, deadlier, more resilient aircraft were other factors in Americans' favor. The planes of early 1942 were a world apart from the planes of mid-1944. For example, in one of the first clashes of the day, on 19 June, thirty American fighter planes shot down thirty-five enemy aircraft. The only plane the United States lost was one Hellcat fighter. The Grumman Hellcat had quickly become the Navy's dominant fighter.

In addition to Rear Admiral Marc Mitscher's task force—fifteen carriers with nine hundred planes—US submarines provided another crucial advantage. On 13 June the American submarine USS *Redfin* spotted a major portion of the Japanese fleet—six carriers (out of a total of nine), four battleships, eight cruisers, and too many destroyers and other ships to count. They were all heading north at full speed. In preparation for a potential battle, Mitscher ordered Task Force 58 to refuel ahead of schedule. Meanwhile Admiral Chester Nimitz at Pearl Harbor increased submarine and aerial surveillance of the area near the Philippines. Two days later an American submarine reported the movement of the Japanese fleet in San Bernardino Strait in the Philippines. Slowly but surely a series of events were leading to a big showdown.

On 16 June Admiral Raymond A. Spruance, who commanded the Fifth Fleet, informed Admiral Richmond Kelly

Turner and General Holland Smith of the situation: "The Japs are coming after us," he told them. "They're out after big game . . . the attack on the Marianas is too great a challenge for the Japanese Navy to ignore."

An hour later Ozawa's first attack sent sixty-nine planes to attack Task Force 58. American radar picked up the planes, and Hellcats were in the air quickly. The results were devastating.

Lieutenant Alex Vracui dove on a flight of thirty enemy planes from two thousand feet above them and continued firing. Vracui was the Navy's ranking ace, with a dozen miniature Rising Suns stenciled on his Hellcat's fuselage. There were about to be six more.

"Scratch one Judy [Navy lingo for enemy aircraft]," he reported. A short time later he radioed, "Splash number six." He had shot down six enemy planes in a matter of just eight minutes.

When Ensign Wilber "Spider" Webb spotted a large patrol of Japanese planes over Guam, he quickly made contact with the carrier USS *Hornet* and told them, "I've got forty Japs surrounded and need help!" He shot down six of them before he veered away.

Ozawa sent a second wave of 110 planes around 0900 and ended up losing 79 of them. About an hour later he sent a third wave of 47 planes and lost 7. Finally, at 1130 he sent 82 planes more. He lost 73, many of which crashed as they tried to land at Guam's Orote Field for refueling.

Americans, of course, also had their own losses. On 13 June, even before the landing on Saipan, Lieutenant Commander Robert Isely, the commanding officer of VT-16, the torpedo squadron aboard the USS *Lexington,* was leading his squadron of Avengers in attacks on Aslito Airfield when he was hit by enemy anti-aircraft fire and crashed in flames. The airfield was subsequently renamed Isely Field in his honor.

Estimates of Japanese plane losses that first day vary. Mitscher, head of the Fast Carrier Task Force, counted 383 planes shot down. Other estimates placed the Japanese losses as high as 476.

More than that, the Japanese lost hundreds of experienced pilots. Even if the planes could be replaced, the experienced pilots could not. It was a devastating blow. In a day's time Japan had placed itself in a precarious position. Now it would always be short of planes, the men who flew them—and the mighty carriers that ferried them around.

Ozawa's flagship, the mighty *Taiho,* the largest carrier in the Japanese fleet, was hit by only one of the six torpedoes fired by the US submarine *Albacore.* Ozawa didn't know that gas fumes were accumulating below decks in the area where the US torpedo had damaged the hull of the carrier, and the *Taiho* continued to move with no apparent damage. More than eight hours later the Taiho exploded and went to the bottom of the sea with 1,650 crew members.

Another submarine, the USS *Cavalla,* with Commander Herman Kossler in charge, was shadowing Japanese ships when he spotted an almost unbelievable sight. At 1052 Kossler raised his periscope and found himself looking at a picture that was almost too good to be true: the carrier *Shokaku,* the pride of the Japanese carrier fleet, which had served continuously since the surprise attack on Pearl Harbor. It was so close that Kossler thought he could reach out and touch her.

He could see three more ships: two cruisers ahead on the port bow and a destroyer about a thousand yards on their starboard beam. He decided to concentrate on the carrier and take his chances with the destroyer. They fired a spread of six torpedoes, and by the time the last torpedo was leaving the tubes, they already had nosed down for a deep dive.

The Japanese destroyer hunted for the *Cavalla* for the better part of three hours, but the sub made a narrow escape. At least one of its torpedoes had found its target: at 1510 the *Shokaku* blew up in an enormous explosion and sank immediately.

WITH JAPAN'S OVERWHELMING defeat becoming obvious, Admiral Spruance, commanding the Fifth Fleet, decided to take the offensive. After conferring with Mitscher, he planned to launch an air attack on the late afternoon of 20 June. It was already midafternoon when Mitscher learned the exact location of Japan's First Mobile Fleet. Ozawa was sailing northwest, away from Task Force 58, but the US Navy command assumed it planned to return for another round on 21 July.

Mitscher's 216 planes from ten carriers were in the air by about 1830—in the amazing space of about ten minutes. "Give 'em hell, boys! Wish I were with you!" Mitscher told his pilots.

But by now the Japanese fleet was already further away than Mitscher had expected. For a few moments he toyed with the idea of calling back the planes, but after rechecking the charts he dumped the idea. After flying almost three hundred miles, the American pilots didn't reach the Japanese fleet until it was almost dusk. Their new position would suck up the last ounce of fuel and force most of the US planes to land at night. But with the sky brilliant with orange and red clouds, the Hellcats struck, and Ozawa launched his last eighty planes to protect his ships.

Lieutenant George Brown led one of the US attack squadrons, and as his TBF Avenger (designated TBF for aircraft manufactured by General Motors) dove toward the carrier *Hiyo,* he flew through a barrage of anti-aircraft fire. His friend, Lieutenant J. D. Walker, watched him descend through the smoke.

Brown's plane took the brunt of the Japanese fire. Shell after shell struck home, and suddenly it began to burn. Brown's two crewmen bailed out to escape the flames, but Brown flew straight toward the carrier. "Brownie pushed on," said Walker, "and pretty soon the flames went out, leaving his plane black and his recognition marks burned away. He reached the dropping point and released the torpedo straight and true."

Brown died in this action, waving a shattered arm to his friends as his plane wavered and plunged into the blackness below. While the Japanese concentrated their fire on Brown, another Avenger, flown by Lieutenant (junior grade) Warren Omark, dropped a torpedo that found its mark. The *Hiyo* spouted flames immediately, and fires broke out from one end of her to the other. She lit up the darkening sky like a giant torch, and then the explosions started, each of them sending columns of fire high into the night sky. The *Hiyo* went down by the bow with her propellers clearly visible, sticking up above the water.

Some of the USS *Hornet*'s fourteen planes attacked the carrier *Zuikaku,* Admiral Ozawa's flagship after the *Taito* was torpedoed, and damaged her so seriously that Ozawa thought for a time that he would have to abandon ship again. But as men were going over the side to escape, the fires were miraculously brought under control and the order to abandon ship was rescinded. The carriers *Chiyoda, Junyo,* and *Ryuho* were damaged but stayed afloat.

As US planes headed back to the carriers, the planes started to run out of fuel, and Admiral Mitscher made the decision to violate the Navy's "lights out" rule to guide the planes home.

The overwhelming danger was that a Japanese submarine might intrude into the picture and spoil everything, but Mitscher had no way of knowing this, and he took an awesome chance. But luck held for Mitscher that night, and no Japanese submarines appeared. Part of the reason for that was the excellent search job US destroyers and aircraft had already conducted in the area. At least two enemy submarines had been destroyed in this sector several days earlier, but Mitscher had no way of knowing whether other submarines might be nearby.

Mitscher's decision to hit the lights was a brave one, and the pilots and their crew remembered it well. In doing do, Mitscher, in his own words, was "facing the worst disaster in naval-aviation history."

As the planes approached, Rear Admiral Joseph "Jocko" Clark, the group commander of four carriers, turned on the deck lights and pointed searchlights into the sky to act as homing beacons. Mitscher ordered all the ships in Task Force 58 to do the same, turning on every light aboard. He also ordered star shells fired into the air and used vertical searchlight beams to guide the planes in. He spread the word that any plane could land on the closest available carrier. In all it was a decision that Clark later called "one of the war's supreme moments."

As one of the pilots, Lieutenant Commander Robert A. Winston, observed, "The effect on the pilots left behind was magnetic. They stood open-mouthed for the sheer audacity of asking the Japs to come and get us. Then a spontaneous cheer went up. To hell with the Japs around us. Our pilots were not to be expendable."

Despite the lights, many planes were ditched that night, and along with them, forty-nine crewmen lost their lives. As the darkness closed in around them, they flew through squall lines and heavy clouds, which made the enclosing darkness ever blacker. Many of the planes had lost their radios, and the circuits were jammed with pilots asking directions.

The returning planes were to be guided in by radio beams, and about a hundred miles out they began to pick the beams up. But knowing where an aircraft carrier was located and making it back to its deck were two entirely different matters. Darkness had settled in before eight o'clock, and the skies were overcast, which hampered the pilots even more.

Roughly halfway back to the carriers the first of the planes began to ditch. The first to go down were those that had suffered damage in the attack, particularly the ones that had lost a wing tank or had gas tanks punctured. An hour after dark the planes started arriving over the carriers—and then real confusion set in. Pilots unused to making night landings plowed their planes into the barriers and fouled up the decks.

Pilots behind them received a wave-off from the signal officer. In desperation the waved-off pilots, seeing their gas gauges hovering near zero, had to find other carriers to take them aboard.

Of the dive bombers from the USS *Bunker Hill,* only one managed to land on a carrier at all. It was piloted by Lieutenant (junior grade) Kenneth Holmes, who landed on the USS *Cabot* at 2120 that night with twenty gallons of fuel left. Holmes's plane was the only one out of twelve *Bunker Hill* dive bombers to return undamaged from the raid.

The *Bunker Hill*'s torpedo bombers were a little luckier. Three of them managed to land on other carriers, although one landed on the *Enterprise* with a resounding bump. When the plane had stopped and the crew disembarked, a plane handler took a reading on the gas tank. It registered zero.

Fighters had far better luck than the heavier planes. The USS *Bataan* launched ten fighters for the strike. All but one returned safely and landed aboard their own carrier.

A pilot who was sent up in a night-flying Hellcat to help guide the planes in said the scene was like "a Hollywood premiere, Chinese New Year's and the Fourth of July, all rolled into one."

Much later Admiral Spruance would analyze the battle in these terms: "As a matter of tactics, I think that going after the Japanese and knocking their carriers out would have been much better and more satisfactory than waiting for them to attack us, but we were at the start of a very important and large amphibious operation, and we could not afford to gamble and place it in jeopardy."

When Mitscher tallied up reports from the carriers late that night, he found that Task Force 58 had lost 100 of 216 planes in the action. The overwhelming majority were lost on the trip home. Only 20 could be identified as shot down by enemy planes or gunfire from the ground. A total of 209 men had gone into the water by the end of the day, and only 101 had been rescued. A final total showed that all but 49 pilots and crewmen were recovered during the next day.

The Japanese lost three carriers—a third of their carrier force—and approximately four hundred airplanes and 445 crewmen. Ozawa was left with only about thirty-five of the one hundred planes that were available that afternoon. Worse yet, he was left with almost no experienced pilots.

Admiral Spruance steamed after the departing Japanese, but he found no crippled ships, despite a report from a plane shadowing the enemy force that some of Ozawa's ships were trailing oil, suggesting that some were badly damaged. He finally turned back toward Saipan when his armada was about 550 miles from the Philippines.

That evening, 21 June, Ozawa called his senior staff officer into his cabin and dictated a letter to Admiral Toyoda Soemu, the commander in chief of the combined fleet, offering his resignation. He expressed the deepest regret that he had lost this opportunity to lead Japan to victory—a defeat he ascribed to his own inadequacy and to the pilots' lack of training. The resulting loss of planes and pilots would haunt the Japanese for the duration of the war in the Pacific.

Admiral Soemu, after consulting with the navy minister in the Tojo Cabinet, refused to accept Ozawa's offer to resign, and on 22 June the remains of Ozawa's defeated and dispirited mobile fleet anchored at Nakagasuka Bay at Okinawa.

With Ozawa's ships out of range, Admiral Spruance ordered Task Force 58 to return to Saipan. The skill and intrepid courage of his aviators had made this day one of the all-time high points in the history of American arms. From this point on to the end of the war, US combat aircraft would never be outnumbered.

chapter 6

★ ★ ★

Smith vs. Smith

THE BIGGEST STORY, by any measure, to come out of the Battle for Saipan—at least where US newspapers and magazines were concerned—would be the controversial "showdown" between Marine General Holland M. "Howlin' Mad" Smith and Army General Ralph Smith.

It was a slow news day when the story first broke, a period of relative quiet on both the European and Asiatic fronts. The Normandy invasion was into its third week, with Allied armies hammering their way through the hedgerows of France. And the American forces in the Pacific were very much in the driver's seat against the Japanese on Saipan, where they were only a day away from declaring the island secure.

William Randolph Hearst's *San Francisco Examiner* unveiled the story on 8 July under front-page headlines that proclaimed, "Army General Relieved in Row over Marine Losses." The article, composed mainly of rumor and innuendo, alleged that Ralph Smith had "openly expressed" a negative opinion concerning battle tactics used by the Marines and strongly indicated an open disagreement between himself and Holland Smith—which was blatantly untrue. A later story in Hearst's

New York Journal-American said that Ralph Smith had accused Holland Smith of a "reckless and needless waste of American lives." This also was untrue.

As the story unwound, Ralph Smith was repeatedly accused of saying that the Marines were much too reckless with the lives of American servicemen—though he never actually said anything at all. The writers said it all for him. Up until the time he died in 1998, at age 104, he still remained mostly silent on the subject.

IN THE BEGINNING, more than two weeks earlier, only three men were involved in making the decision to remove Ralph Smith. They included Holland "Howlin' Mad" Smith, Vice Admiral Raymond A. Spruance, and Rear Admiral Richmond Kelly Turner. What the three of them did on that late afternoon of 24 June would impact many lives.

But as far as anyone knows, they never discussed one of the major problems facing American forces—the fact that both Army and Marine intelligence had vastly underestimated the number of Japanese committed to defending the southern end of Saipan.

An Army report had strongly suggested that no more than three to five hundred Japanese troops were in the area—actually, there may have been close to two thousand. And Holland Smith and his Marine staff were all but certain that the Japanese were on the brink of defeat at Nafutan Point. Holland Smith's orders of the day called for one Army battalion to "mop up" any remaining enemy detachments, a strong indication that it was to be a relatively minor job. The rest of the 27th Division was to turn north in support of the two Marine divisions.

From this point on, the 2nd Battalion of the 105th Infantry had the considerable task of clearing Nafutan Point—with a terrain that was mountainous and full of cliffs, crevices, and caves—on its own. Thinly spread across 2,500 yards, the Army troops at first made little progress.

Robert Sherrod, a correspondent for *Life* and *Time* magazines who would later become a central figure in the Smith vs. Smith episode, toured the area. He found the job at the southern end of the island extremely tough. The coral-rock formations provided natural caves, and one area of about fourteen hundred yards was laced with jagged rocks that largely favored the defenders.

The "mopping up" phase of the battle was, at best, still several days away—a fact that seemed lost on Holland Smith.

MEANWHILE, ON THE night of 20 June the Japanese were busy digging fortifications in the Nafutan Point area, and when the sun rose, the Americans were confronted with a new Japanese defensive position with a large number of machine guns and about a full company of fresh riflemen. As soon as it was light the Japanese opened fire, and several companies of the 165th suffered large losses. The US artillery responded, but it did little damage to the Japanese defenses. Combat continued throughout the day with little progress.

At one point US tanks inadvertently turned and began firing at their own men. Lieutenant Luke Hammond of the 1st Battalion, 105th Infantry Regiment, reported a dead corporal from A Company. He later learned the corporal was killed by American tanks because Lieutenant Colonel William O'Brien, commanding the 1st Battalion, had been unable to reach the tank crews by radio to warn them off.

O'Brien eventually stopped the tanks by running out through a hail of fire, crawling up on the turret of the lead tank, and banging on it with his pistol butt. The tank contacted the other two tanks by radio, and the firing stopped.

That afternoon Sergeant Thomas Baker volunteered to take up a position in his company's rear to defend it against pockets of Japanese resistance the Americans had bypassed. Twice he found and attacked a group of soldiers and killed all of them—a total of two officers and sixteen enlisted men.

WHEN HE RECEIVED Holland Smith's "mopping up" order, Ralph Smith knew immediately that one battalion of men was not nearly enough to clean out Nafutan Point. He contacted Holland Smith by phone, explained the situation, and was given permission to use two battalions. Several days later Holland Smith would criticize the order because it instructed the troops to "hold" rather than attack.

During the night of 21 June the Japanese again dug new positions on a cliff about thirty feet up the side of Mount Nafutan. The approach to the cliff was up a steep, unprotected slope. At dawn on 22 June, as the men of G Company, 2nd Battalion, 105th Infantry Regiment tried to make the ascent, the furious fire they met was almost indescribable. In the space of a few seconds six men were killed or mortally wounded and twenty-one others were less seriously wounded. The 105th fell back.

When Ralph Smith again consulted with Holland Smith, the Marine general blamed the lack of progress at Nafutan on the leadership ability of Colonel Leonard Bishop, commander of the 105th Infantry Regiment. "Colonel Bishop must not be permitted to delay," Holland Smith said. "If he can't do it, send somebody who can!"

Ralph Smith pointed to the difficult terrain and the Japanese positions interspersed in caves and gullies. But he promised constant pressure. He thought the Point could be cleared in a couple more days.

But in Holland Smith's mind that still didn't solve the problem of gaps left in the line between Ralph Smith's 27th Division troops and the Marines. His reference to "mopping up" the area made clear that he thought the 27th Division would have little difficulty in carrying out the order. Instead, part of the line pressed forward while part of it lagged behind as company commanders waited until they had closed their lines and established closer contact with each other. In those cases no movement came until noon or after.

Army thinking at the time dictated that if you gained a lot of ground during the day, soldiers were told to retreat at night and return to their foxholes. This was a practice the Marines hated. Another difference was the approach to warfare that each service took. Army ground forces stressed slow and steady operations with fewer frontal attacks. The Marines, by nature an assault force, emphasized immediate attacks on the enemy after landing.

"Yeah, we regrouped," Sergeant Nick Grinaldo recalled. "They put the Second Marines on the left going up toward Garapan, and the Fourth Marines were on the opposite side. The Marines had all the level ground. The 27th Division got stuck in the mountains fighting—they had to fight cave-to-cave, hand-to-hand a good part of the time."

The 27th had General Ralph Smith—"one hell of a good man," according to Grinaldo. "The major reason he was relieved was because the Marines said the 27th couldn't keep up with them. The Marines had the tank support down in the lowlands, which the 27th didn't have. The Marines also requisitioned half of the 27th's artillery—the 104th and 105th Field Artillery Battalions. There was no way the 27th could keep up with them under conditions like those."

The best weapons the 27th had left were 60-millimeter and 81-millimeter mortars, and half the time they couldn't use them because of the terrain. There were mountains, gulches, hillsides—all with caves dug into them. As hard as they tried, the 27th couldn't stay with the Marines. "You go past a cave that's so small you never even noticed the opening," said Grinaldo, "and the next thing you knew, you were getting shot at from behind."

Angered by the delay, Holland Smith personally called Colonel Bishop and, in effect, read him the riot act: "Colonel, this is General Smith. What's holding you up down there? Sure, the ground's rough, but it's rough all over this island. That's no excuse. How many Japs are in front of you? Well, if there aren't any Japs, how the hell could you be held up? Now listen, Colonel. I want you to push ahead with your battalion and clean up that damned place. If you don't, the Japs will break through and be all over the airfield. Now move out and take it. Do you understand?"

The confrontation between the two generals was about to explode.

ACTUALLY THE FEUD can likely be traced to a confrontation between the two Smiths seven months earlier on the little island of Makin in the Gilbert chain, where soft-spoken

Ralph Smith commanded the 165th Regimental Combat Team in its first action in November 1943.

He came ashore and set up his command post in a tent on the beach, and Holland Smith continued to harass him, for whatever reason. The two of them sat there together batting at mosquitoes while the irascible Holland Smith continued to criticize Ralph Smith. Suddenly there was a crackling of rifle fire, close in and on three sides, and a staff officer came running in, shouting, "Snipers! They've got us surrounded!'"

Instead of getting flustered, Ralph Smith picked up his phone and told his men to have a couple of rifle companies prepare to sweep toward the CP from either direction. Then he hung up the phone and went about his business. In the meantime Holland Smith picked up his carbine and stalked into the bush. After about five minutes he returned, rubbing his hands. "Well, I took care of those bastards," he said.

The sniping continued for about twenty minutes following Holland Smith's announcement that he had taken care of "those bastards." Then Holland Smith turned to Ralph Smith and said, "Get your troops going. There's not another God-damned Jap left on this island."

Ralph Smith's reply was simple and direct: "General, that plain isn't so."

One observer of this episode would take a very special interest in Holland Smith, who he found to be "clearly a bully, something of a sadist, and tactically a chowderhead." Later, in Hawaii, the account was passed to Major General Charles H. Corlett, commanding the 7th Division. The officer recounted what he had seen Holland Smith do at Makin and to air his conviction that Holland Smith was determined to make trouble for any Army general who came under him.

MEANWHILE ATTACKS BY the 27th over the next few days were termed "faint hearted" by Holland Smith when "the means were readily available for complete success if a determined assault had been made." The fact that he had not examined the terrain over which the 27th had to advance seemed to make little difference. Marine casualties, incidentally, had climbed to 6,165 in less than a week of fighting.

It was in this context of all-around poor performance—at least as it appeared to Holland Smith—that he sought the help of Army Major General Sanderford Jarman, who would soon replace Ralph Smith as temporary commander of the 27th Division. He asked Jarman to see Ralph Smith and "appeal to him," Holland Smith wrote, "as one Army man to another, on the grounds that the reputation of the Army was suffering through a lack of offensive spirit."

For whatever reasons it didn't work. On the morning of 24 June the 27th Division failed, once again, to hold up its end of the bargain. The result had been to slow down the pace of the 2nd and 4th Marine Divisions, operating on either side of the 27th, to a virtual standstill.

To Holland Smith these results had been the last straw. As he saw it, the 27th Division had done nothing but stall in its traces since it had arrived. In a scenario that called for speed and swift action, the 27th had consistently faltered and floundered. In his mind it had already contributed to the loss of hundreds of Marines to wounds and death—and the loss of hundreds more if it was allowed to continue. Something had to be done to stop the bleeding—immediately.

The atmosphere was tense that afternoon aboard the cruiser USS *Indianapolis*, flagship of Vice Admiral Spruance, commander of the US Fifth Fleet, where Holland Smith was joined by Rear Admiral Turner of the US Fifth Amphibious Force. They had come to see Spruance about a matter of utmost urgency.

The subject was Ralph Smith, who seemed to have an inevitable habit of lagging behind the Marine divisions engaging the enemy on either side of the 27th—and in Holland Smith's opinion, for no legitimate reason.

"Ralph Smith has shown that he lacks aggressive spirit," Holland Smith said, "and his division is slowing down our advance. He should be relieved."

There was nothing that awful, on the face of it, about being relieved and replaced in the midst of the greatest war in history. It happened to quite a few high-ranking officers in World War II and for a lot of different reasons. But a Marine general who removed an Army general was a bit of a different story. When General Jarman had talked to Ralph Smith beforehand about the gaps in the line, the Army commander had pledged to do better the next day. In fact, according to Holland Smith, Ralph Smith had said if he didn't do better, he would "deserve to be replaced."

"There was no improvement the next day," Holland Smith later claimed. "What had promised to be a swift, effective movement degenerated into a laggard action that almost came to a standstill. The two Marine flanks had to advance slowly to prevent the widening of the gaps between themselves and the 27th in the center."

After hearing the evidence presented by Holland Smith, Admiral Spruance glanced at Admiral Turner, and Turner nodded his agreement. "All right," said Spruance, "relieve him, then."

THAT EVENING THE following message was dispatched from Spruance as commander of the Fifth Fleet: "You are authorized and directed to relieve Major General Ralph Smith from command of the 27th Division. . . . This action is taken in order that the offensive on Saipan may proceed in accordance with the plans and orders of the Commander, Northern Troops and Landing Force."

By the end of the day Ralph Smith was no longer in command of the 27th. He was replaced by General Jarman, who immediately replaced Colonel Bishop with his own chief of staff, Colonel Geoffrey O'Connell, who ordered six batteries of artillery into the fight. This, coupled with a strong suggestion for more aggressive tactics, led to the clearing of Nafutan Point and Ridge 300.

The result was a controversy that lasted far beyond the twenty-four days of the battle of Saipan. It drove a stake into the heart of the 27th Division and soured relations between the Army and the Marine Corps so severely that some feared it might threaten the entire Pacific War effort.

The departure of Ralph Smith was scarcely noted at the time by the rank and file of the division. But on the day Holland Smith removed him as commander of the 27th, Ralph Smith did two remarkable things. He spent most of 24 June with his troops on the front lines, personally investigating the conditions his soldiers were facing—and narrowly escaping death a time or two. (This is something that "Howlin' Mad" Smith had never done; he sat in the secure surroundings of his Charan Kanoa headquarters and let Brigadier General Bobby Erskine go to the battlefield—whenever he could find the time.) And after Ralph Smith received word of his dismissal, he spent most of the afternoon and evening with his successor, General Jarman, explaining an imaginative plan he had formulated for breaking up the long-lasting stalemate in Death Valley.

His plan called for a flanking-encircling operation, with one battalion of the 106th Infantry Regiment remaining at the south end of the valley to hold the Japanese in place, while the other two battalions of the 106th moved east and then north to surround the enemy. The next day, as Ralph Smith was being flown back to Hawaii in the early hours of 25 June, General Jarman was eagerly following through with this plan of attack. And after the battle Jarman would change his mind about Ralph Smith's sacking. Initially agreeing with Holland Smith about the 27th's lack of aggressiveness, he would later state that Holland Smith was too prejudiced to be impartial.

THERE WAS ONE remaining bad apple in the bunch—Colonel Russell Ayers, commanding the 106th Infantry Regiment. Instead of following the route Ralph Smith and General Jarman had indicated, when his men came under fire, he allowed them to retreat to their point of departure at the start of the day, and the would-be offensive ended where it began. General Jarman had threatened earlier to relieve Ayers and ultimately did so on 26 June.

On 28 June a permanent replacement, Major General George Griner of Whiteburg, Georgia, succeeded Jarman. After some troop deployment, the 106th Infantry Regiment made the largest gain yet achieved by any regiment in the fight for Death Valley on 29 June. In the days that followed, the U-shaped gap that had so worried Holland Smith had been eliminated, the

106th had advanced a thousand yards, and by 30 June all three divisions were in a line and ready to complete the conquest of the island.

On 25 June Japanese General Saito sent a message to Tokyo delineating the harsh state of the Japanese defense:

> The fight on Saipan as things stand now is progressing one-sidedly, since along with the tremendous power of his barrages, the enemy holds control of sea and air. In daytime even the deployment of units is very difficult, and at night the enemy can make out our movements by using illumination shells. . . . Due to our serious lack of weapons and equipment, activity and control is hindered considerably. Moreover, we are menaced by brazenly low-flying planes, and the enemy blasts at us with fierce naval and artillery cross-fire. . . . The attack of the enemy proceeds ceaselessly, day and night, and as they advance with the aid of terrific bombardments it becomes apparent that the northern part of the island . . . cannot be held, with our skeleton strength of 20%.

In a week when General Saito was forced to move repeatedly to avoid contact with the Americans and any prospect of a Japanese victory was rapidly fading, he also sent his usual message to the troops: "Positions are to be defended to the bitter end!"

By this time the Japanese high command in Tokyo as well as their subordinates on Saipan were compelled to admit that the situation was critical. The island had been cut in two, and the southern part of it, including the main airfield, was for all practical purposes in American hands. In the face of unrelenting pressure from their attackers, the Japanese were withdrawing to a "line of security" that ran from a point just below Garapan to the south slopes of Mount Tapotchau and then to a point on Magicienne Bay.

With this situation as a backdrop, "Howlin' Mad" Smith soon became nationally known when newspaper and magazine articles quoted him as saying that the commanders of the 27th Infantry had made it "the worst division I've ever seen." He called the soldiers of the 27th "yellow" and "not aggressive." He said he hoped that the Marines passing through the lines of the 27th wouldn't touch off a fight by calling its members "yellow bastards" as they passed through. That actually happened, according to Lieutenant Claude Duval of the 4th Marines. In one attack, the 4th Marines were drawing artillery, mortar, and light arms fire from the left, and the Army had pulled back, leaving the left flank open. The high-ranking Marine officers wouldn't let their troops move over there because a "big to-do" was going on between the generals about the Army division. That area was in the Army division's zone of action, but the 27th had not kept up with the Marines.

"Finally an Army battalion had been forced to move up, and they came up behind us in our lines, and I was really embarrassed for them," Duval recalled. "The Marines cussed them out like nobody's business."

IT SEEMS HIGHLY DOUBTFUL that Ralph Smith's firing brought about any significant change—one way or the other—in the aggressiveness of the 27th Division. But there is absolutely no doubt that it triggered an interservice controversy of alarming proportions, one that seriously jeopardized relations at all levels among the Army, the Navy, and the Marine Corps in the Pacific.

The first signs of strain appeared naturally enough on Saipan itself, where soldiers and Marines still had to fight for the better part of two weeks to secure the island. Army officers were quick to resent the slur on their service implied by the removal of Ralph Smith, and by the end of the battle relationships between top Army officers and Holland Smith's staff had reached the breaking point. After replacing Ralph Smith, General Griner said he came away with the firm conviction that Holland Smith was "so prejudiced against the Army that he could never expect a fair and honest evaluation." A military board was appointed to study the case. Its ruling found that the removal of General Ralph Smith "was not justified by the facts."

A 1986 book on the subject entitled *"Howlin' Mad" Smith vs. the Army* by Harry A. Gailey would sum it up this way: (1) relieving Ralph Smith was uncalled for, and the substitution of a new, untried commander to bring about a quicker victory on Saipan may even have lengthened the campaign; and (2) the slurs cast upon the officers and men of the 27th Division then and later by Holland Smith in his articles and books were totally "unwarranted and unconscionable."

To the men who knew Ralph Smith when the chips were down, like Grinaldo, the truth was simple and straightforward: "I remember that one incident, when our battalion hit Mount Tapotchau, and it became part of the headache between the two Smiths. 'Howlin' Mad' wanted us to attack that ridge, and Ralph Smith gave him a little bit of flak. 'How do you expect me to send those men to their death without any artillery support?' He said it because the Marines had confiscated all our artillery. Holland Smith said, 'You got 81-millimeter mortars,

60-millimeter mortars—use them.' That was one reason that Ralph was relieved—because he wouldn't go along just to get along."

In his book *Coral and Brass*, published four years after the battle of Saipan, Holland Smith had this to say: "Relieving Ralph Smith was one of the most disagreeable tasks I have ever been forced to perform. Personally, I always regarded Ralph Smith as a likeable and professionally knowledgeable man. However, there are times in battle when the responsibility of the commander to his country and to his troops requires hard measures. Smith's division was not fighting as it should, and its failure to perform was endangering American lives. As Napoleon has said, 'There are no bad regiments, only bad colonels.'"

IN THE MEANTIME the fighting continued.

By the evening of 27 June Nafutan Point and Ridge 300 at the southernmost part of Saipan were finally in US hands, but there was one more river to cross for the soldiers of the 27th Infantry Division and the Marines of the 2nd and 4th Marine Divisions. This river was a valley, and they called it Death Valley—for good reason.

This particular valley was actually a terrace-like depression on the eastern slope of the craggy mass that dominated most of central Saipan and culminated in the 1,564-foot peak of Mount Tapotchau. The floor of the valley was less than a thousand yards wide and dominated by the rugged slopes of Mount Tapotchau on the west and a series of tree-covered, high hills—the highest being about 150 feet—on the east that was dubbed Purple Heart Ridge. There was almost no cover in the flat valley except for a line of trees near the southern end and a few small groups of farm buildings here and there. A narrow road ran up most of the length of the valley.

The 8th and 29th Marines had been given the task of capturing Mount Tapotchau. On 21 and 22 June the Marines moved toward the mountain, hiking uphill through the steep valleys and across sharp coral ridges. On the afternoon of 23 June artillery fire suddenly hit the Marine battalions.

"The first salvo hit directly on Marine lines," remembered Sergeant John Orsock. "Whoever it was continued to pound the lines, and a lot of people were being killed by direct hits." Someone finally sent up a green flare, the signal for shells landing short on friendly troops, and the firing stopped. "It was so-called friendly fire," Orsock said, "but we never found out if it was Marine, Army, or Naval gunfire."

The Japanese held the high ground, from which they could watch and anticipate what moves the Americans were likely to make. The force comprised some of the island's best fighting men, though they had taken a beating in the first week of the invasion—and also some of its worst, at least as far as arms went. On its way to Saipan less than three weeks earlier one of the ships on which one regiment had been traveling had been torpedoed; 850 of its men had been lost, and almost all its weapons and equipment, and it too had suffered heavy losses since the assault. But the Japanese owned a valuable advantage: terrain. From their top-of-the-mountain vantage point their gunners could observe the entire road network for a distance of at least two miles. The hills and hillsides were pocked with small and large caves. The wooded area was rough, filled with boulders, and excellent for defensive operations. The Japanese had several light and heavy mortars and some 75-millimeter mountain guns, all well concealed.

Over the next few days US forces would make repeated efforts to advance through Death Valley, often with tanks attempting to hit the Japanese emplacements, but with little success as tank after tank was knocked out by enemy artillery. Intense fire forced any Marine or Army units to retreat south. At the end of the day on 25 June American forces had advanced just two hundred yards farther up the valley.

Meanwhile Marine units began assaults on Mount Tapotchau from that side. By 25 June elements of the 1st and 2nd Battalions had seized the peak, though the fighting was tough over every foot of terrain. Japanese counterattacks to regain their valued observation post were unsuccessful.

Following an artillery barrage on Japanese positions on Purple Heart Ridge, the 3rd Battalion, 106th Infantry Regiment, attacked at midmorning on 27 June, advancing through thick tufts of grass for most of the way, then through sugar cane fields, and onto a low ridgeline that intersected the valley. As soon as the men moved down into the valley they were subjected to a murderous crossfire, but they stubbornly held their position despite being low on water and ammunition. The 2nd Battalion of the 106th soon joined them, and the combined units gained significant ground against the enemy.

"Congratulations on a day's work well done," General Jarman, who was still in command, told the troops. "I have the utmost confidence in our continued success in a vigorous push against the remaining enemy. Keep up the good work."

But the next day, under General Griner, brought no advances. When trucks bearing food and ammunition arrived, more problems immediately developed. Company commanders sent patrols to try to recover the equipment, but a Japanese mortar barrage intervened, killing seven and wounding twenty-two from I and K Companies of the 106th, and two Japanese tanks showed up and opened fire on the 2nd and 3rd Battalions of the 106th, killing twelve and wounding sixty-one.

As soon as the 3rd Platoon moved into the valley the Japanese opened fire and pinned everyone down. When the Japs sent two tanks in, the 3rd Platoon quickly knocked out both of them, and the crews faced withering fire from the soldiers. Despite their success against the Japanese tanks, the platoon was cut off in the valley and trapped for over three hours, and most of the men were killed or wounded. "We were in an open bowl like sitting ducks," remembered Private John Munka. "Finally, everyone tried to get out of there, and they were cut down. Only four or five men of the original thirty-six were not casualties. We didn't have a prayer."

In total, twenty-two company commanders of the 165th and 106th Infantry Regiments were either killed or wounded in action. The wounded included Colonel Gerard Kelley, commander of the 165th Infantry Regiment, and Lieutenant Colonel John McDonough, head of the 2nd Battalion of the 165th. Major Gregory Brusseau of the 165th was fatally wounded, and Colonel Harold Mizony of the 106th Infantry Regiment was also killed in Death Valley.

On the morning of June 27 Lieutenant John Graves was sitting calmly in the battalion headquarters of his 4th Marines battery when a platoon-sized unit of Japanese troops suddenly stormed the outpost.

"I don't know to this day where they came from or what they were trying to do," Graves remembered. "They just kind of barged in, over a little hill, and there must have been forty or fifty of them. They may have been disoriented, but suddenly they were all over us."

A sentry shouted, "Identify yourselves, you bastards!" Then he raised his rifle and started firing. "The Japanese ran into an old, abandoned gun position halfway up the hill and started shooting downhill at us," Graves said. "It was touch and go for a while there. We had a machine gunner and some of us had rifles. If anything moved, we shot at it."

Finally the hill got quiet. Some of the Americans started moving forward, watching for any sign of movement by the Japanese. But Graves didn't see a single enemy soldier move until one threw a grenade right at him. It blew up about six or seven feet ahead of Graves and sprayed him all up and down his left side and blinded his left eye. Graves was trucked back to an Army tent hospital, where a doctor used a flashlight and a magnet to try to remove the pieces of the grenade.

"There was a crummy Japanese air raid going on with a couple of Betty bombers while all this was happening," he recalled. "And a doctor later on told me that they probably messed the eye up worse than it was, but they were doing their best, and it was definitely under adverse circumstances. When they'd done all they could, they put me in a little two-man tent with my head wrapped up, even over my good eye. And there was a kid Marine in the other bunk who was in awful shape. I was pretty sure he was dying. He said he was from Alabama, and he was just so glad I was a Marine and not a 'dogface Army man.'"

"Would you hold my hand?" the young Marine asked. Graves reached over blindly, and the pair clenched hands. He died a short time later.

PROGRESS THROUGH DEATH Valley remained slow but steady, and soon Marines had undertaken the tedious job of clearing out caves along both sides of the valley, often with flamethrower-demolition teams. The 1st and 2nd Battalions of the 106th Infantry Regiment were now positioned in Death Valley, and the bone-weary 3rd Battalion was moved into reserve. By the next day, 28 June, only Hill Able, the final, northernmost promontory of Purple Heart Ridge, remained, and the 27th Division was ordered to attack it. But fierce enemy resistance kept the Army from making much headway, though pockets of Japanese forces in the central part of the island—chiefly to the north of Mount Tapotchau—were attacked anew, and US troops made impressive advances. By the end of the day soldiers of the 106th Regiment had gained close to a thousand yards in the largest one-day gain since the fight for Death Valley began. But Hill Able still remained Japanese property—soldiers who tried to scale the steep southern slope were gifted with hand grenades tossed down into their ranks. That night several Japanese planes attacked just after dusk and continued until midnight but failed to inflict any significant damage.

It was not until the next morning that the hill was taken. At 0715 one company of the 27th attacked from the east and one from the west. They encountered little opposition—the enemy forces had already begun to retreat north to consolidate and form another defensive line across the island that stretched east from the town of Tanapag. By 0940 the hill was secured.

The fight for Death Valley had lasted a week, and when it was over, the casualties were high—1,465 for the 27th Infantry, 1,016 for the 2nd Marine Division, and 1,506 for the 4th Marine Division. In all, almost 4,000 men.

Would the loss have been less severe if Ralph Smith had stayed aboard? No one can say for certain. But the events of the early morning of 6 July—although it was still a handful of days away—would go a long way toward refuting Holland Smith's accusations against the 27th Division.

AFTER SEVERAL DAYS of artillery bombardment Marines on the west coast began moving into the town of Garapan on the east coast. Most of the buildings had been reduced to rubble, and the 2nd Marine Division moved through the streets until, by the evening of 3 July, only four hundred yards of real estate ending at Mutcho Point were untaken. The next day that area was also in American hands. And with the Army in control of Death Valley and Purple Heart Ridge, the U-shaped gaps between the 27th Division and the Marines that had worried Holland Smith so intensely had been permanently closed. Now all three divisions were in a straight line and prepared—they believed—to complete the conquest of Saipan by moving north toward Marpi Point and its unfinished airfield.

"Howlin' Mad" sent a Fourth of July greeting to the American forces:

> The Commanding General takes pride on this Independence Day in sending his best wishes to the fighting men on Saipan. Your unflagging gallantry and devotion to duty have been worthy of the highest praise of our country. It is fitting that on this 4th of July you should be extremely proud of your achievements. Your fight is no less important than that waged by our forefathers who gave us the liberty and freedom that

> we have long enjoyed. Your deeds to maintain these principles will not be forgotten. To all hands a sincere well done. My confidence in your ability is unbounded.

The attack was scheduled to resume at noon on 5 July. The 4th Marine Division and the Army's 27th Infantry Division would pivot around the 2nd Marine Division, moving west across the island toward the coast near Garapan. Once this had been done, the 2nd Marine Division would be relieved to prepare for the upcoming invasion of Tinian.

While the 2nd Battalion of the Army's 105th Infantry Regiment was moving along the beach to check the supposedly abandoned Japanese positions, the Marines set up a CP atop Mount Tapotchau. When they received word that a group of civilians was coming toward them, they discovered they were Japanese soldiers dressed in civilian clothes. Some of the Japanese soldiers were a little careless with their sabers, and the Marines could tell immediately what was going on. The Japanese opened fire with a water-cooled machine gun, and the Marines used their M-1s until they cut them down, though not without some casualties.

"Gunnery Sergeant Gus Bloomenshine took a bullet right through the heart," remembered Corporal Barnes Whitehead. "He was one of the finest men I ever knew. And when another friend of mine got shot through the neck, I made a stupid move, and I got shot myself."

The Japanese bullet went through Whitehead's right shoulder, came out the back of his right arm, and shattered everything in its path. A few days later, when a doctor back in Hawaii looked at an X-ray of the arm in the hospital, he could only shake his head.

"Son," he said, "You'll never use this arm again."

"Get your damn ass out of here," Whitehead responded. "I'll show you what I can do."

The doctor frowned and shook his head again. "All right," he said. "You've got but one chance in hell. But I'll get you a rubber ball, and we'll see what happens."

At first Whitehead couldn't even move one of his fingers. But he started squeezing the rubber ball, and by the time he got to San Francisco he could move all of them a little. He still had a long way to go, but his arm was on its way to being fully healed.

PRIVATE FIRST CLASS RAYMOND RENFRO was as tired as he had ever been. He hadn't slept for more than a handful of minutes in over a week, and if he could have shut his eyes for a moment, he would have been sound asleep. He was half-listening to a conversation between two 4th Division Marines in his rifle platoon who were talking about who would get the other's watch if they didn't make it through the next few minutes. They were under attack, Ray knew that much, but it really didn't matter. Ray felt like screaming at them, but he wasn't sure he had the strength.

"I was utterly exhausted," he recalled. "I didn't know what to do, but I didn't really care." There he was, just sitting on a rock, when he heard a clicking noise—just like when you snap your fingers. The mine was about four or five feet to his left when it exploded.

The last thing Renfro remembered was going up in the air and somebody giving the order to retreat, so they withdrew to the top of the hill they were on. They left Renfro and two or three others lying there, thinking they were dead.

Ray didn't know for sure how long he lay unconscious there, but he slowly awakened. He couldn't see anything because his eyes wouldn't open. He had blood all over his face, but he finally managed to open his left eye. He started feeling around to where he was injured. He still had his arms and legs, and through the gravel and grit in his eye he could make out the men on his left. They looked dead. But there was another Marine on his right. He'd been hit hard, and his whole chest was just laid open. Ray started to talk to him.

"There's nobody here but us," he told the man. "Everybody else is dead." Ray knew from which direction they'd come, so with his help they started slowly up the hill. Eventually several Marines ran down and dragged them to safety.

Someone gave Ray a shot of morphine, and he began to examine where he was hurt. "I had a big piece of shrapnel in my left shin bone, three pieces in my left arm, and two in my left thigh," he said. "My eye still would barely focus from the rock and sand hitting my face. My BAR and helmet, they were all bent up. It looked like they'd been stomped on."

Ray lay there until they put the wounded in a Higgins boat and ferried them out to a hospital ship. "I heard one of the men say, 'Well, this one looks like he's dead.' I waved my hand to let 'em know I was still alive. I must have looked pretty scary. I hadn't shaved in a long time and I was bloody all over, but by God I was alive!"

And there were plenty of Japanese still alive, as the Americans were about to learn.

chapter 7

★ ★ ★

"Something's Coming!"

WHEN SERGEANT JOHN SIDUR of the 27th Division's 105th Infantry Regiment heard the screams of a small baby from somewhere in the back of the cave, he winced.

Lieutenant Colonel William O'Brien had warned him that many of the caves where Japanese soldiers were hiding might contain children, even young babies. "It's a sick job we have to do, John, but somebody's got to do it—and unfortunately it's you," O'Brien told him. He added pointedly that the Japanese soldiers in those caves with guns and explosives had to be eliminated—"no matter what happens."

The two Japanese interpreters who stood with Sidur at the cave's entrance—they had been brought to Saipan from the Hawaiian Islands—seemed to know exactly what they were doing. "You've got five minutes to come out of the cave," they yelled in Japanese. "If you don't come out in five minutes, we will blow the cave up, and everyone in it will die. If you come out, you will not be harmed in any way. You will be taken to a refugee shelter and be given food and water. No harm will be done to anyone. You have my word on that."

The interpreter paused for a moment to listen. At first there were no noises. Then they again heard the cries of a young baby, followed by a masculine voice that said something to the child that ended in a shout.

"No, no," a young man's voice said. A woman began to cry out and moan. Sidur could hear the children screaming.

Those outside the cave wanted desperately to get the children out of there alive, but there was nothing anyone could do unless they got cooperation from the inside, and Sidur knew that this was almost hopeless. The children started screaming even louder and the women were crying. Sidur turned away, shaking his head and feeling helpless.

My God, he thought, *this is the worst job I've ever had.* He wasn't sure how much of this he could stand, but it had to be done.

After a long silence the two Japanese from Hawaii tried one more time. "You have three minutes to come out and you will be cared for. No harm will come to you. You will be given food and water, a comfortable place to sleep. All you have to do is come out of the cave."

The seconds dragged by. By Sidur's watch, six minutes had passed.

"I'm giving you one more chance," the man said. "If you come out now, everything will be fine. Please come out. I beg of you!"

For a long instant there was only silence from the cave.

Finally there was the lonely sound of an infant crying. Then the interpreter signaled the Marines standing by, ready with the explosives. Then there was the thundering boom of satchel charges of TNT going off.

Sidur bit his lip and turned away.

LIEUTENANT ED BALE of Dallas watched the Japanese soldiers push women and children off the cliffs to their death. Bale had earned a Marine commission at Texas A&M and joined the 2nd Marine Division in New Zealand. He had endured the fight at Tarawa, but seeing what was happening on Saipan was somehow even worse.

The Japanese soldiers wouldn't let the civilians even approach American lines. They would throw them off the cliffs first. There were interpreters up there trying to talk the soldiers into surrendering, but the Japanese soldiers killed many of the women who wanted to come into the American positions.

"We were horrified by it, but after a while, I don't think we were surprised," Bale remembered. "I think that after we got over the initial shock, we simply knew there was no way to stop it." If the Marines attempted to stop the slaughter, they would have to kill innocent civilians themselves, and there had been enough civilians killed by Marines inadvertently as it was.

One dead woman, a native of the islands, was killed and left lying on her back at a road junction. No one bothered to move her for days. Instead, they used her as a guidepost for troops moving up the mountainside.

"When they were giving the truck drivers directions to bring supplies up, they'd say, 'Go up to where that dead woman is lying on her back, and then turn left or right,'" Bale said. "It was a horrible-looking sight, but after a while it just became a fact of life."

WHEN THE SUN ROSE on 5 July the Japanese were defeated in every sense of the word—and they knew it. The rapid and virtually uncontested advance by American troops strongly indicated the total collapse of General Saito's plans to establish a final defensive line across the entire northernmost neck of Saipan.

In fact, the 4th Marine Division had already overrun the entire left flank of this proposed line. Japan's 136th Infantry Regiment should have fought to contest this ground, but the remains of that unit were scattered and isolated in pockets—more than a few with children—behind the American lines. All that remained under Saito's control was in the 27th Division's area, and even there the defense was disorganized and confused. Japanese officers captured on that day told of their front-line units being mixed up and the communications badly disorganized. There was little or no organized resistance, no organized supply plan, and very little artillery, if any, remaining.

Three Army tanks appeared at midafternoon, led by Lieutenant Willis Dorsey of Newton, Kansas. They came upon some Japanese massed in a ditch, almost shoulder to shoulder, and opened fire using machine guns and canister, killing approximately 150 of the enemy. This allowed the 105th Infantry Regiment to resume its planned offensive in the area. Earlier Dorsey had performed a similar service for the 3rd Battalion when Japanese machine gunfire from a palm grove slowed them down.

Everywhere the Japanese forces turned they seemed to be facing imminent defeat. They were almost out of food and water. One Japanese report would tell of troops being without drinking water for three days, holding out by chewing the leaves of trees and eating snails.

What Japanese General Saito termed "the bitter end" was rapidly approaching for himself and an estimated seven thousand men still under his command.

LIEUTENANT JOHN GRAVES of the 4th Marines was having ongoing trouble with his injured left eye. They had carried him into a hospital on a stretcher. He was getting around, but he had to hobble a little because of problems with the eye. The hospital was on a hill overlooking Pearl Harbor, and the first thing he saw was a nurse he had dated in San Diego. Her nickname was Hobbie, and she somehow managed to find him a spot in the senior officer's ward.

Graves would be there for a month or so, and they still couldn't get the eye to function properly. It got infected, and they sent him to another hospital in Long Beach, where one of the two ophthalmologists on the staff wanted to take it out. By now he too simply wanted to get rid of the damn thing. But the other doctor had seniority, and the two doctors had a sort of rivalry going. So they kept him there and tried one thing then another, hoping something good would happen. And the eye finally "calmed down," although he still couldn't see more than a little daylight out of it.

At the Long Beach hospital he had a roommate who had been a rookie second lieutenant with the troops attacking Tarawa. This was where the Marine Corps learned that landing boats couldn't usually cope with coral reefs. The roommate's name was Warren, and he was assigned to bring forty or fifty men to shore in an LCVP (land craft, vehicle, personnel), better known as a Higgins boat. The landing was hotly contested, with Japanese machine gun and mortar fire everywhere.

Warren signaled the coxswain to lower the ramp, which the coxswain gladly did. Then Warren hollered, "Follow me!" and led the men out into about eight feet of water on the other side of the reef, with bullets coming in thick and fast. Warren was struck in the legs and paralyzed from the hips down, but he could tell that story—laughing like hell—and Graves would laugh with him.

WITH THE JAPANESE hovering on the ragged edge of defeat, Holland Smith had every reason to believe that the remaining enemy troops would stage a banzai attack of some sort as a grand finale. "With this thought hard in my mind," he would later write, "I had issued a special Corps order on 2 July, warning all units to take special precautions against nocturnal mass attacks and to button up their lines each night by physical contact."

He followed up by visiting the 27th Division's command post on the afternoon of 5 July and warning General Griner that a banzai attack would probably come down Tanapag Plain late that night or early the next morning. Holland Smith was very familiar with past banzai attacks against the Marines on Guadalcanal and especially on the Arctic island of Attu in 1943, when a defeated Japanese garrison stormed American lines. American losses were 580 troops killed and about a thousand wounded.

Even with Holland Smith's warning, there was no serious alert to what was coming. Staff officers at the 105th Infantry Regiment's command post believed that what enemy resistance remained would be minimal the next day.

All the information available indicated that the Japanese had been reduced to a small force incapable of withstanding an attack. Most of the men were led to believe that all that was left to do was a matter of two or three days of mopping up a not very formidable force. It was the first night they could remember on the island when there wasn't artillery fire all night long. Usually there were star bursts and star shells that would light up the landscape. But on this particular night, aside from the fact that it was raining and dark in the earlier part of the evening, there was no such support.

The night was highly uncomfortable for men on the front lines. Rain came down in torrents. Foxholes flooded, and sleep was next to impossible. Sidur lost his helmet when he was caught in the midst of a furious downpour while trying to hold onto his M-1.

Tucked away in the lining of the helmet was the only photo he had of the girl he intended to marry when he got home. The photo blew away in the gusty wind, and although Sidur tried his best to pick up his helmet, it rolled away and was lost.

When Colonel O'Brien and his radioman, Sergeant Ronald Johnson, finished digging their slit trenches that night, O'Brien took his wallet out of his pocket. He opened it and sat for a while looking at a picture inside it. Then he handed his wallet to Johnson and pointed to the picture.

"This is what I'm fighting for," O'Brien said.

Johnson looked in his wallet and saw a photo of O'Brien's wife and young son.

BY THE AFTERNOON of 5 July the Japanese on Saipan were in desperate shape. After three long weeks in which the American invaders had fought hard, suffered heavy casualties, and lost a lot of good men, they were now in a position to make full use of the Aslito Airfield and to pound the remaining Japanese with long-range artillery and naval gunfire until they surrendered or died.

The headquarters of General Saito, commander of all the remaining Japanese forces on the island, was located in a cave a thousand yards from the village of Makunsha. The gaunt general and his half-starved staff gathered to make what plans they could—there wasn't much left to save. Saito had been wounded by a piece of shrapnel, and he looked very old and disheartened. But he had a new plan, and he told them about it.

Before dawn the following morning, 6 July, the Japanese would stage one last glorious attack on the invaders and die proclaiming the everlasting life of their emperor. In a material sense there was nothing to be gained from the attack except death. The Americans were everywhere and had won the battle. All the Japanese could do now was attempt to extract seven lives for each of their own in a massive banzai attack against the "American devils."

If any American could have read the letter General Saito sent to all Japanese officers on Saipan on the morning of 5 July, they would have known in advance what to expect:

> I am addressing the officers and men of the Imperial Army on Saipan.
>
> For more than twenty days since the American Devils attacked, the officers, men and civilian employees of the Imperial Army and Navy on this island have fought well and bravely. Everywhere they have demonstrated the honor and glory of the Imperial forces. I expected that every man would do his duty.

> Heaven has not given us an opportunity. We have not been able to utilize fully the terrain. We have fought in unison up to the present time but now we have no materials with which to fight and our artillery for attack has been completely destroyed. Our comrades have fallen one after another. Despite the bitterness of defeat we pledge "seven lives to repay our country."
>
> The barbarous attack of the enemy is being continued. Even though the enemy has occupied only a corner of Saipan, we are dying without avail under the violent shelling and bombing. Whether we attack or whether we stay where we are, there is only death. However, in death there is life. We must utilize this opportunity to exalt true Japanese manhood. I will advance with those who remain to deliver still another blow to the American Devils and leave my bones on Saipan as a bulwark of the Pacific.
>
> As it says in the **Semjinkum** [a volume of Battle Ethics], "I will never suffer the disgrace of being taken alive" and "I will offer up the courage of my soul and calmly rejoice in living by the eternal principle."
>
> Here I pray for you for the eternal life of the Emperor and the welfare of the country and I advance to seek out the enemy.
>
> Follow me!

If those he commanded had literally followed the example of General Saito, there would have been no attack. The exhausted, wounded general, feeling that he was too aged and infirm to be of use in what he was asking for, held a farewell feast of saki and canned crabmeat and then committed suicide.

His guest for the occasion was Admiral Nagumo Chuichi, the architect of the 1941 attack on Pearl Harbor, who did likewise.

Cleaning off a spot on the rock, Saito sat down. Facing the misty east and saying "*Tenno Heika! Banzai!*" (Long live the Emperor!), he drew his own blood first with his sword. Then his adjutant shot him in the head with a pistol.

As General Saito and Admiral Nagumo conducted their own honorable deaths, Japanese soldiers, sailors, and some civilians gathered in the fields and woods north of the US lines near Makunska. By nightfall on 6 July able-bodied Japanese soldiers were converging on a set of rendezvous points. The troops had been told that anyone incapable of reaching the assembly points on his own would be shot or allowed to commit suicide.

About an hour after darkness fell on the early evening of 6 July an American soldier patrolling the road near the command post of the 3rd Battalion, 105th Infantry Regiment, discovered a lone, armed Japanese soldier lying asleep. When the American took the Japanese prisoner and sent him routinely back to headquarters for interrogation, his testimony was sufficient cause for alarm.

An all-out attack by all remaining Japanese forces on Saipan, the soldier said, had been ordered for early the next morning. This information was then conveyed to all major US units of the division as well as to Holland Smith's headquarters. The basic message was to prepare for the worst.

Over the next hour or more, mixed or muddled communications became commonplace. As soon as the word reached Colonel William O'Brien, commander of the 1st Battalion, 105th, and Major Edward McCarthy, commander of the 2nd Battalion, 105th, both attempted to reach a higher authority about

An artist's conception of the 27th Infantry Division smashing through Germany's—supposedly impregnable—Hindenberg Line in the fall of 1918. *(27th Division History)*

The 105th Regiment of the 27th Infantry Division on parade in 1941 shortly before leaving camp at Fort McClellan, Alabama. They were the first full US division to go overseas in World War II. *(27th Division History)*

John Sidur and a couple of buddies pose at their newly erected tent at Fort McClellan in the wilds of Alabama. *(27th Division History)*

John Sidur, a private first class at the time, poses for a picture in his "dress khakis." *(27th Division History)*

John Sidur shows off his collection of medals, including the Purple Heart he was awarded many years later. *(Courtesy of the New York State Military Museum)*

General George C. Marshall, US Army Chief of Staff, is greeted by members of the staff of the 27th Division at Fort McClellan, Alabama. Marshall congratulated the 27th for its splendid record in both war and peace. *(27th Division History)*

Alex Vracui, the Navy's ranking air ace, shot down six Japanese planes in the Marianas Turkey Shoot in a matter of eight minutes. *(US Navy)*

The biggest story to come out of Saipan—at least as far as the newspaper and magazine coverage was concerned—was the blowup that caused General Ralph Smith (left) of the US Army to lose his job as commander of the 27th Infantry Division. He was relieved of command by General Holland M. "Howlin' Mad" Smith (right) of the US Marine Corps. *(US Army and US Marine Corps)*

Major General George W. Griner, who assumed command of the 27th Infantry Division on June 28, 1944, after Major General Ralph Smith was relieved from duty. (*US Army*)

Taking cover behind the "King Kong," a medium tank, these Marines try to locate the source of automatic rifle fire cracking above them. *(US Marine Corps)*

Marines dig up a 123-pound bomb found in Garapan. Buried with noses protruding above ground, the bombs could be set off by almost any US vehicle. *(US Marine Corps)*

A bazooka-man and his assistant cautiously search for targets on the outskirts of the destroyed capital of Garapan. (*US Marine Corps*)

At Mount Tapotchau's peak men from the 1st Battalion, 29th Marines, prepare positions by building foxholes from the ground up rather than digging in. *(US Marine Corps)*

A ragged Marine sits on a sixteen-inch naval shell while returning several days' worth of topsoil to Saipan. *(US Marine Corps)*

Captain Frank Olander, commander of G Company, 105th Infantry: in a deadly game of "baseball" with live hand grenades, "We cut the Jap attack to ribbons, but we left many, many dead men on the field." (*27th Division History*)

Lieutenant Colonel William J. O'Brien, commander of the 1st Battalion, 105th Infantry, after slaughtering several dozen Japanese soldiers during the *gyokusai*, seized a machine gun and shouted in the face of the enemy, "Don't give them a damned inch!" until he was cut down by masses of enemy troops. When his body was found the next day he was surrounded by thirty dead Japanese soldiers. He was awarded the Medal of Honor. (*27th Division History*)

Captain Bernard A. Toft of the 249th Field Artillery Battalion picked up wounded future Medal of Honor recipient Sergeant Thomas Baker and carried him for a while until Toft himself was critically wounded. Later, when Toft realized he was dying, he asked Sergeant Robert Smith, also of the 249th Field Artillery, to stay with him until he died. "Please don't let the Japs take me alive," Toft said. "I've seen what they are capable of doing." Smith stayed with Toft until his death. (*27th Division History*)

Sergeant Thomas Baker, A Company, 105th Infantry, killed dozens of enemy soldiers over a period of several days but was grievously wounded in the process. Unable to move by himself, he asked for a freshly loaded .45-caliber pistol containing eight shots—and a lighted cigarette. Then, leaning against a tree trunk, he waited for the enemy. When his body was found, his pistol was laying empty beside him and eight Japanese soldiers lay dead at his feet. He was posthumously awarded the Medal of Honor. (*US Army*)

Private First Class Harold C. Angerholm made repeated trips through an area swept by heavy hostile fire in an ambulance-equipped Jeep to singlehandedly load and evacuate forty-five wounded men of the 3rd Battalion, 10th Marines. He was mortally wounded by an enemy rifleman and posthumously awarded the Medal of Honor. (*US Marine Corps*)

Sergeant Grant F. Timmerman, of the 2nd Marine Tank Battalion, blocked with his body a Japanese hand grenade that otherwise would have fallen through his tank's open turret, probably killing the other crewmen inside. In giving up his own life for his comrades, he was posthumously awarded the Medal of Honor. (*US Marine Corps*)

Marines look over piles of dead Japanese soldiers following the *gyokusai*. (*US Marine Corps*)

The ravaged remains of a sugar treatment plant at the town of Charan Kanoa. (*US Marine Corps*)

A battle-weary Marine leads a Saipan family toward a temporary home. The defeated Japanese army killed thousands of civilians. *(US Marine Corps)*

Hundreds of Saipan civilians committed suicide by flinging themselves—and their children—down these jagged coastal rocks. (*US Marine Corps*)

Although Tinian was highly valuable to the United States for its flat terrain, not all of the island's terrain was easy going. (*National Archives*)

The open terrain of central Tinian permitted a rapid advance by the 4th and 2nd Marine Divisions. In four days the Americans had pushed their lines ahead by as much as ten thousand yards. As General Cates expressed it, the Marines were "heading for the barn." (*US Marine Corps*)

The USS *Colorado* took heavy damage and casualties during the support phase of a mock attack during the Tinian invasion. (*US Naval Institute*)

Ushi Point Airfield in the northern portion of Tinian, which was expanded with lightning speed by hundreds of US Seabees, would play a major role in the American A-bomb attacks on the Japanese mainland. (*US Marine Corps*)

Photo of Lieutenant David Braden's stricken B-29 taken moments after a crash at sea. *(Shannon Braden/Kimberly Chamlea Collection)*

Lieutenant David Braden was a survivor of two B-29 crashes at sea. *(Shannon Braden/Kimberly Chamlea Collection)*

Lieutenant Norman Westervelt *(front row, third from left)* and Lieutenant Gordon Nedderson *(front row, fourth from left)* were killed in one of the B-29 crashes at sea. *(Shannon Braden/Kimberly Chamlea Collection)*

As the "father of the atomic bomb," General Curtis LeMay was called "Old Iron Pants" because he was such a tough cookie. He was "ecstatic" when he heard that the first fire raid on Tokyo had killed eighty-three thousand people and left 1 million people homeless. He was also called the "George Patton of the Air Force." There is no question that he put the United States on the path to winning the war. *(US Air Force)*

Colonel Paul Tibbets waves from his B-29, the *Enola Gay*, the plane that dropped the atomic bomb on Hiroshima, as he prepares to take off from Tinian. (*National Archives*)

The ruins of Hiroshima after the B-29 raid. "Hiroshima was no longer a city . . . to the east and to the west everything was flattened." *(National Archives)*

Sergeant Harold Haberman of the 2nd Marine special weapons company lost count of the Japanese he killed during June 15 and 16. He had a bazooka and started firing at the enemy, and he didn't stop until he had killed—literally—everything in sight. *(US Marine Corps)*

Mr. and Mrs. Harold Haberman slice their wedding cake, but the worst was yet to come for the young married couple. *(Haberman Family Album)*

When the fighting was over, the newly completed Saipan Cemetery held 3,426 American servicemen who were killed in action. A total of 16,500 were wounded in the twenty-four-day battle. *(US Marine Corps)*

After narrowly escaping death as a machine gunner/radio operator in an amphibious tank, Private First Class Wayne "Twig" Terwilliger played for five Major League Baseball teams during a sixty-three-year career as a player and a coach. Here he poses for a picture with the immortal Ted Williams during a stint with the Texas Rangers. (*Terwilliger Collection*)

Ordinarily Corporal Canara Caruth spent his time guiding a Marine amphibious tank across Saipan, but here (second Marine in photo) he catches a few winks of sleep on a pile of rocks. *(US Marine Corps)*

reinforcing an existing five-hundred-yard gap in the American lines, but both received word that no one was available for this assignment. A call also went out to division headquarters, but it too received a negative response. If any response was made, it would have to be with whatever troops the two battalion commanders could put together themselves.

Consequently O'Brien's 1st Battalion of the 105th took up positions ahead of the front lines and dug in east of the railroad tracks. McCarthy's 2nd Battalion also moved to a defensive line straddling the coast road that ran fifty yards from the beach.

Near the front line the men knew that something big was about to happen.

The sound the Japanese troops made as they prepared for the assault was a heavy, steady roar that seemed to shake the countryside. "We began to hear this buzz," said First Sergeant Mario Occinario of the 1st Battalion, 105th. "It was the damnedest noise I ever heard, and it kept getting louder and louder."

O'Brien conferred with McCarthy, and defenses were tightened somewhat between the 1st and 2nd Battalions. O'Brien moved his machine guns nearer to the railroad tracks. But both commanders knew that gaps still existed in their lines, and neither one had the personnel to cover the smaller openings, much less the large and dangerous five-hundred-yard gap.

O'Brien again called regimental headquarters to ask for reserves, but the request was denied. Lieutenant Colonel Leslie M. Jensen contacted division headquarters and repeated the request, but it again was denied.

Normally the battalion established a perimeter defense for the night with soldiers facing outward in a rough circle to protect themselves. But there were not enough men to create a solid defensive line, and the perimeter was not closed on all sides. The Japanese sent patrols to probe the front lines and quickly uncovered these gaps in the American defenses.

Because of this, these refusals to send extra men to cover the gaps would prove to be a major mistake, as the Japanese were allowed to penetrate between the 1st and 3rd Battalions and then virtually annihilate the 1st and 2nd Battalions. Filling the lapses in the darkness would have proved extremely difficult because all units were stretched extremely thin by this time. The sound the Japanese were making rose in intensity until everybody could hear it. "It was like the sound of bees inside a hive," remembered Sergeant John Sidur, who was now on the front lines with the 105th Infantry's 2nd Battalion. The 2nd and 3rd Battalions were positioned across the so-called Tanapag Plain along Saipan's western shore. The two battalions would bear the harsh brunt of the coming assault.

"It was the sound of the enemy forming up to attack," Sidur recalled. "If you listened carefully, you could almost tell they were repeating the same word over and over again, but it was hard to tell what it was."

It was "*Banzai! Banzai! Banzai!*"

chapter 8

★ ★ ★

To Die with Honor

AT APPROXIMATELY 0445 on the morning of 7 July between three and four thousand Japanese troops flung themselves at the thin American perimeter several hundred yards north of Tanapag along the northwestern coast of the island.

A short time earlier Sergeant Ronald Johnson, Lieutenant Colonel William O'Brien's radio man, had seen strange, shadowy figures and silhouettes moving back and forth far up in the hills in the predawn darkness. Now he knew exactly what they were. The shadowy silhouettes were Japanese soldiers, remnants of Saipan's defenders, moving through a gap between the 1st and 3rd Battalions of the 27th Division's 105th Infantry Regiment on the left and the Marines on their right flank.

Johnson didn't know that the Japanese troops on Saipan had been ordered to attack the American camp in a massive banzai charge, with the avowed purpose of killing as many of the "American devils" as possible. The goal for each individual was seven American deaths for every Japanese soldier who had died in the struggle for the island.

Despite all that has been said and written about the less-than-satisfactory state of the Japanese soldiers' weapons and equipment, each individual's willingness to die honorably and to attempt to take seven American lives as a repayment for his country's loss stands as a remarkable achievement. "Here was a determination which was seldom—if ever—matched by the fighting men of any other country," the Marine Corps would later acknowledge.

As Major Yoshida Hiyoshi, a captured intelligence officer, explained the Japanese soldier's philosophy about death: "They knew at the outset that they had no hope of succeeding. They simply felt that it was better to die that way and take some of the enemy with them than to be holed up in caves and be killed."

They had a name for what they were doing. It was *gyokusai*, which means "to die with honor."

The *gyokusai* would also claim the lives of many other small groups of Japanese. Some were soldiers, and some were not. They came together to be killed by shots from the Americans or by self-inflicted hand grenades. In preparation for their final stand they celebrated by drinking the best Japanese whiskey and smoking their finest tobacco.

Among the remaining Saipan defenders was a group of about twenty members of the Japanese Imperial Navy, including Mitsuharu Noda, who had been a paymaster for Admiral Chuichi Nagumo. Shouting together, the men resolutely marched toward the enemy lines. "We weren't going to attack our enemies," Noda remembered. "We were ordered to go there to be killed. It was a kind of suicide, but that last taste of Suntori Square

Bottle whiskey was truly wonderful. We didn't crawl on the ground, though bullets were coming toward us. We advanced standing up. We were even able to smile."

Above the sound of singing and shouting, there were explosions that grew more pronounced as they moved along. The men in Noda's group had only a few weapons. "Some had shovels; others had sticks," he recalled. "I had a pistol. I think I was hit by a machine gun. Two bullets in my stomach, one passing through me, one lodging in me. I didn't suffer pain. None at all. But I couldn't stand up either. I was lying on my back. I could see the tracer bullets passing over."

Noda saw a group of four or five men, all of them Japanese, crawling toward each other on their hands and knees. One of them held up a grenade in his right hand, he said, and called out to Noda.

"Hey, sailor there!" he said. "Won't you come with us?"

"I have a grenade," Noda said. "Please go ahead."

Noda heard "Long live the Emperor!" and the explosion of a hand grenade a split-second later. "Several men were blown away, dismembered at once into bits of flesh," he said. "I held my breath at this appalling sight. Their heads were all cracked open, and smoke was coming out. It was a horrific way to die. Those were my last thoughts as I lost consciousness."

Despite his intentions, Noda was one of a tiny handful of Japanese who survived the largest banzai attack in modern history.

Most of the marchers, however, were Japanese soldiers. Those who were wounded or unable to walk and bear arms were killed or took their own lives before the banzai charge began. Every military survivor was armed with something, although there were not nearly enough rifles to go around. Many officers gave away their pistols and kept only their sabers. Daggers and hunting knives were parceled out. When these were exhausted, some men armed themselves with shovels, the limbs of trees, or bamboo poles with sharp sticks—anything that would serve as a spear.

At 0400 on 7 July the entire remaining Japanese force had headed south from the village of Makunsha, traveling through what they called Paradise Valley to reach the US forces. But the Americans had a much more fitting name for it: the Valley of Hell.

The Japanese force had sent out patrols all along the front that quickly probed—and just as quickly discovered—the wide gaps between the American lines. They knew exactly where they were going, and they were determined to get there.

Almost immediately the Japanese soldiers split apart and followed three principal routes toward the Americans. One main force moved along the water's edge and railroad tracks that ran south and parallel to the sea, where they would strike with deadly fury at the isolated positions of the 1st and 2nd Battalions of the 105th, dug in along the railroad tracks. Meanwhile a second large column on the left flank marched down Hara-Kiri Gulch and struck at elements of the 165th Infantry Regiment and the 3rd Battalion, 105th, at their positions above the gulch, the first point of high ground inland from the beaches. Finally, a smaller third column in the middle split the three-hundred-yard gap between the 1st and 2nd and continued south, mostly unimpeded.

From Makunsha it had taken the main body of Japanese about forty-five minutes to get to the combined perimeter of the 1st and 2nd Battalions of the 105th Infantry Regiment.

Shortly before 0500 hundreds of Japanese troops stormed the two battalions in what would subsequently be called the Old or First Perimeter with such force that they overwhelmed the Americans.

FROM THE HIGH GROUND of Hara-Kiri Ridge Lieutenant Donald Speirling, executive officer of G Company, 2nd Battalion, 105th Infantry Regiment, looked down on the three-pronged Japanese attack developing below. He heard what he thought was the sound of a truck motor, then discovered a bevy of Japanese tanks with hordes of Japanese troops following along behind them.

Captain Bernard Tolf, battalion forward observer for the artillery, called back and forth across the railroad tracks to Colonel O'Brien, trying to get clearance to call the artillery into action, but the noise became so loud that neither party could hear. Tolf conferred with Captain Louis Ackerman, the leader of A Company, and the two decided to try a series of interdiction fire by the artillery along the railroad and roadway south of Makunsha.

The use of artillery was effective, and the firing was almost constant. The bombardment caused no great casualties, but it touched off complete disorganization in the advancing column. Every few steps the Japanese had to stop and dive for cover, and men who had held their positions until now were dispersed and never managed to get back together again. Japanese officers urged their men out of the ditches, collected stragglers, and herded them back into the road.

But the artillery didn't stop the attack. The 2,666 rounds of ammunition the Americans fired only slowed it down. The enemy column inched ahead, with Japanese soldiers singing songs and shouting encouragement to one another, relentlessly moving forward in the dark. The left flank began climbing the hills toward the American positions.

Above them from Hara-Kiri Ridge and its surrounding terrain American troops could see the massive destruction of their comrades unfolding below, but they could do little to halt the Japanese assault. They too were under attack.

Lieutenant Arthur Hansen of G Company, 2nd Battalion, 105th, watched as comrades in the 1st and 2nd Battalions were overrun and the Japanese ran willy-nilly over the ground formerly occupied by American troops. Hansen's carbine couldn't reach that far from the top of an outcropping of Hari-Kiri Gulch. As he watched, however, an engineer with G Company managed to drop a few Japanese with his M-1.

Lieutenant George O'Donnell, also of G Company, later observed that the Japanese were "like a crowd moving after a big football game, with everyone trying to get out at once." It was raining at the time, and O'Donnell and his men were having a hard time keeping the Japanese from overrunning them. They had a field day firing until their ammunition started running low. The nearest any Japanese got was about ten yards, and the Americans were hitting most of them at several hundred yards.

It reminded Tech Sergeant J. F. Polikowski of G Company's 1st Platoon of Yankee Stadium after a big victory. The crowd of Japanese milled out on the field, pushing, shoving, yelling, and shouting. There were so many of them that the Americans could just shut their eyes, pull the trigger, and hit someone.

Sergeant Edwin Luck, the squad leader of the 1st Squad, 1st Platoon of G Company, 105th Infantry Regiment, was at a listening post near the road on a hillside overlooking Hara-Kiri Gulch when he saw Japanese soldiers struggling to carry a large Hotchkiss-type machine gun and trying to get across the road about two hundred yards away from him. The gun was so heavy that it took two soldiers to carry it.

Luck took aim and killed one enemy soldier, and when others came to help, he started picking them off, one by one. "I believe I killed or wounded about nineteen or twenty Japs that morning," he said later. "That's not bad for an old crow hunter from upstate New York."

Luck was finally wounded by an incoming mortar fragment that struck him in the upper left chest. The splinter went into the shoulder bone and completely immobilized him. He was lucky enough to get picked up and taken to a field hospital in Charan Kanoa, where he underwent surgery. Then they moved him to the hospital ship USS *Relief*, and he ended up in Kwajalein, where it took a couple of months to recover. Luck found out later that he was one of only two men from his G Company who survived.

With its two machine guns knocked out and a lack of other ammunition, the troops of Captain Frank Olander's G Company, 105th Infantry Regiment, watched the Japanese creep as close as fifteen yards to the company's foxholes. When the enemy started tossing hand grenades, the men scooped them up and threw them back. It was a dangerous—and deadly—game of catch.

Within a period of about thirty minutes the game had resulted in heavy casualties on both sides. Five G Company members were seriously wounded, including Olander. After his left arm was almost blown off by an exploding grenade, he had a rough tourniquet placed on his arm above the break and continued to lead the defense of G Company's position.

The company was unable to stop the Japanese from infiltrating the rear of Hara-Kiri Gulch. Their gunfire killed Private First Class Elmer Bornich and wounded two other G Company men. The company was hemmed in on three sides and almost out of ammunition. Then the enemy started placing heavy knee-mortar fire on the position. Three men were hit, and Olander collapsed from loss of blood.

Lieutenant O'Donnell took command and quickly had his men move back about a hundred yards. Moving the wounded back with him, O'Donnell ordered the remaining men to dig in alongside L Company, 3rd Battalion.

"My own company didn't give an inch," Olander remembered. "It stayed put and we fought it out. It cut the Jap attack to ribbons, but we left many, many dead on that field."

AFTER THE JAPANESE—including the Imperial Army's last three tanks—overran the two battalions of the 105th and the 10th Marine Artillery Battery placed at the rear of the 105th, they spread out. Part of them focused on the 3rd Battalion's Command Post, where they quickly interrupted communications. They also overran the 10th Marines' 3rd Battalion. But when they turned on the 105th Regimental CP they came away with heavy losses.

When the Japanese knocked out the neighboring artillery battalion, Private First Class Harold Agerholm of the 4th Battalion, 10th Marines, volunteered to help evacuate the many wounded. Commandeering an abandoned ambulance Jeep, he made repeated trips under intense rifle and mortar fire, single-handedly loading and evacuating forty-five seriously wounded men. He worked tirelessly, disregarding his own safety, for a period of more than three hours. Despite unrelenting enemy fire, he ran out to aid two wounded Marines but was himself gunned down by a Japanese sniper. He would receive the Medal of Honor posthumously.

AT THE FIRST PERIMETER the harsh sound of rifle, machine gun, and antitank gunfire echoing through the darkness awakened Lieutenant Luke Hammond of the 1st Battalion, 105th Infantry Regiment. From his foxhole it sounded as though "everything we had and everything the Japanese had was being thrown back and forth at a very short range." Enemy bullets zipped overhead, and tracers streamed over his foxhole. Hammond dug deeper and prayed. It had just stopped raining, and he and his comrades were wet and cold.

Sergeant Nick Grinaldo of C Company in the 105th opened his eyes in the dawn of 7 July with Japanese soldiers shooting down at him with small arms. He turned and saw his lieutenant go down after a Japanese bullet knocked off the bottom of his jaw. Grinaldo got to his feet and had run a couple of steps when his rifle was shot out of his hand. When he bent to pick it up, he couldn't close his fingers. He'd been shot through the shoulder and didn't know it. Only when another soldier helped him get to his feet and he saw a trickle of blood on his shoulder did he know he had been hit.

Private First Class David Boynton of A Company, 105th, twenty-one years old and from Honolulu, was caught up in the midst of the first charge by the Japanese when the sun came up. He stayed in his foxhole beside the railroad track, repelling attack after attack.

Wounded by a grenade, Boynton was last seen standing in his foxhole with blood running down his face, yelling, "Come on, you yellow bastards, and fight!" No one saw him fall, but his body was found later in the foxhole. The bodies of Private Frank Gooden and Private First Class Leon Pittman, both of A Company, were found nearby.

Sergeant Felix Giuffre, A Company, 1st Battalion, 105th, had seen three of his comrades—Sergeant Edgar Theuman; Private First Class Clement Mauskemo, a full-blood Cherokee; and Sergeant W. A. Berger—killed beside him. Giuffre had also caught a bullet in his leg as he tried to escape. Seconds later he stumbled across Private First Class William Priddy, a BAR man from A Company who was trying his best to kill three Japanese soldiers trapped in a ditch, but he couldn't get his BAR to fire. Giuffre grabbed the gun, unjammed it, then killed all three enemy soldiers. He gave the BAR back to Priddy and never saw him again. Priddy was killed a short time later, and Giuffre was wounded severely in the head and lost consciousness.

Sergeant Anthony Auzis, with A Company, 1st Battalion, was wounded in the leg and arm, but he was crawling around searching for ammunition when he came across Giuffre, who was unconscious and suffering from two wounds. Although it was all he could do to drag himself along, Auzis somehow picked up Giuffre and carried him a short distance south down the railroad tracks. Then Auzis was hit in the leg, so he laid Giuffre down at the edge of a minefield just north of Tanapag and managed to crawl on to the village, where he was hit in the back by a large shell fragment. That afternoon he would be removed to a base hospital.

Giuffre awakened later in the day and tried to pull himself along, tearing out chunks of ground with his hands as he moved. He was wounded a second, third, and fourth time by enemy fire before he was rescued and evacuated later that afternoon. He would survive the battle.

At the rear of the assault formations hundreds of sick and wounded Japanese—men swathed in bandages, men on crutches, and scores of walking wounded—tried to help each other. Some carried weapons, but many had none at all.

Hit from three sides, the 105th's headquarters was cut off quickly with no chance of spreading the word. The 1st Battalion CP straddled the railroad tracks just behind the foxholes occupied by three rifle companies and D Company of the 1st Battalion. Fully half the CP's men were killed or wounded in a matter of minutes.

Private First Class Cassie Hill of A Company, 105th, was struck by a rifle bullet in his upper arm, shattering the bone and leaving him unable to fire his rifle. So he gave the weapon to Private First Class Armin Kunde, who was sharing the same foxhole. At that point Hill and Kunde became a team, with Hill using his one good arm to load and keep Kunde's rifles operational.

They held their position until they were completely out of ammunition, then they moved south, with Hill methodically stripping ammo from dead and seriously wounded men and collecting quite a batch. When Hill was hit in his good arm he was unable to do anything but struggle along, carrying the rifles under his arms, and sometime later his leg was shattered by a bullet. With three crippling wounds, he was finally forced to quit. Much later that evening he would be evacuated to a field hospital.

The fighting soon devolved into small groups of men fighting for their lives against an onslaught of thousands of enemy soldiers. In the midst of it Colonel O'Brien, leader of the 1st Battalion, 105th, ran up and down the line of foxholes with a pistol in each hand, slapping his men on the backs and urging them to hold the line. When he saw that they couldn't hold out, he ordered a retreat south to Tanapag village, where he had heard that a new defensive perimeter was being established.

By then hundreds of O'Brien's men were dead. But the last message he was able to send was met with such skepticism that the 165th CP didn't even record it in its journal—they were certain it was a Japanese trick. It was not until Lieutenant Colonel Joseph Hart climbed atop a hill and looked down on the plain below that he realized what had happened. Hart was regimental commander, and O'Brien was his best friend. He only needed one look at the burning vehicles and dozens of dead Americans lying on the ground to assess the scope of the destruction.

As the sky grew lighter Lieutenant Luke Hammond could see objects moving about thirty yards ahead of him. He saw men from the front-line battalions falling back, and he caught a glimpse of O'Brien talking to someone on his field telephone.

"Hold the line, and stay up there," Hammond thought he heard O'Brien say. Then O'Brien threw down the phone and yelled at a soldier running by, "Where in the hell are you going?"

The soldier waved his arms and said, "I have no weapon!" and ran on.

O'Brien turned to Hammond and shouted, "As long as one of my men is up there, I'm going to be with them!" Then he was gone.

"We've got to fight and hold this line," Hammond told his men. "We've got to hold the 1st Battalion CP at all costs." He crawled into the concrete cistern near his foxhole and looked out at the enemy. Fifty yards away he saw a huge mass of people—hundreds of yelling Japanese approaching.

Several other soldiers jumped into the concrete cistern. "Okay, let's hold here," they said and immediately began to fire at the enemy.

Just thirty yards away Hammond saw two Japanese soldiers jumping among the dead and dying Americans and swinging their samurai swords at them. He and several others fired at them, and they went down. Then he turned his carbine toward the other Japanese. Targets were plentiful and so close there was no excuse for missing, so Hammond gave some of his ammunition to Captain John Bennett, a naval liaison officer, who had run out. Hammond figured the two of them could use it to better advantage if he shared.

Hammond left the cistern and moved to a position behind a concrete wall, firing at Japanese no more than thirty yards away. He felt a slight jar and heard a plunking sound as a bullet smacked into his helmet. The pain was slight and he couldn't tell exactly where the wound was, but blood was streaming down from under his helmet.

He calmly emptied his carbine at the enemy, then allowed one of the cooks from the Headquarters Company to apply a bandage to the wound on the side of his head. He put his helmet on, reloaded his carbine, and started back along the railroad tracks, dodging bullets and looking for an aid station.

Still waving a pistol in each hand, O'Brien continued to run back and forth along the front line until a bullet hit him in his right shoulder. He shook off attempts to evacuate him but eventually allowed a bandage to be applied to the wound by medic Sergeant Walter Grigas. As Grigas applied the dressing, O'Brien leaned on his right knee, firing his pistol with his left hand and yelling, "Don't give them a damn inch!" He paused just long enough to tell Grigas, "Get the hell back where you belong!"

Out of ammunition for his pistols, O'Brien jumped into a foxhole, snatched a rifle from a wounded man, and emptied the gun in the direction of the Japanese. Then he ran to a Jeep parked in the middle of the 1st Battalion perimeter and took control of the .50-caliber machine gun mounted on it. He fired until that too ran out of ammunition.

O'Brien grabbed a saber from a fallen Japanese and continued to stand atop the vehicle, flailing away at a small army of assailants and hollering, "Don't give them a damn inch!" until he was cut to pieces. When his body was recovered the next day thirty dead Japanese were piled around him.

Captain Ben Salomon, a dentist from Los Angeles, had started duty that morning as regimental dental officer of the 2nd Battalion, 105th Infantry Regiment. When the doctor who usually cared for the wounded was hit, Salomon volunteered to replace him in an aid station close behind the front lines. Fighting was heavy, and the Japanese soon overran the defenses and then the aid station, where Salomon was working to save the lives of approximately thirty wounded soldiers who had walked, crawled, or been carried there.

When Salomon saw a Japanese soldier in the act of bayoneting a wounded American soldier lying near the tent, he drew his pistol and fired from a squatting position, killing the enemy soldier. As he turned his attention back to the wounded men, more Japanese soldiers appeared at the entrance of the tent.

Rushing them with a rifle, Salomon kicked a knife out of the hand of one, shot another, and bayoneted a third.

Recognizing the danger of their position, Salomon ordered the wounded to make their way as best they could back to the regimental aid station while he attempted to hold off the enemy until his patients had made it to safety. He grabbed a rifle from a wounded man, and when four American soldiers were killed while manning a nearby machine gun, Salomon seized control of it. According to eyewitnesses, Salomon fired the gun so quickly and accurately that dead Japanese kept piling up in front of the gun and obstructing his view. He had to move the gun at least four times to maintain a field of fire.

When an Army team returned to the site a couple of days later, they found Salomon's body slumped over the machine gun. Lying before him were ninety-eight dead enemy soldiers in front of his position. He had seventy-six bullet wounds and countless bayonet wounds. He was belatedly awarded the Medal of Honor by President George W. Bush some fifty-eight years later in 2002.

In less than half an hour of combat the 1st and 2nd Battalions were overrun as the Japanese tide swept through them and they tried in vain to regroup. The fighting had quickly degenerated into hand-to-hand combat, with every American soldier battling for his life against overwhelming odds. Any survivors stumbled south toward Tanapag before the onslaught.

Private First Class William Hawrylak had been back with A Company, 1st Battalion just one day when all hell broke loose. He had gone AWOL from the hospital where he was being treated for previous wounds to rejoin his comrades in arms. That morning he received a saber thrust from a Japanese officer that came close to cutting off his entire buttocks. Although bleeding heavily and unable to walk and with nearly every other American near him either dead or dying, Hawrylak continued to fire his submachine gun.

When Staff Sergeant Dominic Daurio of Valley Falls, New York, Hawrylak's squad leader, ordered him to vacate his foxhole because another Japanese wave was imminent, Hawrylak yelled, "Hell no! I like it here. Besides, I got no ass. How can I walk?"

Daurio unceremoniously picked up Hawrylak and carried him toward the rear. Halfway down the beach Daurio got help from another man, but Hawrylak was bleeding so profusely that he finally had to be laid on the ground. Daurio gave Hawrylak a sulfa pill when they stopped, then placed him in a foxhole for his own protection. Hawrylak refused to stay in the foxhole and spent the next several hours crawling around the perimeter, collecting discarded ammunition and cleaning weapons for men still able to load and fire. He was eventually evacuated and survived the battle.

Lieutenant John Mulhern of Portland, Maine, would be remembered as the only officer of B Company, 1st Battalion, 105th Infantry Regiment, to survive the *gyokusai* without injury. As he retreated that morning Mulhern picked up a wounded soldier, Private Anthony LaSorta from San Jose, California, who had a broken leg caused by machine gunfire. Mulhorn attempted to take him to the rear, but as soon as he put LaSorta on his back, an enemy machine gun opened fire and blew LaSorta to pieces. A few moments later, when Mulhern struggled to his feet, he was amazed to find that he didn't have a single scratch.

The men of the 105th were losing many officers as organization collapsed around them, ammunition ran desperately short, and Japanese troops eagerly scooped up rifles and ammo from dead Americans. The toll of dead and critically wounded officers steadily grew as the assault raged on.

Lieutenant Robert McGuire, an H Company platoon leader, was wounded in the initial enemy assault that morning. When he saw his company's machine guns being overrun by the Japanese, he ran to the front line and took control of one of the guns, continuing to fire it into repeated charges by the Japanese. No one knows how many times he was hit before he was killed, but he was riddled with bullets. One of the H Company men approached him and urged him to leave the gun and go to the rear so that his many wounds could be treated.

"I'd rather stay here," he said. He died shortly after.

A stray bullet hit and killed Lieutenant George Dolliner of Battle Creek, Michigan, a member of the 1st Battalion, 105th Infantry Regiment, as he led his men during the American withdrawal from the front lines early that morning.

"We called him 'Daddy,'" said Sergeant Michael Mele, who was also from Battle Creek. "He was an inspiration to us all. I was beside him when he got it. He died instantly. If the Army ever had a braver officer, we'd sure like to meet him."

First Lieutenant Hugh King of Hewlett, Long Island, who had assumed command of B Company, 1st Battalion, 105th, when Captain Richard Ryan was killed, died when a mortar shell struck him as he was directing traffic and shouting encouragement to his men. Moments earlier Sergeant James Rhodes of Tell City, Indiana, had been killed when a grenade hit him squarely in the face.

Twenty-one men from B Company, 105th, were killed in the fighting at the First Perimeter that morning, including one entire squad commanded by Sergeant Barney Stopera. The squad had stood its ground even after its ammunition was gone, with

Stopera leading them in hand-to-hand fighting against rapidly increasing numbers. After the battle every member of the eight-man squad was found dead in a tight group. About thirty dead Japanese lay around them.

In the 2nd Battalion both E and F Companies suffered severe casualties early in the fighting. F Company alone lost twenty-three men, and E Company suffered sixteen fatalities. Lieutenant John Titterington, F Company's commander, was hit early in an initial charge by the Japanese, but he dragged himself from one machine gun to the next until he could find someone else to take over.

A company clerk would find Titterington at about 0830 and urged him to take time off to get his wound dressed, but Titterington declined. "I've got to go, I guess," he said, "but if I do go, I'm going to take a helluva lot of those son of a bitches with me." True to his word, he died at the machine gun.

AT 0700, SOON AFTER the Americans first reached Tanapag, they were attacked by the left flank of the Japanese, which had come down along the cliffs and knocked out the 10th Marines artillery positions. Two officers, Captain Earl White, commander of F Company of the 105th, who had been badly wounded and was now limping along on one leg, and Lieutenant Hugh King, who had assumed command of B Company, 1st Battalion, 105th, after Captain Paul Ryan was killed earlier in the day, took charge of the situation. Directing the men to dig in where they were and make a stand, they managed to stem the wild rush to find cover. King was killed while directing this operation, but the men had found a place where they could put up a fight.

By 0800 what would later be called the Second Perimeter was set up around Tanapag as survivors from the 1st and 2nd continued to straggle in before the enemy advance. They did what they could to set up defensive positions on the edges of the village and moved the wounded into the small wooden and concrete buildings in its center. There were almost no medical supplies and few medics, and much of the first aid was one wounded man doing what he could for another. The medics constantly risked their lives moving between first aid stations to administer to the wounded.

Directed by Major Edward McCarthy, the only officer of the 2nd Battalion, 105th, not killed or wounded that day, the Second Perimeter took up most of the village of Tanapag. It was a desperate, hastily built affair requiring a lot of bullet-dodging work. The men who organized it had an almost impossible chance of digging in and protecting themselves, but by a near-miracle they accomplished their task. Small houses built by the Japanese and constructed of concrete offered the wounded who could get inside protection from small-arms fire. Other houses, made of wood, provided air spaces between the bottom floor and the ground where soldiers from the 105th could protect themselves from stray bullets.

Trenches ran throughout Tanapag. Although they were shallow in spots, the Americans improved them when they weren't firing until they had fairly good foxholes. The trenches were not closed circles. Large gaps existed throughout their length, and many of them were not covered by American fire. Groups of enemy soldiers could—and did—infiltrate the ditches, but the majority were killed before they did any harm. Most of the wounded found their way into these ditches and spent hours huddled there. The men charged with defending the Second Perimeter were also dependent on this trench system for cover.

With these makeshift emplacements as their only protection, the surviving men of the 1st and 2nd Battalions of the 105th Infantry Regiment were swept up in the midst of a furious assault as the Japanese struck with every kind of weapon—rifles, pistols, machine guns, grenades, samurai swords, and knives on sticks.

Private John Purcell of Schenectady, New York, in E Company of the 105th, was stationed at the Second Perimeter. In the afternoon he lined up eight rifles along a stretch of trench covering a clearing used frequently by charging Japanese. Then he ran from one rifle to another, pulling the triggers as the Japanese attacked. In between enemy thrusts he hurriedly reloaded the rifles, prepared for the next charge, collected loose ammunition, and filled clips with bullets. "I felt like the proverbial one-armed paperhanger with the seven-year itch," he remembered. His action helped to save the American line, which was under continuous sniping by the Japanese against a beach position that sheltered many American wounded. For his heroism Purcell would be awarded the Silver Star.

Not long after the Second Perimeter was established, Private First Class Charles Emig of A Company, 105th, took up a position along the line of small houses where the wounded were lying. He and a few other men discovered that Japanese soldiers had infiltrated some of the houses where the wounded lay. They decided to clear them out. For the next four or five hours Emig moved from window to window inside the house, firing at any enemy who lifted his head.

When enemy mortar barrages began falling they came dangerously close to the wounded men, and Emig decided to move them to a ditch where they would be safer from mortar fragments. He covered the exit of most of the wounded, but he was shot down and killed as he crossed a window opening to help one of the last few soldiers.

The longest and by far the most crucial period for the survivors of the 1st and 2nd rifle companies of the 105th Infantry was securing the thin Second Perimeter against the Japanese attackers. Private First Class Mark Winter was one of those protectors. He had been seriously wounded earlier and was hit again shortly after getting inside the Second Perimeter. He was unable to move under his own power, but he managed to talk someone into propping him up into a firing position.

From that point on, he fired his carbine slowly and deliberately for much of the morning and managed to hit several Japanese. When he finally ran out of ammunition, he hailed a soldier and asked for an M-1 rifle lying nearby. The soldier protested, telling Winter he shouldn't be firing from such an exposed position that was well above ground level.

"I'll stay here and fire until I get the last Jap—or they get me," Winter said. Later in the day he was killed on the spot where he lay, but not by a sniper—he was hit by artillery.

As the day wore on, the number of injured soldiers steadily grew. Some were so badly wounded that they could take no part in defending the Second Perimeter. They did what they could by remaining quiet, although many were in such extreme pain that they wanted to scream.

Sergeant Attilio Grestini of B Company, from Cohoes, a mill town north of Albany, New York, had remained active all morning in a rifle position near the northeast corner of the Second Perimeter. When a sudden burst of artillery fire fell near him, one shell blew Grestini's left arm completely off and mangled his left leg at the hip. He lay there for an hour or more without uttering a sound, biting his lips to keep from crying out. Staff Sergeants John Sidur and John Goot, B Company, found him and insisted on trying to help him, carrying him on a rifle to the center of the Second Perimeter, where he refused any further assistance.

Instead, he somehow applied tourniquets to his arm and leg, then sat quietly for the rest of the day. He had neither medical treatment nor drugs to ease the pain. He was later transferred to a hospital ship, survived the war, and later moved to Chicago and raised a family.

Sidur also saved Corporal Wilfred "Spike" Mailloux when he found him seriously wounded an hour or so after the incident with Grestini. Mailloux had met Sidur in Cohoes, where they both lived in 1940. At the time Mailloux was sixteen and Sidur was twenty-two. When Sidur spotted Mailloux in a muddy ditch, bleeding profusely from a stab wound delivered by a Japanese officer with a long knife, he didn't recognize him at first. Then he thought, *Boy, he really looks familiar.* Mailloux had been injured when the enemy overran the 1st and 2nd Platoons of the 105th Infantry Regiment.

As the Americans continued to fight, Sidur too was wounded in the arm. Late in the afternoon, after the attack subsided and he left Tanapag with his comrades, he had to use one end of the rifle to lean on. He managed to walk out very slowly with the rest of his platoon. On his way a couple of Japanese jumped up, and the wounded men fully expected to be killed right there. "For some reason they didn't shoot," Sidur said. "They let the Americans pass." Later on Sidur would wonder whether the Japanese were actually trying to surrender.

SOON THE SECOND PERIMETER was surrounded, and all along it a ragged, thin line stretched in a half moon from beach side to beach. The fight was a series of all-out clashes, much of them hand-to-hand, as wave after wave of suicidal Japanese hurled themselves against the exhausted American soldiers. Over the next four hours a gutsy stand would be made that would constitute one of the great defensive maneuvers in American military history.

With nearly all the commissioned officers killed or wounded during the attack, the sergeants, corporals, and sometimes privates were left to assume the roles of leadership. The senior sergeants especially assumed command of their units.

Sergeant John Domanowski, B Company, First Battalion, 105th, was shot in one arm during the initial banzai attack. About midmorning, as he made his way back to the rear along the beach, he stopped to rest under a tree. A Japanese soldier hiding in the tree shot him in the other arm.

Domanowski found a spot on the beach where there were some bushes and small trees and decided to stay there. His left arm was useless, and the pain was severe. As he lay there on the beach, many other wounded men were brought in from the front lines for evacuation. He saw a group of soldiers heading for the water, where it was about three feet deep. "They were desperate men who wanted to hide, but the Japanese saw them and opened fire on them with machine guns," he remembered. "You could hear the bullets hitting their skulls. I thanked God that I stayed in those bushes."

Early in the attack, under heavy fire and armed with a bazooka, Sergeant Thomas Baker, A Company of the 105th, was among those who picked up the standard of leadership. Baker destroyed a Japanese emplacement firing on his company and, a short time later, single-handedly attacked and killed two groups of Japanese soldiers. Wounded by a grenade that almost blew off his whole foot, Baker continued to man his position until all his ammunition was gone.

Although barely able to move, Baker left his foxhole in search of more ammunition. He encountered Private First Class Frank Zielinski of A Company, 105th. Wounded himself, Zielinski picked up Baker and carried him about 150 yards until he was wounded for a second and third time. Captain Toft, who had been instrumental in launching the first artillery barrage against the Japanese, lifted Baker up and carried him until enemy fire tore into his stomach.

Another soldier offered to carry him, but Baker turned him down. "I've caused enough trouble already," Baker said. "I'll stay here and take my chance. Just give me a cigarette. I'm done for anyway."

Tech Sergeant John McLoughlin of Troy, New York, also of A Company of the 105th, propped Baker against a tree trunk and gave him a .45-caliber pistol filled with eight rounds of ammunition. Sergeant C. V. Particelli, also from Troy and A Company of the 105th, lit a cigarette and handed it to Baker. As Patricelli turned away, he looked back at Baker for an instant and saw him holding a .45 in one hand and a cigarette in the other. Baker looked cool as a cucumber.

A day and a half later, after the battle was over, returning Americans would find Baker's body—the burnt-out cigarette butt in one hand and an empty pistol in the other. Surrounding him were eight dead Japanese. Like his commander, Colonel O'Brien, Baker was awarded the Medal of Honor for his heroism in battle.

Captain Toft somehow made it from the field, but the stomach injury grew worse as the day wore on. He sensed he was dying. Sergeant Robert Smith of the 249th Field Artillery, sharing a foxhole with Toft, tried to reassure him. "No, I'm dying," Toft said. "Please don't let the Japs take me alive."

Smith knew what the enemy was capable of doing to a wounded man, so he stayed with Toft until he breathed his last.

Later that morning a Japanese swordsman jumped into Smith's foxhole with his saber half out of its sheath. Smith lunged up with his bayonet and rammed it into the enemy's gut. When he withdrew the bayonet, the Japanese soldier half-jumped, half-stumbled away. Smith shot him just to make sure he wouldn't be any more trouble.

AT TANAPAG, FACED WITH dwindling ammo, a lack of water, and a critical shortage of medical supplies, the Americans fought off the incessant attack with every available man, wounded or otherwise, engaged in the action.

Those who realized their buddies were running out of ammunition ducked from trench to trench picking up rifle bullets from the dead and wounded and carrying them to the men on the firing line. Three soldiers from E Company of the 2nd Battalion of the 105th—Staff Sergeant Homer Simms of Decatur, Illinois, and Privates First Class Thomas Daley of Brooklyn and Gerald Laucella of Schenectady—performed yeoman service in retrieving shells. Simms and Daley worked together: Daley collected the ammo, and Simms put it in clips.

In addition to collecting ammo, Laucella began grabbing first-aid packets and turning them over to medics. As he bent down to pick up a packet, Laucella spotted two Japanese soldiers trying to penetrate the American lines. He shot one, then killed the other as he tried to get away.

Several minutes of mortar fire from the Japanese scattered and disorganized the Americans but caused no casualties. Then the Japanese charged. The result was a massacre. The men of both the 2nd and 3rd Battalions of the 165th mowed down the attackers without suffering a single casualty. At least 300 enemy soldiers were killed in the initial charge. After that, they kept coming in groups that grew steadily smaller and smaller. When the attempts finally failed, more than 160 Japanese bodies were counted in the space of a few feet.

At approximately 1130 two American artillery barrages mistakenly struck a group of about a hundred American soldiers who had left the Second Perimeter to try to make contact with the regimental CP and bring up help for the badly wounded. Several of them were killed and others wounded. The rest of the men panicked, and most of them splashed into the lagoon just below Tanapag. Some swam to the outlying reef 250 yards from the shore. Others blindly followed suit and dove into the water. Several of the wounded drowned while trying to reach the reef.

Seventy-one men made it to the reef and were eventually picked up and rescued by a destroyer. About twenty-five others decided to turn back and return to shore, then banded together and established what became known as the Little Perimeter. It was about a quarter of a mile from the First Perimeter, and only a few feet of sand separated it from the ocean. About fifty other soldiers would join them as the day wore on.

The Second Perimeter and the Little Perimeter were like small, isolated islands surrounded by a sea of enemy soldiers.

There was no effective communication between the two, and neither made contact with any other Marine or 27th Division officers for most of the day.

ABOUT NOON THE first signs of help came too late in the form of a platoon of medium tanks, which lumbered up the road from the 105th Infantry CP. The problem was that none of the tanks had a radio frequency, and neither Major Edward McCarthy nor anyone else had a way of communicating with them.

The tanks rolled to a stop on the north side of the bridge that crossed Bloody Run and sat there for more than two hours. During that period they laid down an almost steady stream of fire on anything that resembled a Japanese hiding place. At one point McCarthy got inside one of the tanks and used the radio to plead for help, but he was unable to receive any intelligible answer.

McCarthy decided to lead a group of thirty-five men, mostly walking wounded, to fight their way south to the regimental CP. He commandeered one of the tanks, and he and his men followed it down the road. They would lose half their men along the way, but when they finally reached the CP at 1500 he reported with full details on the situation at Tanapag. All available tanks were ordered to Tanapag and the Second and Little Perimeters.

IN THE EARLY AFTERNOON scores of men from the 105th Infantry Regiment were still running into the village of Tanapag in search of shelter. Dozens sprinted to the waterfront, then turned with nowhere else to go to make a last stand at the edge of the beach, taking advantage of rows of ditches and concrete facilities that the Japanese had erected as beach defenses. They lay there for hours fighting off the Japanese, who came down the shoreline and over from the road. They fought off assault after assault.

When the Japanese tried to come down the beach and move behind the ragged perimeter, Private Willie Hokohana of E Company, 105th, set his BAR in the crotch of a tree. Hokohana, a big Hawaiian, was just an ordinary rifleman, but he had picked up the BAR when one of his buddies was wounded. The weapon had been badly damaged, but Hokohana repaired it. He gathered a part here and a part there from other BARs until he had a working gun. He had carried the salvaged weapon back toward the Second Perimeter and picked out a tree with a trunk split about four feet above the ground. He settled his BAR in the crotch and started firing.

Hokohana held his position most of the day, firing at the Japanese as they came along the water's edge. All told, he would be unofficially credited with killing about 140 Japanese before darkness obscured his view. He was exposed to a tremendous hail of small-arms fire and mortar shell fragments, but he suffered only one minor wound during his hours of firing.

Sergeant William Baralis of Troy, New York, joined Hokohana in defending the beach and the perimeters. A pitcher on the A Company, 105th, baseball team, he gathered up as many grenades as he could find and threw about 150 of them, killing close to a hundred Japanese before an enemy bullet struck him in the spine. He died the next day in a field hospital.

By about 1800, as the sun was setting, they had managed, against all odds, to hold the Second Perimeter amid the slaughter. The fury of the *gyokusai* had subsided to a great extent, and the ranks of the Japanese had been decimated. The stonewall defense the 105th had put up had stopped and dispersed the enemy, but Japanese soldiers still lurked behind every bush and tree, in every ditch and furrow, and under every sort of construction. From these vantage points they continued to pour fire on anything that moved. The two patchwork American perimeters were still holding tight, weathering the storm like islands in a hostile sea.

Months—and even years—later the vast majority of men in the 105th Regiment admitted to being scared to death throughout the nightmarish day of 7 July. But one young man in C Company didn't seem to know the meaning of fear.

He was Private Celso Flores, an eighteen-year-old fondly called "the Kid" by nearly everyone in his battalion. He had always complained about his choice of shots at the Japanese, but that was before he took part in the first counterattack and they heard him yell as he fired his rifle: "Holy cow! Just look at them! Oh boy! Oh boy!"

Nobody knows for sure how many Japanese Flores killed that day, but from his shouts it must have been a dozen or more. He was one of the last Americans to leave the Second Perimeter. Although he was wounded, the older members of the company almost had to drag him away. "I'll never get as many shots as this again," he told them.

There were also occasional incidents when laughter—at least when it was over—was the only real response.

Private First Class Marcus Itano of C Company in the 105th had a near-deadly experience as he took cover with a body of men he thought were Americans. He started out with a large group who were going to try to break through the Japanese lines to get back to their own lines. That was how confused the situation had become in the afternoon of 7 July as the day wore on.

They were just getting ready to leave when a heavy artillery barrage hit them. Some of the men were killed and badly shot up—about half of them. They started to run and got hit again. Then everyone headed for the water.

Itano ran about fifty yards, keeping pretty low, and when he looked up he spotted about twenty men ahead of him. They were lying prone on the beach with their backs to him and seemed to be looking at something across the way. They had on the same green uniforms—just like his own.

He thought he'd join them, so he ran right into the center of the group and lay down. Nobody paid any attention to him. He must have laid there for two or three minutes. Then he poked the man next to him to find out what they were looking at.

When the man turned toward him, Itano found himself face to face with a Japanese soldier. He had a grenade on his shoulder strap, and as Itano jumped to his feet, he pulled the grenade loose and yanked the pin. Then he dropped it and ran like hell.

He stepped on heads and backs and everything else getting out of there. The grenade went off, but he didn't turn around to see how much damage it did.

THE LAST MAN left the Tanapag area and the Little and Second Perimeters at about 2200. When the battle was finally over two battalions of the 105th Infantry Regiment—the 1st and the 2nd—had essentially ceased to exist. There were more than nine hundred deaths and casualties from their combined strength of twelve hundred men.

Every officer in the 1st and 2nd Battalions of the 105th was killed or wounded except for Lieutenant John F. Mulhern of B Company, 1st Battalion, and Major Edward McCarthy, commander of the 2nd Battalion.

A total of 1,694 Japanese bodies were found in the areas defended by the 105th and 106th Infantry Regiments.

chapter 9

★ ★ ★

The Aftermath

On 8 July, while handfuls of the Japanese who had staged the *gyokusai* were still alive and capable of trouble, Marines of the 2nd and 4th Divisions moved north toward Marpi Point in the northernmost section of Saipan to conduct a final sweep to clean out the few remaining points of enemy resistance.

Marpi Point had originally been the American objective for Day 9 of the invasion, but it took until Day 23 to wrest it from a scattering of Japanese. Most of the survivors were hidden in caves, and when they were ordered out, most of them killed themselves with hand grenades.

If civilians were thought to be in the caves, Americans would try to persuade them to surrender. But most of these overtures were also answered with an explosion of grenades.

"We rarely saw any live Japanese," remembered Chester Szech, a Marine corpsman. "Every time we saw Japanese, they were already dead. When they approached a cave, they would tell the occupants to come out and surrender. If they didn't come out, we'd turn the flamethrower on them, and that would be the end of it."

That wasn't always the case. Gunnery Sergeant Keith Renstrom of the 25th Marines would recall the "glorious feeling" of saving about twenty civilians on the brink of starvation in one cave. Renstrom laid aside his Thompson submachine gun and happily poured water into the mouths of the crowd before sending them off to a refugee camp.

THERE WAS ONE pint-sized Marine, however, who earned the name the "Pied Piper of Saipan" for his humane heroics to save literally hundreds of refugees—both enemy soldiers and civilians—from certain death. Private First Class Guy Gabaldon single-handedly talked more than a thousand Japanese soldiers and civilians into coming out of their caves and pillboxes and surrendering.

Gabaldon, who stood barely five-feet-four, joined the Marines when he was seventeen years old and became a scout and observer with the 2nd Marines. As a Mexican American youngster in the Boyle Heights neighborhood of East Los Angeles, he had grown up with a Japanese family and played every day with two little Japanese boys. At the age of twelve he had moved in with a Japanese family named Nakano, and he spoke a lot more Japanese than English—a skill that precious few other Marines had. Most importantly, he knew that what he told the Japanese on Saipan was true.

After Japan attacked Pearl Harbor on 7 December 1941, the Nakano family was among more than 100,000 Japanese Americans who were sent to internment camps across the country. These internments upset Gabaldon, and they were a primary reason he joined the Marines in 1943.

"The first night I was on Saipan I went out on my own," Gabaldon recalled. "I always worked on my own, and I brought back two prisoners, using my backstreet Japanese."

His commander, Colonel John Schwabe, scolded him, but Gabaldon went out again and came back with twelve more Japanese. Schwabe had first threatened a court martial, but now he gave Gabaldon explicit permission to continue.

"He would go up to the mouth of that cave and jabber, jabber, jabber—and pretty soon somebody would dribble out," Schwabe said.

With his pockets full of ammo and rations and a few grenades hanging from his belt, he took off for enemy country. He was nervous, but he knew this could be either a terribly foolish move or it could earn him the recognition he needed to be an official interpreter.

He told no one what he was going to do, not even his closest friend. It was about 2100 when he shoved off for Japland. His greatest danger just starting out was getting shot by his own men, so he had to be extremely careful.

He crawled for more than an hour until he came to a cave and smelled shouya and seafood, favorite foods of the Japanese. He crept as close to the entrance as he could and listened to several hushed Japanese voices. They were talking about the "coming defeat of the American devils" when the Japanese fleet returned. They had no idea that the US Task Force 58 had shot down their ships and planes.

Gabaldon quickly came up with a plan. As the sun was about to rise, he would toss two fragment grenades in succession into the dugout, then a smoke grenade. The smoke emerging from the cave was accompanied by Japanese soldiers with their hands high in the air. He told the soldiers he had many Marines with him and warned them that if they did not surrender, he would kill them.

He counted twelve prisoners. Several later gave valuable information that increased the Marines' effectiveness throughout the rest of the campaign. This became the start of his "freelance" operation on Saipan.

Gabaldon always warned the Japanese that they would die if they chose to stay hidden—and he later admitted that he had killed thirty-three of those who had tried to resist him. He told them that Marines were not the torturers that they had been repeatedly portrayed as. The people in the caves would be given food and medical care and had no reason to fear the Americans if they surrendered.

Often civilians were with the Japanese soldiers—in many cases women and children. They were hungry, and many were suffering from leprosy, dengue fever, and shellshock. Fear of the Americans would cause thousands of women and children to blow themselves up with grenades or jump to their death from high cliffs.

Gabaldon's successful efforts, in fact, may have reached as high as 1,500 saved Japanese, although in a book he wrote later he merely claimed a total of "over 1,000." Major James High, a Marine officer, was there when Guy brought in a total of 800 prisoners at once. "Everyone in the regiment was talking about it," High recalled.

Gabaldon's exploits would become a matter of public record in 1957 when Ralph Edwards put together a segment for NBC's *This Is Your Life*, which brought a new wave of fame. Then Hollywood producers became interested in the story, and in 1960 a film entitled *Hell to Eternity* was released. Jeffrey Hunter played the part of Gabaldon, whose ethnicity was changed to Italian American.

Out of this came a move to nominate Gabaldon for the Congressional Medal of Honor, and Colonel Schwabe officially recommended him for this one. He had already received the Silver Star, and in 1960 the Pentagon upgraded that to a Navy Cross, the second-highest honor in the Navy's arsenal of awards.

"It is particularly significant that for the most part Gabaldon captured these prisoners entirely by himself," Colonel Schwabe's recommendation said. "Furthermore, most of these activities were strictly voluntary and far and above the call of duty."

A documentary film, released in 2008 and entitled *East L.A. Marine,* posed the question of whether Gabaldon's Hispanic heritage played a part in him not receiving the medal. Other sources have blamed his tough and outspoken nature. Some claimed that his feats didn't measure up to those of other heroes on Saipan.

Guy Gabaldon died on 31 August 2006. Almost all the Marines who championed his cause have also died, and as of 2017 he has not received the Medal of Honor.

GABALDON'S SKILL AT TALKING the Japanese out of their hiding places was not the norm. Most of the time it was the other way around. "We saw hundreds of bodies, lying in the surf or lying dead on the rocks below," remembered Private Clifford Howe of Havre, Montana, serving with the 1st Battalion, 165th Infantry Regiment. "It made even the most hardened American soldiers sick to see this."

Marpi Point was a long plateau where the Japanese had built an auxiliary airfield. Its landscape contained a honeycomb of caves, the last refuge of hundreds of Japanese troops and civilians. At the edge of the plateau there was a sheer eight-hundred-foot drop to jagged coral below that bordered the sea. Marines learned to call the precipice "Suicide Cliff" or "Banzai Cliff." Whole families gathered there at the edge of the cliff, then leapt off. Another cliff, 265 feet above the ocean, was also the site of many Japanese suicides. When the suicides ended, the areas below them were stained red with human blood.

"You wouldn't believe it unless you saw it," said one Marine who was part of a group working with ropes to pick up the bodies of two Americans who had been killed there. There were hundreds of Jap civilians—men, women, and children—up there on the cliff. In the most routine way they would jump off the cliff or climb down and wade into the sea. "I saw a father throw his three children off and then jump down himself," said the Marine.

Corporal Canara Caruth, the commander of a 2nd Armored Amphibian tank attached to the 2nd Marines, saw a woman throw her children over the cliff, then jump after them. Some photographers took her picture when she was falling. "I guess she thought we were going to take her babies and eat them," Caruth recalled. "I saw a lot of terrible things at Saipan, but I think that was the worst thing I ever saw."

Sergeant Tom Tinsley recalled, "Some children were killed by holding their feet and beating their heads against the rocks. Any civilians that didn't kill themselves, the Japanese soldiers would kill with hand grenades. Some used swords to cut off the heads of the children. The bottom of the cliff at Marpi Point was a horrendous mass of bodies, both military and civilian. This was a hell of a price to pay for an island not any larger than Fort Smith, Arkansas."

SERGEANT DAVID DOWDAKIN of I Company, 3rd Battalion, 2nd Marines, described the bloody, disturbing events at the northern end of Saipan in the aftermath of the *gyokusai*.

"We dug in a double line on either side of the road—one facing toward the cliff and one facing toward the sea," said Dowdakin. "We were keeping our normal watch on at night so that half of us would be awake at any time, and after so many days of this routine, we were suffering badly from sleep deprivation.

"The first night I awoke to find a Japanese soldier crouched beside me. I shot him as he cracked the fuse on a grenade. Then I went back to sleep listening to the cries of women and children nearby," he said.

The second night, Dowdakin added, everybody awoke at once to find themselves under attack. Dowdakin opened fire and cut down a man who seemed to be struggling with smaller people. "Then I realized the man was killing his children with a knife," he said. "A figure in a skirt leaped over the double concertina wire and kept running full tilt to the cliffs and leapt over. There was another burst of fire from the BAR man next to me, and he hit a teenage boy squarely in the head. It was obviously a terrible mistake, but it was too late now to do anything about it.

"At dawn we sat eating our C-rations calmly," he said, "in the midst of what could truthfully be described as a slaughterhouse. Two women and several children sat among us. We gave them C rations, but they wouldn't eat them. They drank all our water."

MARINE SERGEANT GRANT TIMMERMAN was a tank commander in the 2nd Tank Battalion supporting the 6th Marines. During mop-up action the day after the *gyokusai*

Timmerman was advancing with his tank ahead of an infantry unit, firing steadily until a series of enemy trenches and pill-boxes halted him.

He noticed a likely target and immediately ordered the tank stopped. Aware of the danger from the muzzle blast from his 75-millimeter gun, Timmerman stood up in the exposed turret and ordered the infantry to hit the dirt.

At that moment a Japanese soldier threw a grenade that would have dropped through the open turret into the tank, doubtlessly killing or wounding all or most of the inhabitants. Timmerman blocked the opening with his body and held the grenade against his chest, taking the full force of the explosion. His Medal of Honor action saved the rest of his crew, but he willingly sacrificed his own life in the process.

Another Marine, Private First Class Harold C. Agerholm of the 4th Battalion, 10th Marines, made repeated trips through a highly dangerous area in a Jeep converted into an ambulance to evacuate about forty-five seriously wounded men before a hidden Japanese rifleman shot him to death.

SOME QUESTIONS STILL REMAIN unanswered almost three-quarters of a century later. One of them is a report that a Marine artillery unit—the 3rd Battalion, 10th Marines—repulsed an attack by Japanese forces at the height of the *gyoku-sai* by firing its artillery at point-blank range, decimating the enemy and thus sparing many American lives.

As war correspondent Robert Sherrod, writing for *Time* magazine in the 19 July 1944 issue, phrased it: "The artillerymen fired point-blank into the Japs with fuses set at four-tenths of a second. They bounced their high explosive shells 50 yards in front of the guns and into the maniacal ranks. . . . When the order came to withdraw, they sent this answer back, 'Sir, we would prefer to stay and fight it out.' They did."

Not according to General George Griner, commander of the 27th Infantry. In a September 28 letter addressed to the editor of *Time,* he said the Marine artillery battalion did not stop the attack. It fought very courageously and suffered 136 casualties, but it was likewise overrun. The number of enemy dead found at its position was 322.

Captain Edmund Love of the 27th Infantry had this to say: "It is doubtful that the Marines ever fired a round from any one of their artillery pieces during that morning. Men of the 1st and 2nd Battalions, 105th Infantry, who were in front of those guns are adamant in their statement that no rounds were fired. Officers of this battalion later investigated the sites of the two batteries nearest them. They testified that the ammunition was piled neatly and the only used brass was also stacked in neat piles. Not a round had been fired since the registration of the night before."

After a brief and gallant fight at close range in which these Marines killed 322 enemy soldiers at a cost of 136 killed and wounded, the positions were overrun, according to Love. The brevity and surprise are attested by the fact that the guns captured by the enemy and recaptured later by the 106th Infantry Regiment were found intact without even one single breechblock removed.

THE FACTS, AS FAR AS "Howlin' Mad" Smith was concerned, were simple enough. He reported to Admiral Spruance that the Japanese banzai attack—unquestionably the largest of its kind in the Pacific War—had included only "300 enemy supported by two or three tanks."

It stretches the imagination considerably that the same military commander who traveled the front lines on the afternoon of 6 July, warning people about the strong possibilities of a banzai attack, could now write it off as consisting of only three hundred men. (By 1948, when his book, *Coral and Brass,* was released, Smith had reexamined the incident and come up with a more realistic figure of fifteen hundred to three thousand Japanese attackers.)

General Griner immediately protested Smith's report and ordered a careful count of the bodies. What he found were 4,311 Japanese corpses. Fully aware that Smith would claim that a large percentage of the dead had died of wounds suffered earlier in the campaign, Griner cited figures given in the tried-and-true Army field manual.

"I viewed personally upwards of one thousand enemy bodies," Griner said, "and nowhere did I find marked decomposition of bodies which would indicate that the enemy had been dead for more than thirty-six to forty-eight hours. I call your attention to the Army field manual on military sanitation and hygiene which states, 'At temperatures of 85 degrees Fahrenheit, maggots will begin forming on bodies in approximately forty-eight hours.' There were no maggots on these bodies when I viewed them."

There is no way to ascertain exactly how many Japanese were involved in the banzai attack. That is precisely the reason the estimate of fifteen hundred to three thousand is most often used.

Although this figure is not specific, it serves to correct the first early report that the total was 300 to 400. That erroneous figure as well as a larger one of 1,500 participants put forward by Japanese Major Yoshida are almost certainly wrong by at least several hundred—and possibly by 1,000 or more. American soldiers and Marines reported figures of 50, 75, 100, 150, and so on. This was in addition to a sector-by-sector count of enemy dead that revealed that 2,295 enemy soldiers were killed in the combat area of the 1st and 2nd Battalions of the 105th Infantry Regiment as well as 2,016 in the combat area of the 1st and 2nd Battalions of the 106th Infantry Regiment.

One mass-killing episode, related by Lieutenant Kenneth Hensley of G Company, 6th Marines, is an example. Hensley was in command of four amphibian tractors and twenty-four riflemen on 9 July, when the incident occurred.

"We closed to about a hundred yards from the fifty or sixty enemy on the reef, and motioned them to come to the boat," he said, "but they motioned us away. One officer armed with a rifle and standing on a rock . . . aimed his rifle at the boat several times. We covered this officer with machine guns and closed with the LVTs to about fifty yards.

"The Jap officer fired at the leading boats, and a machine gun—apparently about a .50-caliber—opened fire on the boats, putting two holes completely through one LVT. Many of the enemy threw hand grenades from the reef and fired rifles at the leading boats. Immediately all boats opened fire with small arms and annihilated the fifty to sixty enemy on this section of the reef."

In addition to their reef sweeping, Hensley's men also cleared a pocket east of Tanapag village on 9 July. One hundred Japanese bodies were counted there.

On the night of 8 July and into the early morning hours, a large cadre of Japanese emerged from their hiding places, and the 165th Infantry Regiment killed approximately 75 in front of its positions. The next night 150 more were killed. The 6th Marines, meanwhile, reported killing "50 or more" enemy soldiers as they attempted to sneak through the lines.

When darkness arrived on 8 July, from positions overlooking the coastal flats the 23rd Marines observed large straggler groups of Japanese moving toward Marpi Point, and they brought their long-range machine guns and 75-millimeter guns to bear on them. When the carnage was over, the 23rd Marines had this to report: "Over 500 Japanese were killed."

But it seems likely that the 1st Battalion, 2nd Marines, could claim to have racked up even more dead Japanese that day. They killed an estimated eight hundred enemy soldiers—more, in fact, than they had killed during the rest of the Saipan operation put together. As one company commander observed, "Hunting was exceptionally good."

Exactly how many Japanese were killed during the climactic *gyokusai* attack and the mop-up that followed will likely never be determined.

EARLY ON 8 JULY the Marines of the 23rd Regiment started moving toward the caves that flanked the north coast near Karaberra Pass. Instead of giving the 27th Army Division the task of officially securing Saipan, Holland Smith had recalled his 2nd Division to the front, along with the 4th Division, to do what mopping up was necessary.

"I don't think the Japs have much fight left in them," Lieutenant James Leary remarked after a steep climb up the hill and a pause on a flat-rock outcropping.

"That's just the way I like it," said Private First Class Carl Matthews, Leary's runner. "I'm plumb tired of fighting." Matthews's words were more drawn out than usual, even given his East Texas accent, but nobody seemed to notice. Matthews was having a hard time walking, much less talking. There was something wrong with him, but he couldn't tell what it was. It seemed to have something to do with a siege of relentless shelling he had gone through. He continued to perform his duties, but he was aware of blacking out for several seconds at a time.

When it was time to move on again Matthews stood up first, leaning into the wind unsteadily. Leary also stood up, and a split-second later the rattle of a machine gun below them broke the silence. Matthews ducked instinctively just as he saw Leary fall.

From somewhere up above him he heard someone calling for a corpsman.

"It's no use," he yelled. "The lieutenant's dead."

JAPANESE ATTACKS STILL CAME without warning. The day after the *gyokusai,* when everything was supposed to be settling down, the enemy attempted to move men through Karaberra Pass in order to stage another assault. Warned early that the Japanese were coming, A Company of the 2nd Marine Division established a defensive line and waited for the charge. Sometimes, if the Japanese drank some saki before the assault, they'd try to make a run at the Americans. They did this time.

As the Japanese attacked, some of them yelled, "Babe Ruth no good!" "Roosevelt son of a bitch!" and "Japanese drink Marine blood!"

The Americans responded with, "Tojo eats shit!" and "Hirohito eats shit!"

Some Japanese made their way around a cliff and attacked from the sea. One young Marine, Oklahoma-born Private First Class Ralph Browner—who was only sixteen years old, five-foot-six, and 125 pounds—found himself on a lonely section of beach with the ocean about two yards to his left, a cliff five yards to his right, and the beach behind him, about twenty yards deep. Browner had a .30-caliber machine gun, his carbine, and several grenades. He heard the sound of dripping water behind him.

He turned to see three Japanese soldiers in loincloths emerging from the water brandishing knives. He shot each one squarely through the head. A fourth soldier appeared and lunged at him, and Browner put a bullet through his chest.

Firing the machine gun freehand, Browner pulled the pins on a couple of grenades and threw them with his other hand. When the fight was over he had killed approximately forty of the Japanese. He was awarded the Navy Cross.

THE CASE OF Private First Class Carl Matthews was extremely puzzling at first. But under repeated questioning by doctors and nurses, his problems were slowly uncovered. During a period of close-in shelling, a short round of artillery had fallen close to Matthews. "It did something to my head," he recalled. "It was like my brain was bigger than my skull all of a sudden. My entire body felt like a giant firecracker had exploded and slammed against me."

When that happened Matthews passed out completely. Observers said he simply sat down on the ground and didn't move. Another soldier picked him up and took him to a regimental hospital. He was transferred to a hospital ship. But his memory was faulty, and his eardrum was busted. He didn't remember anything for eight days. When he finally woke up he was in New Caledonia, and another patient heard him talking.

The soldier said, "Hey, Matthews, is that you?"

It was Corpsman Winiford Moore of Dandridge, Tennessee—from Matthews's unit. He had been blinded from a bullet wound in the head, but he knew Matthews by the sound of his voice. Matthews's nerves were in such a state that he vomited all over the floor.

For a few months following that day Matthews moved in and out of unconsciousness. There were periods he could remember and periods when he could remember nothing. Blood vessels in his brain were ruptured, and the seepage of blood produced a condition similar to a stroke. It took many months for him to return to normal.

Each overloaded hospital ship had beds for 480 men, but the flood of wounded was such that patients were put on cots, sofas, and borrowed bunks of ship personnel—and still there was never enough space. Only about one man of every five wounded could be taken aboard hospital ships. The rest were forced to sweat it out on the crowded bunks of transport ships. Matthews was lucky: because of his strange and recurring illnesses, he rated a bed.

The types of wounds most men suffered were from artillery and mortars, which caused an estimated 65 percent of the wounds. Saipan had been an artillery fight, punctuated by brutal, close-in fighting and more and larger banzai wounds than veterans in the Pacific had ever experienced.

When men on hospital ships succumbed to their wounds, as many did, they were lowered over the side of the ship.

Matthews saw eight or ten dead men buried at sea. They had weights tied to their feet so they'd go down in a hurry.

SERGEANT TOM TINSLEY'S Marine regiment had moved to the top of a hill and dug in for the night. The next morning they moved down the hill and relieved the Army units that were left from the banzai charge. It was a far from pleasant experience.

They had to move bodies in order to dig a foxhole that first night on the coastal plain, and for the next few days the stench of rotting flesh was almost unbearable. "The flies were so bad you couldn't eat without them getting in your mouth," remembered Tinsley. In this one small area there were 3,000 or more dead in a tract of ground that contained only a few acres. "It reminded me of Custer's last stand," he said. "I think there were 918 US military men killed or wounded in the area."

As Tinsley and a battalion runner named Tex were returning to the Regimental CP, a Jap who was dug into the railroad bank opened fire on them, but because he was firing across the railroad tracks, he couldn't depress the gun low enough to hit either Marine.

"He did put a hole in the canteen I had on my back," Tinsley said, "and I found out I could dig a foxhole in the hard clay with my feet and bare hands. Our command post was just on the other side of the railroad tracks, and Tex was really getting nervous. I did my best to calm him down.

"He can't hit us here, and if he moves to where he can see us, we can hit him," Tinsley told him. But Tex just couldn't take it. He was determined to make a run for the CP. "Later on, after he got back, he showed me five bullet holes in his dungarees and a bullet burn across his stomach near his navel. "You were damn lucky," Tinsley said. "You pull a stunt like that again, and I'll shoot you myself!"

By late in the evening they had advanced to the top of the ridge, and the regimental commander ordered them to retreat to the forward slope of the hill behind the ridge. Tinsley was bunking with a young private first class named Leonard Allen, an eighteen-year-old recruit from Selma, Alabama, whom Tinsley had adopted as a foxhole buddy.

"But I was so dog-tired," Tinsley said. "The rain had kept us wet and muddy for weeks. I think it rained every day and night we were on the island. At any rate, I passed out cold."

A group of Japanese troops decided to charge their line just at dawn the next morning while Tinsley was still sound asleep. They came racing over the ridge yelling, "Banzai! Marine, you die!" When they found the Marines weren't there, it was too late—they were like lambs led to the slaughter.

"The machine gun in front of the two-man foxhole where Allen and I were was credited with killing over fifty Japanese troops," Tinsley remembered. He slept through the battle, and when he asked Allen why he didn't wake him up, he just kind of shrugged.

"We had the situation well in hand," said Allen. "And you needed the sleep."

When the battle of Saipan was declared officially at an end, it wasn't actually over. Small pockets of resistant Japanese remained hidden in caves, and their presence posed a threat to workers who were rapidly turning the island into an important base for bombing runs over the heart of Japan.

In no time Holland Smith went back on his vow "never to use the 27th Division again." During the period between 9 July and 4 October, when the division was finally evacuated, the Army killed about 2,000 more enemy soldiers and captured 3,000 civilians. Of the 30,000 Japanese troops on the island, only 921 were taken prisoner. Some 20,000 Saipan civilians died.

For the record Holland Smith would never again command US soldiers in the field. It was probably because of opinions similar to those expressed by Brigadier General Clark Ruffner in a letter to Lieutenant General Robert Richardson, commander of all Army troops in the Central Pacific. Ruffner accused "Howlin' Mad" of being "highly prejudiced against the Army, as demonstrated in his manner, language, overbearing attitude toward Army commanders, and his biased remarks and actions in all Army matters."

General Ralph Smith, who had earned a Silver Star for two instances of bravery with the infantry in France in 1918, went on to become military attaché at the US Embassy in Paris. Upon retiring from the Army in 1948 he served as a fellow at Stanford University's Hoover Institute on War, Revolution, and Peace. After he passed his hundredth birthday and became the oldest surviving general officer in the US Army, he was asked how he achieved such a magnificent age. "I get up every morning and I'm still here," he said. "That's how I got this way."

THE JAPANESE WERE the first to admit that losing Saipan was a blow that was beyond recovery. As Fleet Admiral Osami Nagano, supreme naval adviser to the Emperor, later put it, "When we lost Saipan, hell was upon us."

Vice Admiral Shigeyosh Miwa, who commanded the Japanese submarine force that attacked Pearl Harbor, stated it even more bluntly after the war: "Our war was lost with the loss of Saipan," he said. "It meant [that the United States] could cut off our shipping and attack our homeland."

Vice Admiral Shigeru Fukudome, who had served as chief of staff of the Imperial Japanese Navy, expressed similar feelings. "With the loss of the Marianas," he said later, "I felt that the last chance had slipped away from us."

Their assessment was accurate. It was truly the beginning of the end for Japan, although only a handful of American civilians realized the importance of what had happened. In the frantic flood of war news and the continuation of the assault against Japan, it is doubtful that most US citizens even understood the importance of the fall of Saipan.

"I have always considered Saipan as the decisive battle of the Pacific offensive," Holland Smith would write later. "Iwo Jima and Okinawa were costlier battles and carried us closer to Japan, but their capture was made possible only by our earlier success at Saipan."

Before Saipan, America and Japan both possessed powerful carrier-based air support, but after Saipan—because of the Marianas Turkey Shoot—only the Americans prevailed. Before Saipan, except for a few tenuously held airbases in China, the Japanese homeland was beyond the range of US land-based bombers. After Saipan, land-based American bombers could strike Japanese cities every day. Before Saipan, US submarines were based some 2,400 miles from Japanese home waters. After Saipan the distance was reduced by about half.

And most importantly, before Saipan the Japanese government that had triggered the war against the United States at

Pearl Harbor was still in power. After Saipan the government of Hideki Tojo was forced to resign, and the new government was ordered to consider the possibility of ending the war.

DESPITE ALL THIS, some Japanese soldiers refused to concede and continued to operate in the remote high country around Saipan's Mount Tapotchau for more than a year. One case involved Captain Oba Sakae, who vanished into the hills with 350 Japanese soldiers as the battle was ending. Oba spent several months organizing his forces and stealing supplies to keep them alive.

In spite of numerous Marine sweeps through the area, Oba somehow always managed to escape. Nevertheless, his soldiers suffered from constant hunger as well as a loss of men whenever they encountered US troops.

The situation remained unresolved for more than a year until the Americans sent other Japanese officers to persuade Oba that the war had indeed ended. Three months after Japan surrendered, Oba led his small remaining group of forty-six men down out of the hills, and they gave themselves up.

TODAY THE TUMULT of war seems far away in Saipan, which is now a part of the US Commonwealth of the Northern Marianas Islands.

The wreckage of Garapan, once the island's capital, remained unpopulated for close to twenty years after the war. But in the 1960s and 1970s the area was redeveloped into large resort hotels and expensive condominiums. Today thousands of tourists flock there each year, many of them from Japan.

Garapan now has a resident population of about 3,600 persons. It is also home to the American Memorial Park, which honors the US soldiers and Marines who died in the battle.

Among the fields that lie inland from the hotels, occasional reminders of the war are still found. It is relatively common to find weapons, canteens, and unexploded shells left behind by the 100,000 Americans and Japanese who fought for twenty-four days on Saipan.

Kuentai, a Japanese organization that has located the remains of several 27th Division soldiers on Saipan, reported in February 2016 that it had found the dog tag of a member of the division, Private First Class Thomas Davis, who received the Silver Star in June 1944 for risking his life to rescue a wounded comrade under heavy fire. The dog tag was found sticking out of the soil in a farm field on Saipan.

Ironically, Davis, who served in the 165th Infantry Regiment of the 27th Division, was killed some ten months later on Okinawa by a Japanese sniper while again helping a wounded soldier. His body was brought home four years later and was reburied in Roachdale, Indiana.

Officials said that Tom Davis of Victoria, Texas, a fifty-seven-year-old machinist who was named after his uncle, would receive the dog tag.

chapter 10

★ ★ ★

Tinian's Rolling Plains

THE ISLAND of Tinian, three and a half miles southwest of Saipan, might very well have been made for the B-29 Superfortress. Within a few weeks after US forces landed, about five hundred of the massive bombers would be grazing on Tinian's rolling plains. And when the B-29s started to roll, there would literally be hell to pay in Japan.

It was true that most of Tinian was edged with jagged limestone cliffs that ranged from the height of a man's head to about a hundred feet. Gaps in the cliffs were few and far between. They allowed Japanese defenders to concentrate their defenses on some of the most likely landing sites, a distinct problem for a Marine landing force.

But once you got beyond the limestone cliffs, almost the entire length of Tinian was actually one long plateau—as flat as a pancake—rising up from the surrounding ocean. At the time of the Tinian invasion on 24 September 1944, most of that long, flat plateau was devoted to neat, checkerboard fields of sugar cane, and two sprawling airfields took up much of the rest.

While the bitter fighting for Saipan was unfolding, US forces had ample opportunities to scrutinize Tinian from every possible angle. At thirty-nine square miles, the island was as large as Saipan, and American artillery systematically pounded it every day for almost two months. It is highly doubtful that any enemy island was more thoroughly reconnoitered during the entire Pacific War.

In the words of Admiral Raymond A. Spruance, the assault on Tinian was probably the "most brilliantly conceived and executed amphibious operation" in all of World War II.

From a strategic standpoint it was the flatness of Tinian's terrain that made it such a desirable target. One of the main objectives of the entire Marianas campaign was to obtain bases for long-range bombers, and Tinian's rolling plains and gentle slopes offered far better sites than Saipan. The Japanese themselves had already constructed one airfield on Tinian that boasted a runway almost a thousand feet longer than the one at Aslito Airfield on Saipan.

In a matter of a few months—with the help of fifteen thousand men of the Naval Construction Battalion, or Seabees—two Tinian airfields, known as North Field and West Field, were destined to become the busiest in the world as the home base for the newly formed 20th Air Force.

THE BEACHES OFF Tinian Town, the largest settlement on the island, located on the southwest shore facing Sunharon Bay, obviously offered the most convenient place for the Marines to land. They were designated as Orange, Red, Green, and Blue, and they boasted beaches some 2,100 yards wide with only a few small breaks.

This was also where the Japanese fully expected the US forces to come ashore and where most of the island's nine thousand Japanese troops—approximately half Army and half Navy—were congregated and well prepared. They were deeply entrenched with many 25-millimeter guns in place and sizable infantry defenses. Two coastal defense batteries also covered Tinian Town, and the waters around it were known to be heavily mined. Convenient or not, serious consequences had to be considered. Holland Smith, before he departed to take a new noncombat job, warned that it could be another Tarawa.

Another potential site was Yellow Beach on the northeast shore of Asiga Bay, about one-third of the way up the island. It consisted of short, sandy stretches of twenty or twenty-five feet, with the longest expanse about 125 yards wide.

Two other possible sites were located on the northwest shore near the two airfields. These White 1 and White 2 Beaches, each less than two hundred feet wide, were generally considered by the Japanese as simply too small for a regimental landing with two battalions abreast. Nevertheless, American planners felt they had no alternative but to seriously consider the White beaches, even with their shortcomings.

Ultimately, the planners chose the narrow White Beaches on the northwest coast. In so doing they accepted the risks that troops, equipment, and supplies might back up and stagnate hopelessly at the water's edge. That risk was heavy. Despite the fact that the assault troops of the 2nd and 4th Marines would be worn and weary after a long and difficult struggle to take Saipan, all the Marine and Navy commanders finally agreed: it had to be the White Beaches or else.

With Saipan secured and the preparations for the next landing at midpoint, a change of command within the Northern Troops and Landing Force took place. On 12 July Holland Smith was relieved and ordered to take command of Fleet Marine Force, Pacific, a newly created unit for all Marine combat forces in the Pacific theater. It would be an administrative but backwater position, with little or no dealings with troops in the field. The new commanding general for the Northern Troops and Landing Force was Major General Harry Schmidt, who was relieved of his command of the 4th Marine Division by Major General Clifton Cates. Schmidt was a smart, tough leader and strategist with thirty-five years of service as a Marine.

THE JAPANESE FORCES on Tinian were under the command of Colonel Kiyochi Ogata, commander of Japan's 50th Infantry Regiment. Ogata was well aware that an invasion of the island was coming, and he was luckier than General Saito, his counterpart on Saipan, in that his troops were fully trained and well equipped. Ogata had headed his regiment since August 1940, and before arriving on Tinian they had served in Manchuria. In the process Ogata had developed a high degree of spirit among his troops.

Ogata's plan for defending Tinian was basically the same as the one used on Saipan. The enemy was to be destroyed at the water's edge if possible. If not, he was to be subjected to a counterattack on the night after the landing. If expelling the enemy proved impossible, the Japanese would fall back on prepared positions to the south and defend them to the last man.

For once the Americans were close enough to their next objective to pound it with their guns from a fire support base on Saipan. On 20 July, while the combat on Saipan was at its height, US Army 155-millimeter "Long Toms" started bombarding Tinian daily, and the number of artillery pieces grew as the battle for Saipan wound down. Meanwhile Rear Admiral Harry Hill's gunships were also busy over Tinian, while carrier planes and Army P-47s flying from Aslito Airfield added to the bombardment.

Beginning on 16 July the US naval bombardment began. On 23 July Admiral Hill stepped up his preparatory fire with a total of three old battleships, two heavy cruisers, three light cruisers, and sixteen destroyers. The ships were set up to fire in such a way that Tinian would be shelled from every point on the compass, and the naval artillery plan was carefully designed to give the Japanese no indication about where the amphibious assault would take place.

The day of the assault, 24 July, was called "Jig Day" in Marine terminology, although few, if any, people know today exactly how the name originated.

At daybreak a flotilla of ships and landing craft carrying the 2nd Marine Division set out from Saipan's Tanapag Harbor in a well-calculated feint on Tinian Town. The battleship USS *Colorado* and the destroyer USS *Norman Scott* were struck numerous times by Japanese guns, while they sat offshore pounding Japanese fortifications, with the Navy suffering sixty-two killed, including *Norman Scott*'s captain, Commander Seymour D. Owens, who was posthumously awarded the Navy Cross for his actions that day. In addition, 245 sailors on the two ships were wounded before the Japanese shore battery was silenced. Except for those considerable losses, the feint attack was highly successful. In the process Tinian Town was reduced to ashes and piles of burning rubble.

The Japanese fell for the American ruse hook, line, and sinker. A message from Tinian to Tokyo said that "more than a hundred landing barges had been repulsed" in an attempt to get ashore at Tinian Town. Instead, elements of the 4th Marine Division and the Marines' 8th Regimental Combat Team were pouring ashore at the other end of the island in the *real* H-Hour.

Marine casualties for that first day ashore were relatively low, and enemy opposition was spotty—moderate small arms and mortar fire—although occasionally fierce. Those Marines who did make contact with the enemy were impressed with the caliber of the Japanese garrison. The average enemy soldier on Tinian was better trained with much superior marksmanship than those on Saipan.

The 2nd Division took the main beach area. Private First Class Charles Pase had fought at Tarawa and Saipan, and he was still a month short of his eighteenth birthday when he and the rest of the 8th Regimental Combat Team hit shore. The Marines were in relatively flat country, right down next to the beach. The hole through which they moved inland was so small that the Japs didn't even bother to defend it. It couldn't have been more than fifty or a hundred feet wide. "It was tiny," Pase remembered. "It was the kind that you take your girlfriend down to and go skinny dipping."

Despite its size, the entire Regimental Combat Team made it through that opening in a matter of a few hours. The infantry got in, moved out, and gave them a hundred yards of clearance. "They pulled those big guns in—the machine guns and the Pack Howitzers. I don't know how many men we lost, but I don't think it was more than about a dozen," Pase said.

As soon as the 4th Division got ashore, they gave the 2nd Division the protection they needed to make a safe landing on a big beach, which is exactly what they did. In fact, the landing was so well carried out that the 4th Division got a Presidential Unit Citation for it. "Of course, it was dangerous," Pase said, "and the colonel that handled it deserves all the praise he can get. He got us ashore, and we did all of our fighting *after* we were ashore, not just trying to get there."

The 4th Marines took full advantage of the sea power turned loose on Tinian to rush its assault elements ashore in slightly more than 500 LVTs and 130 DUKWs (amphibious trucks). These vehicles penetrated Japanese defenses at White Beach, and although enemy mines and machine guns slowed the advance temporarily, the Marines had the mobility to roll inland in a hurry.

General Clifford Cates had learned from his experience at Guadalcanal how important it was to get his tanks, half-tracks, and light artillery ashore well before sundown. He also landed enough barbed wire to cover the extended perimeter so that the Japanese couldn't surprise his troops. The hurry-up tempo of off-loading never paused for a moment. By nightfall Cates had 15,000 Marines ashore on the narrow beaches, and the cost in lives had been amazingly light—only 15 Marines were killed and 225 wounded.

"The Japs were hell bent and determined," Pase said. "They were willing to sacrifice every Jap on the island if they could stop us. Well, they sacrificed every Jap they had, and they still didn't stop us!"

Men who fought their way through oceans of sugar cane on Saipan couldn't believe the amount of cane they now encountered on Tinian. The land was almost exclusively cane fields, and the Japanese knew how to hide themselves perfectly under a few sheets of cane. The open fields were hazardous enough—they offered clear fields of fire to anyone dug in on the far side—but you could only see a few feet ahead in the unharvested fields.

PRIVATE FIRST CLASS BILL STEEL of the 3rd Battalion, 2nd Marines, had been wounded at Tarawa and wounded again at Saipan. When he got ready to get off the boat at Tinian, he was scared to death—this was his third campaign, and everybody said it was the worst. "I urinated all over myself; that's how scared I was," he remembered.

"It's like a guy going to his death in the electric chair or something," Steel said. "They feed you steak and eggs at about four o'clock in the morning, like it was a ritual of some kind." Once he got ashore, however, he was all right.

That first night on Tinian Steel's unit came ashore near the Ushi Point Airfield. Their first job was killing pilots, air crewmen, and mechanics. All the Japanese had been shot up and just left there. The Japanese were all wearing dungaree flying suits—that was how the Marines knew they were in the air force. They moved across the island, swung around to clear out everything on their left flank, then started down the island with their front line all the way across it.

"We didn't really know at the time what was going on," Steel recalled. "We'd never heard of the Manhattan Project or the atomic bomb, but this was the airport they would use when the time came. I was back home by then. The Navy gave orders that people who had been wounded twice could go home, and I got on the list. I got back to the States on December 7, 1944."

COLONEL OGATA WAS furious that he'd misjudged the main thrust of the Marine landing, and he tried his best to reverse the situation that night by sending several thousand of his troops, led by tanks, in an attack on the American perimeter. The assault came after a heavy artillery barrage, but once again General Cates was too smart for them. Star shells fired from offshore destroyers helped backlight the Japanese attackers, and Marine tanks, half-tracks, and machine guns exacted a hefty toll on Japanese infantry entangled in barbed wire.

When it was over the Marines had held at every point. After sunrise they counted fifteen hundred dead Japanese surrounding their perimeter.

"We've broken their backs," said Cates.

Early that morning the 2nd Marine Division landed on White Beach and maintained the momentum of the previous day. The two divisions moved out together and quickly reached the east coast of Tinian. There they turned southward and began moving down the island. A few Japanese units fought hard to stop them, but many of Ogata's surviving forces retreated rapidly to the south.

"ABOUT HALF THE TIME at Tinian our troops never had any officers around," remembered Private First Class Carl Peltier of the 2nd Marines, who grew up in Texas. He was one of only twenty-two survivors in his 81-millimeter mortar platoon, which hit the beach at Saipan with sixty-two men. A total of forty members of the platoon had been either killed or seriously wounded.

"Those guys who were left knew what we had to do that second time around, and we did it," said Peltier. "One time a lieutenant showed up, and we were all excited. But the first night he was there, he was sitting around talking to us when a sniper got him. He didn't die right then, but he died a short time later. Then we were right back with no officers.

"Most of the guys were still privates who came in as replacements. Since I was a private first class I caught a lot of flak about it. I was small too—a feather merchant if there ever was one—who was barely five-feet-four and weighed 125 pounds after a full meal." Peltier had just turned nineteen, but he was already savvy enough to know how to swipe BARs and Thompson submachine guns from the Army people. "We used to hide them in our 81-millimeter mortars," he said. "Nobody had the nerve to look down those guns."

One time he found himself sitting just two foxholes away from a Japanese. When the interloper was discovered, the Marines all quickly dove in their foxholes. "They sent out a patrol and they got him, but he was well camouflaged," recalled Peltier. "He was in the middle of a cane field, and he was inside a concrete box that looked a little like a coffin—and when the patrol got through with him, it really *was* a coffin. God knows how long that Jap had been there without any food or water or anything else."

Peltier said he didn't like being called a hero, but when he found out later on that his men were the most-decorated 81-millimeter mortar platoon of World War II, he did enjoy calling himself "a survivor." "I earned that," he said, "because of Saipan and Tinian."

CORPORAL ROY ROUSH of the 6th Marines heard by way of the grapevine that there was another man named Roush who had recently joined his G Company on Tinian.

When he heard the news he wanted to meet the guy. Because there weren't a whole lot of people named Roush, he started asking where this new guy was.

"He's over there in the other end of the company line," he was told. Roush number one intended to look up the man and introduce himself, but before he got around to it there was a brief banzai attack, and Roush number two suffered a bullet wound. "He was carried out, and I never actually saw the guy," said Roush. "But we had a first sergeant that was, well, kind of a stumblebum, and he thought the wounded man was *me*, and he sent a telegram to my parents, and it was never corrected."

The telegram sent to his parents said, "Sorry to inform you that Roy William Roush was injured in the Battle of Tinian." In a few weeks he started getting letters from his folks and a lot of other people, asking how he was, where he got hit, and so forth.

"I finally figured out what had happened, but I still don't know if the parents of Roush number two ever got the word. And I got to wondering what would've happened if Roush number two had been killed. Would that first sergeant have done the same thing? Would he have sent a letter saying 'Sorry to inform you that your son, Roy Roush, was killed in action on Tinian'?"

FROM 27 TO 30 July both Marine divisions made rapid advances toward the plateau that dominated the southern tip of the island. For two days General Schmidt used an "elbowing" technique. On the first day he held back the 4th Division while the 2nd Division surged forward. On the second day the roles were exchanged. On the 29th this technique was abandoned, and both divisions were ordered to advance as rapidly as possible.

"The first of August about 2:30 in the morning we had the Japanese pushed back into a small area," remembered Platoon Sergeant Joe Brown of the 2nd Marine Division, a native of Wichita Falls, Texas. "We were fending off banzai attacks all that night. We had a breakthrough, and they came in at us hard with demolition and hand grenades."

The rest of his platoon—those who weren't wounded—had fallen back and left Brown and Lieutenant Stacy Davis all alone. "He was in the hole with me, and he had a machine gun and was firing at 'em when my little carbine misfired," said Brown. "This little Jap came up while we were on our knees in the foxhole. He made a stab at me, and when he did, I got hit by his bayonet. It went in my right arm and slid up under the bones in my shoulder."

Brown was able to grab the muzzle of the rifle, catch the Japanese around the legs, pull him down, and crawl on top of him. Brown still had the rifle in his hands. "I don't know how I held onto it because the wound in my arm was about eight or ten inches long, but I got the stock of the rifle in my hand and beat him with the hand that was numb. I beat him until I was sure he was dead meat. Then I crawled back toward my foxhole through the intermittent fire."

Meanwhile Lieutenant Davis's machine gun was out of ammo, but he kept knocking Japanese soldiers down all around Brown with a rifle until Brown reached safety.

"You got 'em, Joe; you got 'em!" Davis yelled between shots.

"Hell yeah," Brown said. "I got 'em!"

For Brown and his section it was the first banzai attack they had experienced. "I wasn't involved in the big banzai on Saipan," he said, "because we were in another part of the field. But the Japanese were fanatic fighters, and life really didn't mean anything to them. They'd either kill themselves or do something to make you shoot them. They weren't about to let you take them prisoner."

Brown was taken to an aid station and later was put aboard the USS *Relief*, a hospital ship. After a scare with gangrene in his injured leg, he spent twenty days in treatment in Hawaii for a torn ligament, then was flown home to Texas.

PHARMACIST'S MATE H. L. OBERMILLER came ashore with the Marines. A few nights later, when his unit bivouacked, they stretched a trip wire about a foot off the ground so the Japanese would hit it and set off an alarm. One night some civilians came through. The sentry shot at them, and you could hear people running.

"I started back there, and they threw me a light, and I found a little girl," remembered Obermiller. "She was about a year and a half or two years old, and she was tied to an old man's back with a rope." The old man had been shot, and the bullet had gone through him and hit the little girl. Her left kidney was outside her body. Obermiller cut her loose and protected her from the rain that was falling and did what he could to dress her wound. "I sent her down to the aid station in the morning when the sun came up," he said. "I frankly don't know how she could have lived. It's an incident that has haunted me for a long time."

As on Saipan, a Japanese banzai attack was repulsed on Tinian with heavy losses for the Japanese. Colonel Ogata personally led the attack, which was directed primarily at units of the 8th Marines atop a high cliff. For a full half-hour the attackers charged the Marine lines, but at no point did they penetrate. Every charge was turned back with mounting losses.

According to some reports Ogata was killed during the charges by American machine gunfire, and his body was seen hanging dead over a section of the Marines' barbed wire. Other reports said Ogata was seen alive on 2 August, a day after Tinian was declared secured—but that "security" was often fleeting. The 8th Regiment of the 2nd Marine Division spent three months mopping up—in which they killed 542 enemy soldiers and themselves suffered 38 killed and 125 wounded.

After the banzai assault, daybreak revealed over 100 enemy dead in one small area about seventy yards square. Interrogation of prisoners later revealed that the Japanese attackers participating in the assault had numbered between 600 and 800. With the defeat of this last counterattack, organized Japanese resistance quickly came to an end. Altogether the capture of Tinian had cost a total of 328 Marines killed and 1,571 wounded in action. Over 5,000 Japanese were buried, and 252 were taken prisoner. Exactly what happened to the approximately 4,000 remaining Japanese defenders is not known. A large number of them undoubtedly committed suicide in caves, and some may have escaped in small boats to other islands.

Coming so soon after the long, tedious battle for Saipan, the fight for Tinian was almost like a sprint. As General Cates put it later on, "The Marines were heading for the barn."

It took seven days to capture Tinian, and during those days word had finally spread among the Marines. There was something far greater on Tinian than mere cane fields. There were also airfields—and that was why Tinian's capture was so enormously important.

chapter 11

★ ★ ★

Coming Home

ALTHOUGH THERE would be greater losses of human life and spilled blood at Okinawa and Iwo Jima, the two epic and final struggles of the Pacific War, the battles of Saipan and Tinian made America's victory in the Pacific inevitable. The struggle cost US forces a combined grand total of more than fourteen thousand killed, wounded, and missing in action.

But there were also wounded men who never acknowledged their wounds. In the ranks of the hundreds of thousands of US troops engaged in the battles, countless GIs, some as young as seventeen and eighteen years old, suffered irreparable and undiagnosed inner damage to their spirits and souls. They suffered from an ailment that has affected hundreds of thousands of war veterans over the years, but in the 1940s it was an unknown. Some people called it "the shakes." To some people it was like the end of the world.

We know it today as posttraumatic stress disorder.

SEAMAN JAMES SAUNDERS came from a sharecropper farm at Blackwell, Texas, and he had just turned seventeen when Japanese planes attacked Pearl Harbor. "We were all mad as hell," he remembered. "I wanted to do something to get back at the Japs, but my dad said I had to wait."

Saunders's only brother was a couple of years older than James, and two days after Pearl Harbor he joined the Navy. He was aboard the submarine USS *Scorpion* when it was lost with all hands after striking a Japanese mine in January 1944. By then James had dropped out of high school. On 15 January 1943, like his brother, he enlisted in the Navy.

"They gave me a choice of what I wanted to do," he said. "What I really wanted was to be a fighter pilot, but that didn't work out. My next choice was submarines, but that didn't work out either. I finally just told them, 'Just give me a gun and head me west.'"

He was sent to gunnery school for about six months, then he joined the first crew of the USS *Miami*, a brand-new cruiser nicknamed "The South Seas Debutante." Next stop was Eniwetok, where the crew joined the task force of the US Third Fleet.

But on his way to his first island mission James caught a severe case of "jungle rot" in the Philippines and came close to dying from it. "I just rotted from my belt up," he said. "My hair all came out until my head was as slick as a peel, and I had a fever like you wouldn't believe. It lasted twenty-three days, and a man is supposed to die when he has a fever that high, but I didn't. There were fifty cases of it on our ship. Twice a day they bathed me in sulfa drugs. They made a white paste out of it and put it in my ears. It finally eased off, but a doctor told me I'd have trouble with my ears all my life, and I did. If anybody's got their back turned to me, I can hardly tell what they're saying. There was a bunch of the boys that never got over it, but somehow I did."

His first assignment was the Marianas campaign. "I'll never forget the racket those guns made on the *Miami*," he said. "When we opened fire on the beach, the noise was almost unbearable. One young kid got so scared, he hid in a locker. He was only about seventeen, but he just couldn't take it. They had to ship him back to the States.

"Then came Saipan. We were shooting at targets on Saipan," Saunders said, "and we zeroed in on one of the biggest towns there. There was a big sugar factory there with a railroad running through it, and there was a train pulling out of that factory, and I asked for permission to fire on that train. We hit it, and about fifty yards of those rails went straight up, and that engine rolled just like a football. Two of those five-inch shells hit it just about five or six feet from the track, and I mean it did some stopping."

Saunders and his gun mates also sank a Japanese ship. "I put 608 rounds in her—at least my three gun mounts did," he said. "We were pretty sure it was a cruiser, but the reports varied, and it may have been a destroyer. I was mount captain, and I could see every one of those orange blossoms when those shells hit. It took about six minutes to sink.

"When the Marines landed on Saipan we were close enough; we could see everything," Saunders recalled. "And I saw 4,200 Marines fall to enemy bullets in the space of a few hours. There wasn't a whole lot of cover when they went ashore, but by the time our howitzers and field artillery got through with them, they'd blown everything to pieces."

When the atomic bomb went off in Hiroshima ten months later the *Miami* was about a thousand miles away. "I remember that little tsunami or whatever they call it from the Hiroshima blast," James said. "It was about fifteen feet high when it hit us. We called it a tidal wave."

Saunders made it back to the States after stops at Guam, Truk, Yukosuka, Japan, and, finally, Tokyo. "There wasn't anything there," he remembered. "The city was absolutely ruined. It was the stinkiest mess I've ever seen. The Tokyo River was running just as black as tar, and little kids by the thousands and thousands lined the bank of the river fishing, catching little fish about three inches long and eating them raw off the hook."

The *Miami* came home after that. By then Saunders was barely functioning. "They checked me over physically before they would discharge me," he said. "They wanted to operate on me for this and operate on me for that. They wanted to put me in a hospital, but I said, 'No way, I'm going home.'"

When James got back to the States he went to another doctor, who told him, "I tell you what, Saunders, you're in pretty good shape for a man about 135 years old." He had just celebrated his twenty-first birthday, two days after they dropped the atomic bomb on Nagasaki.

"It's something I don't think any human will ever get over," James said decades later of his wartime experiences. "I still have 'mad fits,' I call them. I still have those nightmares. I had a dream one night that was the silliest dream I ever had. My wife punched me one night, woke me up in the middle of the dream. In the dream I was on my hands and knees in the bed, and I had a coat hanger in one hand and a handsaw in the other, and there were six Japanese Imperial Marines after me."

EARLY ONE SUNDAY MORNING in 1945 Private First Class Raymond Renfro stepped off the train at Wichita Falls, Texas, and entered a world he hadn't seen in a long time. His mother, father, and little brother were there on the station platform, and they were all shouting and waving.

"Well, we all had to cry," he remembered. "Especially my mother. I still had a patch over my right eye, but it was just good to be home. It was especially good to be alive. I was proud of what I did, and I'd do it again if I had to. I'm not ashamed of what I did. I did it for my family, for God and my country."

The patch over Renfro's eye covered up the ravaged remains of the area where his right eye had been. But Ray was satisfied to have good vision in the left eye that remained. "I was lucky that my left eye had been real strong all these years," he said. "I had 20/20 vision in it. I just felt lucky to be alive. So many of my friends didn't make it, but I was lucky—a lot luckier than my brother."

Renfro's older brother, Robert, was stationed at Clark Field in the Philippines when the Japanese attacked it. He escaped and joined a guerrilla force. After being captured in early April 1942 he was put aboard a Hell Ship, where many Americans died on the journey to Japan. Ray's parents didn't know for many months whether Robert was alive.

"He went through unbelievable torture, and he talked to me some about it, but he didn't tell me nearly all about it," Ray said, "and the truth of the matter is, I didn't want him to. Robert died in July 2005. His health had broken down so totally, he just couldn't make it any longer. He had heart surgery, and his kidneys were bad. He just wore out. But he didn't hold any grudge against the Japanese. He traveled back over there and visited the place where their camp was.

"He even talked with one of his guards, and that just somehow seemed to make everything all right," said Ray, "and he wrote it all down. But then when he got it all down, he had so many bad thoughts in his mind that he had to have psychiatric help to get it under control.

"I came home a totally changed person from the kid that went over there. I had nightmares all the time. I had some really, really awful bad dreams. There were so many of my friends that didn't make it, and like so many other people have said before, 'They are the real heroes.' None of us were very old, and we took chances that nobody in our families had ever taken before. I'm just lucky to be alive."

AFTER I WAS wounded that last time, I had what I just called 'the shakes.' Even long after I was out of the Army, they scared the hell out of me," recalled former Staff Sergeant Nick Grinaldo decades later. "And they just got worse and worse even, when I was back home in Troy. For years I'd wake up with these screaming fits. Christ, I got two Purple Hearts, and I cherish them both, but there were times when I'd give 'em both back if I could just get away from the shakes.

"Was it posttraumatic stress disorder? I don't know, but it's something like that. I just don't like to think too much about it because I still get them sometimes. I've been holding up pretty good, but you never know. I get the shakes, and I'm afraid I'll have repercussions."

It took Grinaldo a good while to settle down when he returned home. "I had a reputation of being very temperamental—a very tough boy. I'd had to kill people who might have been just as nice a guy as I was, and it bothered me.

"My wife put up with an awful lot," he said. "I told her not to come near me when I was like that because I might kill her."

I'D SAY I HELD my feelings in a lot when I left the Marines," said former 4th Division Marine Jack Gilbreath. "It wasn't something I could talk about then, and I suppose it wasn't a good thing. I'd say it took me maybe twenty years to get over it. It took me ten or twelve years to get over my nightmares. I'd gradually see something on the news, and I'd talk to my wife about it."

Years later one of the stories Gilbreath, who grew up in the Texas countryside, had in mind involved two young women that he and several other Marines encountered as the girls climbed a cliff, apparently thinking of ending their own lives.

"They were beautiful girls, and they were just about my age—about eighteen or nineteen years old," said the small-town Texas native. "They had no clothes on other than just bell-bottom Japanese pants, and they each had a little purse around their neck and under their arm."

Many Marines had had unfortunate experiences with people who hid grenades under their clothing, and one Marine apparently thought the girls might have had a grenade inside their purses, so he decided to take a look.

"When he snatched one of the purses off the girl's arm and opened it up," Gilbreath said, "it was full of condoms. We realized that the girls were women of the evening. The Japanese called them 'comfort women' and had captured them from other places. Everyone laughed, but I found it sort of sad." Gilbreath said he turned away, mildly embarrassed.

"I think about the women and children who were killed, and I get too sentimental," he said. "I wasn't a really religious young man, but I thought about the persons I'd killed. That's the reason you want to forget these things, and I have. I've overcome them, but sometimes I think I shouldn't go to these reunions because they bring back a lot of old memories.

"I wish the world could be more calm and figure out a way of settling differences instead of going to war," said Gilbreath. "There's got to be a better answer. These wars are just not getting it. It seems like one leads to another one. I've begun to believe that every president of this country seems to think they've got to have a war of their own to justify their existence."

THERE WERE BIG PARTIES to celebrate the peace in San Diego where I was," recalled 2nd Marine Private First Class Olian Thomas Perry. "Right there in the middle of downtown, people were pulling their clothes off and going swimming in the fountain. I got so embarrassed, I went on back to camp. It got too rough for me, even after I'd had two or three drinks.

"Yeah, the war was over, but you didn't forget those boys that were with you who didn't come back," Perry said, "and you don't forget your feelings about the Japanese. Those feelings were a real hard thing for me to deal with for a long time. I couldn't even think of buying a Japanese car or anything like that. I'd think about the death march and the way the Japs treated the men they captured, and it tore me up."

For years after his discharge his dreams would jar him awake at night. "My wife said I had nightmares where I would get to hitting her," he remembered. "Nightmares that the Japs were getting in my foxhole. I finally got over them, and I don't have them anymore. Gradually, when I quit having nightmares,

I kind of forgot it. I guess I came to the conclusion that the Japanese were just trying in their own way to survive too, and I managed to put it out of my mind."

WHAT DO YOU DO when you wake up with the cold sweats of what is now recognized as posttraumatic stress disorder some seventy years after it afflicted you? What do you do when a casual talk with a friend triggers an attack that makes you want to run away and hide someplace? Harold Haberman, who lives in Denver, knows firsthand how it feels.

He talked about his ride onto the embattled Saipan beach aboard an amphibious tractor loaded down with .30-caliber machine gun bullets and bazooka ammunition. "All hell broke loose," Haberman remembered. "All around me boats were being blown out of the water. I can't tell you how frightening that was, but I got into shore. For two long nights without food or sleep, me and a buddy held our Ka-Bar knives at our chests and listened to the Japanese running everywhere around us. We could hear them coming, and I was ready, but I was lucky—none of them fell on me."

Several days later Haberman's battalion was ordered to attack Mount Tapotchau, the heart of the Japanese artillery defense. In the midst of the battle he was told to remain with a supply of reserve ammunition cached in a huge hole in the ground. All day and all night artillery and mortar shells burst on every side of him.

"A large chunk of steel missed my head by inches and lodged in the dirt beside me," Haberman said. "That night the Japanese counterattacked. I lost many of my close friends, and I still feel guilty today that I wasn't with them." A runner eventually came for him, and he loaded the ammunition onto a trailer and took it to the front lines, passing scores of dead and wounded.

Out of a thousand men in Haberman's battalion, only about two hundred survived the battle of Saipan.

But a strange new enemy lay in wait for him when he reached the States. At first he did what many returning Marines did. When he docked at San Diego he felt the thrill of being "back in the good ol' USA." He boarded a bus for Denver and was soon reunited with Irene Roth, a girl he hadn't seen in three years. They were married in December 1944, two days after Irene celebrated her twentieth birthday.

But there were signs that something was amiss with Harold. It was hard for him to be around civilians. Then, in August 1945, President Truman announced the unconditional surrender of Japan. The war was over. He and Irene went to downtown Denver for the wild celebration. "I was treated like a king," he said. But something was wrong.

Haberman was called back to duty when the Korean War broke out. He trained replacement Marines headed for Korea. By the time the conflict ended, he'd spent a total of nine years in the Marine Corps. He and Irene had two sons, Paul and Dan, and Haberman found work as a house painter. In 1956 he founded his own painting and decorating company. The family moved into a new ranch house in south Denver, and everything seemed to be going great.

But after an especially stressful time at work, Harold came down with an awful feeling he couldn't explain: "The only way I can describe it is dread and fear, like something awful was going to happen. It would hit me hardest in the mornings. I would wake up in seizures, and Irene would hold me until I calmed down."

The condition grew steadily worse. He didn't want to leave the house. He dreaded the thought of going to work. At home he would refuse to answer the door. "I would go with Irene shopping, and the walls would be closing in on me, and I'd get so scared I'd run away."

Although it was hard, Haberman took care of his family and his business, and he moved on to other things. He fell in love with the beauty of wood grain and made so many tables and lamps that he started selling them at local craft shows. He started making clocks. He polished precious stones. He built model airplanes. But nothing pushed the fear inside him away for good.

He sought help from more than fifteen psychiatrists over a period of forty-plus years. They diagnosed depression and treated him with antidepressants that made his symptoms worse. Twice he ended up in a mental health hospital.

Finally, during the Vietnam War public attention forced the military and medical communities to deal more directly with the psychological aftermaths of war. The old terms of shellshock and battle or combat fatigue were finally renamed posttraumatic stress disorder and recognized by the American Psychiatric Association as a legitimate anxiety disorder in 1980.

The turning point for Haberman came when he visited a Veteran Service Officer and rejected her observation that his problems were connected with his military service. Her response was firm and unequivocal. "I'm tired of you macho Marines coming in here with that bullshit!" she said. "When you hit that beach you were afraid. But you laid that fear aside, and because you were trained to be a Marine, you went and did what you were trained to do. Every morning when you had to get up out of that foxhole and go at it again, you laid that fear back—and now, in later years, the fear is there, and you don't know why or where it is, but it's making you afraid." Haberman gradually improved and stopped having those dark episodes.

But there were many thousands who weren't so lucky.

chapter 12

★ ★ ★

Tinian and the B-29

THE 8TH MARINES took over Ushi Point Airfield in the northern part of Tinian. In a few short days armies of Seabees—fifteen thousand of them—would tackle their largest job yet. When they were finished they had made Tinian the focal point of the largest assignment the Construction Battalion had ever handled. They hauled, blasted, and packed down enough coral to fill three Boulder Dams in what would become their most magnificent job yet—making the airfield home to about five hundred B-29s.

Ushi Point Airfield and Gurguan Point Airfield, when enlarged and expanded, were renamed North Field and West Field, respectively. They became vital bases for the XXI Bomber Command, which, during the spring and summer of 1945, would unleash its long-range bombers from Tinian against the Japanese homeland with devastating impact.

When young David Braden was twelve years old and growing up in Dallas, his uncle was in the Army Air Corps at Randolph Field in San Antonio. "My uncle took me up in one of those little pea-shooter planes, and from that moment on, I knew I wanted to fly," he said.

A little later in life Braden was a student at North Texas Agricultural College, today the University of Texas at Arlington. He was planning to go on to Texas A&M to finish his degree program, but World War II came along, and it didn't quite work out that way. "The day I turned eighteen I signed up for the Air Force Reserve and was called up the following February of 1943," Braden recalled. "They sent me to the University of Tennessee and kept me there for two months, then I went to Nashville to be classified as a pilot, bombardier, or navigator."

The military needed pilots desperately because of the war raging in Africa and Europe, but Braden learned that he had some problems with his vision. He was found to be nearsighted in one eye and farsighted in the other. Essentially, they said, he was cockeyed and couldn't fly a plane with that kind of eyesight. "It almost broke my heart when I found out I was being classified as a navigator," he said.

But Braden overcame his disappointment and went to preflight school and aerial gunner school at Fort Myers, Florida, where he won his gunner's wings, went into advanced navigation, and graduated there to become a commissioned officer. "I was one of the top people in my class," he said, "probably because of my engineering background."

The next stop on his list was Boca Raton, Florida, for a month in top secret training to become a radar bombardier. "When I say 'top secret,' they really meant it," he said. "Our classrooms were surrounded by a barbed-wire fence with an armed guard on duty at the entry to the compound. Training flights were out over the ocean." Then it was on to Clovis, New Mexico, where he joined the combat crew of Lieutenant Norman Westervelt and was introduced to a magnificent airplane called the B-29.

Braden had never seen a B-29 before and hadn't even known it existed because it was a super-secret airplane at that time. He found out that anytime a B-29 took off, the crew was fully armed, and a guard was aboard in case they had to make an emergency landing or anything unforeseen happened. "The B-29 was a high-tech, superb airplane," Braden said. "But it had a lot of problems initially with overheating engines. Losing engines was very common."

So was ditching in the ocean. It happened to Braden on his third mission in a B-29. Two of his closest friends—Lieutenant Westervelt, who was piloting the plane, and Lieutenant Gorden Nedderson—were killed in the crash, but a Navy PBY (a light cargo plane with no armor) rescued Braden.

"All this started changing rapidly when General Curtis LeMay was appointed chief of the XXI Bomber Command," Braden said. "We called him 'Old Iron Pants' because he was a tough cookie. Curtis LeMay was the George Patton of the Air Force, but we respected him tremendously. There is no question that he put us on the path to winning the war."

LeMay saw the poor results the crews of B-29s were having and tried some experimentation. On one particular mission he mixed incendiary bombs with high-explosive bombs. He liked what he saw and decided to try a low-altitude mission. "We were going in at five thousand feet with 197 planes, and we were each going to carry ten tons of incendiary bombs. It was the first incendiary bombing raid on Tokyo," Braden recalled. "This was the start of winning the war in the air over Japan."

When the B-29s approached the city the pilots could see that the city was on fire. Pathfinder planes flying an hour ahead of the bombers had set fires on four corners of the bombing area to mark the spot. "But as we got closer and more and more planes dropped their bombs, a firestorm started," Braden said. "Before it was over sixteen square miles of Tokyo were reduced to ashes. It was like looking at the mouth of hell." That first fire raid on Tokyo killed 83,000 Japanese, and 1 million people were left homeless.

"LeMay was ecstatic," Braden remembered. "We flew twenty-four of those fire raids in all. I flew on seventeen of them. The planes from the 313th Wing on Tinian started an operation called Operation Starvation. They just about stopped all the shipping that took place in Japan. The Japanese couldn't get any raw material at all and very limited food or medicine.

"In the meantime we were going up in daylight and dropping leaflets on ten targeted cities which said, 'We advise you to plead with your rulers to capitulate and unconditionally surrender, and we advise you to evacuate your town because we are coming up here Sunday afternoon at two o'clock and we are going to burn it to the ground.'

"We did exactly that. I don't know whether they evacuated or not, but we performed as scheduled."

THE NATION'S SCIENTIFIC profession went to the Army," said Philip Morrison, a scientist who worked on the Manhattan Project helping to build the plutonium bomb, the one dropped on Hiroshima, and who was now at Tinian to assemble it with a team that included Albert Einstein, the pacifist, as its head. "We beat on the doors and said we must be allowed to make this weaponry or we're going to lose the war. Once we did that, we didn't stop. I didn't stop. I worked a seventy-hour week making bombs."

The man chosen to fly the plane with the first atomic bomb was Colonel Paul Tibbets, who was born in Quincy, Illinois, and had already compiled an admirable record with the B-29.

On 26 July 1945, the cruiser USS *Indianapolis* arrived at Tinian with the firing mechanism and uranium bullet for the first bomb. Once the top-secret cargo was delivered, the *Indianapolis,* one of the fastest ships in the US Navy, struck out for the Philippines.

On 30 July, traveling alone, she was torpedoed and sunk by a Japanese submarine. Marine Sergeant Ed Harrell, who came from a little place called Golden Pond, Kentucky, was one of a small handful of Marines aboard the *Indianapolis* as a corporal of the guard. He described the instant the two torpedoes struck, almost simultaneously, just as he was retiring for the night.

"I began to doze off, and all of a sudden a massive explosion shook the ship," he recalled. "I'm still wrapped in my blanket, and all that water begins to come on me. I'm real close, within thirty-five feet of a main torpedo that cuts through the bow of that ship.

"All the debris is falling and much of the flash of that is in the air," Harrell said. He began to realize that the bow was no longer where it was supposed to be, and he could hear the sound of the bulkheads collapsing below. As people emerged from the forward superstructure of the main deck Harrell could see that they were horribly burned. Flesh was hanging off their hands, arms, and faces, and they were screaming and begging for help.

Harrell tried to make his way back to the quarterdeck, but when he reached it, he could plainly see that the ship was already listing to starboard. There was no question the ship was sinking. "There's an old saying that there are no atheists in foxholes," he said. "If you believe in a higher power, you begin to pray, and certainly I began to pray. I'm looking out, and what I see is eternity."

It took exactly twelve minutes from when the first torpedo hit the ship until it went down. Harrell climbed the rail and jumped into the water feet first and swam away from the ship. When he looked back, the bow was already underwater and the fantail was high in the air.

"The screws are still turning, and boys are still trying to get off," he said. "Some of them are jumping from pretty high up. Some of them are actually jumping into the screws. I could see them jumping, and you could hear them screaming."

About three hundred men went down with the ship.

It was three and a half days before the survivors were discovered. Almost six hundred had perished of burns, exhaustion, dehydration, and madness. And sharks hung around the edges of the men who were clinging to bits of flotsam, makeshift rafts, and a handful of lifeboats.

"I would say that sharks ended the lives of better than half the men," said Harrell. It was the costliest wartime tragedy the US Navy ever experienced. Out of the 1,196 crewmen, only 317 survived.

"A Marine buddy of mine happened to run into Mochitsura Hashimoto, the commander of Japanese submarine I-58, that had done the damage," said Harrell. "They shook hands, and the Marine told Hashimoto, 'After all these years and all that has happened, I forgive you,' he said."

"I forgive you too," Hashimoto replied.

"Forgive me?" said the Marine. "For what?"

"I lost my whole family at Hiroshima," Hashimoto said.

BAD WEATHER POSTPONED Tibbets's flight on 3 August, but on 5 August meteorologists were predicting several days of clear visibility ahead. At 0030 Tinian time on 6 August the crew left the mess hall and headed for the plane. Flight Surgeon Don Young handed Tibbets a pillbox containing twelve cyanide capsules, one for each member of the crew. They were to be passed out in case of emergency. The crew could use them or not—it was up to them.

The bomb was called "Little Boy," and Colonel Tibbets named his plane the *Enola Gay* after his mother. When Tibbets climbed into its cabin and prepared for takeoff, he felt he was about to become a part of "the greatest single event in the history of warfare," he wrote later. The four-and-a-half-ton bomb made the plane seriously overweight, and the *Enola Gay* needed every inch of the runway to take off. At 0245 Tibbets pulled back on the yoke, and the plane headed toward the Japanese islands. Six and a half hours later Little Boy was released over Hiroshima. The *Enola Gay* was ten miles away, but shock waves buffeted the plane.

Tibbets was shocked almost speechless. As his plane left the area, he turned and saw a massive mushroom cloud that seemed to be coming right at them. "We were not prepared for the awesome sight that met our eyes as we turned for a heading that would take us alongside the burning, devastated city," he said. "The giant purple mushroom . . . had already risen to a height of forty-five thousand feet, three miles above our altitude, and was still boiling upward like something terribly alive.

"Even more fearsome was the sight on the ground below," he said. "At the base of the cloud, fires were springing up everywhere amid a turbulent mass of smoke that had the appearance of bubbling, hot tar . . . The city we had seen so clearly in the sunlight a few minutes before was now an ugly smudge. It had completely disappeared under this awful blanket of smoke and fire.

"I think this is the end of the war," Tibbets told copilot Captain Robert Lewis as they headed back to Tinian.

THE SECOND BOMB, called "Fat Man," was bigger and more powerful than Little Boy. Philip Morrison and his crew of scientists had just finished loading the "man-made meteor" into a B-29 named *Bockscar* to be flown to its target by Major Chuck Sweeney.

"It weighed 10,300 pounds—at least 1,000 pounds heavier than Little Boy," Sweeney remarked when he saw the bomb. "Ten feet, eight inches long, five feet across with its high-gloss yellow enamel and black tailfins. It resembled a grossly oversized decorative squash," he said. "I could see that many people had signed the bomb or left poems and messages with varying degrees of vitriol."

On 9 August the second bomb was dropped on Nagasaki. On 10 August Japan surrendered.

chapter 13

★ ★ ★

Dismay in Japan

WITH THE FALL of Saipan, the people of Japan learned to their shock and dismay just how badly the Americans outnumbered and overpowered their forces in the Pacific. For the first time millions of Japanese began to wonder whether the war was actually being lost. The Sons of Heaven began to seriously question what they had come to think of as their divine mission.

On 20 July 1944—just eleven days after Saipan was declared secure—General Hideki Tojo resigned as prime minister and chief of the Imperial General Staff. General Kuniyaki Koiso replaced him as prime minister, but because of a strategic rift between the Japanese army and the navy, he was forced to share authority with Admiral Mitsumasa Yonia, the navy minister.

The war was steadily closing in on Japan on almost every front. Many fine restaurants and geisha houses were shut down, and the geisha were told to find war work. With fuel becoming more scarce, the Japanese authorities imposed travel restrictions on the average citizen; anyone wanting to make a long trip needed to acquire a police permit.

Dining cars on trains were closed down, and the average citizen was unable to obtain rice. City dwellers traded off family possessions for black market food to supplement the lean rations of mixed, unhulled grain they received each month. Aluminum, copper, tin, and other materials the government needed were almost nonexistent.

Meanwhile the late summer of 1944 dragged on, weighed down by stories of valor, sacrifice, suffering, and a giant airplane, which the people of Japan had come to call "B-san"—the B-29s. News reports of the B-29 bombings in Western China had made the rounds in Tokyo and other important Japanese cities, and the Japanese press roundly poked fun at them.

In a raid near Kyushu one B-29 had been forced to make an emergency landing near the front lines. The captain of the plane had called for help, but the Japanese intercepted the message and got there first, destroying the B-29 on the ground. On 3 July, as Marines and soldiers were fighting tooth and nail at Saipan, Japanese newspapers carried photos of the bombing above the caption "B-29 in Flames." Other stories had emerged from the same area during the rest of July, August, and September, accompanied by stories announcing that forty B-29s had been destroyed in the raids, when the actual count was only four.

On 30 August B-29s raided the Yawata Steel Works at Kyushu, and the Japanese air force and anti-aircraft fire shot down three of the planes. One of them was recovered, patched up, and brought to Tokyo, where a massively attended public exposition was staged. Tens of thousands of Japanese flocked to see the B-29, and government posters on display boasted that this was one of a hundred planes shot down by defenders. This was patently untrue, but by this time the Japanese people were well aware of the B-29.

On the afternoon of 1 November 1944, a solitary B-29 appeared high in the skies above Tokyo. It was the first US plane to fly over the Japanese capital city since Jimmy Doolittle's B-25s in April 1942. The big silver plane circled slowly for a while, and Japanese fighters sent out to attack it could get no closer than 7,000 feet. The B-29 was sailing along at 32,000 feet, while the Japanese fighters' maximum altitude was only 25,000 feet. At the time the B-29 was impervious to any type of gunfire at such altitudes.

But what the Americans wanted was an airbase from which they could launch fighters to accompany B-29s to Japan and back. They found it at Iwo Jima. After one of the bloodiest battles in American history, US casualties totaled 26,000, with 6,821 dead. Japanese casualties totaled 22,000—almost the entire defending force on the island. When the battle ended, only 216 Japanese survived to be taken prisoner.

The fall of Iwo Jima had no immediate effect on the Japanese people—it was just another lost island, as Saipan and Okinawa had been—but from Japan's Imperial Headquarters it was viewed as a serious, if not fatal, setback. It was the only remaining base that the Japanese had for launching aerial attacks against the B-29 installations on Saipan and Tinian. In Tokyo officials knew that Americans were lengthening and improving the existing Tinian airstrips. By the summer of 1945 B-29s would have an intermediate base for emergency landings at Iwo Jima and—much more importantly—a base for fighters to use to accompany B-29s to Japan and back.

The United States also found a man who didn't mind going into the history books as an outright advocate of massive firebombings of civilian populations. His name was General Curtis "Bombs Away" LeMay. He is credited with perfecting a highly effective—but intensely controversial—strategic bombing campaign against Japanese cities.

Air Force officers designed and built a typical Japanese village in Utah and practiced bombing it with a new incendiary device made with jellied napalm. It was an almost perfect instrument for destroying small Japanese houses, whereby small bombs, weighing about six pounds, could be dropped in huge numbers. They would fall on roofs and explode, and the napalm would stick tightly to the surface of the roof. The resulting fire was next to impossible to extinguish.

This was how LeMay would incinerate the major cities of Japan.

On 25 February 1945, LeMay began this new type of bombing. A total of 231 B-29s were involved, and they dumped 450 tons of fire bombs on Tokyo. They destroyed sixteen square miles of territory and 28,000 buildings. Only the deaf and blind were still convinced that Japan was not losing the war.

The planes came in very low, at around five thousand feet, scattering their incendiaries in all directions. The tests in Utah had proven that the type of fire-fighting equipment used by the Japanese could never contain the fires created, but not even the Americans had anticipated their effectiveness. High winds caught the fires, and the heat made the winds whirl faster and faster until a firestorm was created. The flames would jump an entire block, spreading the fire faster than it could be contained. Entire sections of the city erupted in flames and then collapsed into rubble, burying thousands of people in the ash and carnage.

LeMay called it a "diller" of a raid. According to official US Army Air Force records, the count of the dead stood at 83,000 Japanese civilians killed, but facts strongly indicate that as many as 200,000 people may have died—about three times the death toll at Hiroshima five and a half months later.

They called it "slaughter bombing," which is what it was. An area of sixteen square miles had been completely gutted. Not only in Tokyo but also later in Nagoya, Osake, and Kobe. A total of 300,000 houses were burned to the ground.

When Emperor Hirohito toured Tokyo some ten days after the raid, he was sick and shocked at what he saw. At this point, regardless of what his generals and admirals told him, he realized the war was lost and every effort must be made to end it.

Standing in the way was an obstacle that probably only the Japanese fully understood. They feared that America's definition of "unconditional surrender," according to the Potsdam Declaration, included getting rid of the Emperor, the most sacred and revered figure in the world as far as the Japanese people were concerned. The thought was unbearable to the Japanese, so they hesitated . . . and waited.

For more than a week the body crews hauled off the dead killed in the air attacks. They found them clustered in air raid shelters, in the canals, and along the river banks. Entire streets and alleys were impassable because of piles of bodies.

Meanwhile the spirit of the kamikaze had spread with alarming speed, taking over all the Japanese armed forces. More US Navy personnel were killed and wounded in the battle of Okinawa than in any other engagement, and it was all because of the kamikazes—suicidal pilots who deliberately crashed into American warships. The kamikaze spirit was on the rise everywhere, even in the civilian population.

Soldiers with satchel charges hurled themselves under tanks, and soldiers in small boats crept up on ships at anchor, clambered aboard, and charged the decks with sabers until they were cut down. One-man suicide submarines were ramming ships. All across Japan, civilians were being taught how to make suicide attacks when American troops landed.

By April destruction in Japanese cities was so massive that the Cabinet approved a program turning large areas of Tokyo, Nagoya, and Osaka into farming zones. The agricultural workers would be women, children, and the elderly, who would be housed in temples and public buildings until proper housing could be built.

Early in April the government created the National Volunteer Force, headed by the prime minister of Japan. It was to be a people's army in which every citizen would spring to the nation's defense. Women, the young children, and the elderly began learning to drill and use such primitive weapons as the pike and such modern ones as high explosives.

The mobilization moved with surprising speed. The national medical association took over the civil hospitals and medical facilities, distributing doctors, nurses, and technicians from one area to another as needed. Units of a thousand men were established around Tokyo to begin building defense positions as part of the National Volunteer Force. Civilians were to take a major role in the projected hand-to-hand fighting on the streets of Japan when the American devils invaded.

As these plans were announced, the government headed by General Koiso collapsed. As nearly as can be determined, Koiso quit because he could no longer pretend that he knew how to stop the American juggernaut. Admiral Kantaro Suzuki replaced him, but only after first refusing the appointment. He had no political knowledge, he said, but this was precisely the reason why Emperor Hirohito wanted him. The war could be stopped only if the Cabinet was in the hands of men who owed nothing to the militarists.

"We need you," the Emperor told him, setting a precedent by making such an outright request. Also brought into the government were a large number of civilians, including Shigenosi Togo as foreign minister, whom the Emperor knew was opposed to many of the excesses of the militarists. An antimilitary segment of society was gradually being formed in the highest councils of government, but there was still the important question: What do we do if the Allies choose to unseat the Emperor?

On 8 May 1945, when news reached Japan that Germany had surrendered to the Allies, it brought no banner headlines to Japanese newspapers. The report of the surrender was terse and contained no details. All it meant was that Japan was standing alone against the rest of the world.

Japanese armies were on the retreat everywhere. Troops in the Philippines were holding out with rifles and machine guns. In Burma Japan's forces were falling back to the east. In China the last offensive was abandoned in May, and the Japanese were retreating toward the coast. By the end of May fifty thousand Japanese troops had been killed on Okinawa; in June another sixty thousand would die.

Not only had the Soviet Union spurned Japanese attempts at open talks for peace as an intermediary, now it seemed likely that the USSR was actually joining the fight against Japan, with Russian troops massed at the borders of Manchuria and Korea.

On 22 June 1945, the Emperor called a meeting of the Supreme War Council. It included the prime minister, minister of foreign affairs, army and navy ministers, and army and navy chiefs of staff.

"We have heard enough of this determination of yours to fight to the last soldiers," Hirohito said. "We wish that you, the leaders of Japan, will strive now to study the ways and means to conclude the war." And he added bluntly: "In doing so, try not to be bound by the decisions you have made in the past."

The audience was stunned into silence. The Emperor had shattered all precedents. Never until this very moment had he spoken a word that implied criticism of the all-powerful military. The men he was addressing didn't know what to do. None of these leaders was willing to say anything, and the meeting was adjourned.

By this time the atomic bomb was a reality. It had been perfected in July, and some of President Harry S. Truman's advisers suggested that he refrain from dropping the bomb; instead, they said, he could simply describe it. The American military strongly objected: not only would it give away the American hand, they said, but the Japanese most likely wouldn't believe it anyhow.

So the United States dropped the atomic bomb on Hiroshima. The explosion annihilated the center of the city. The official death toll was about 80,000. Other sources suggested that 200,000 would be more appropriate.

A Japanese journalist described the scene:

> Everything standing upright in the way of the blast—walls, houses, factories and other buildings—were annihilated and the debris spun round in a whirlwind and was carried up in

the air. . . . Horses, dogs and cattle suffered the same fate as human beings . . .

Beyond the zone of utter death in which nothing remained alive, houses collapsed in a whirl of beams, bricks and girders. Up to about three miles from the center of the explosion, lightly built houses were flattened as though they had been built of cardboard. Those who were inside were either killed or wounded. Those who managed to extricate themselves by some miracle found themselves surrounded by a ring of fire. . . .

By the evening the fire began to die down and then it went out. There was nothing left to burn. Hiroshima had ceased to exist.

Doctor Michihiko Hachiya was the director of the Hiroshima Communications Hospital, which was fifteen hundred yards from the center of the blast. He began keeping a diary the evening the bomb hit:

Suddenly a strong flash of light startled me—and then another. . . . Through swirling dust I could barely discern a wooden column that had supported one corner of my house. It was leaning crazily and the roof sagged dangerously.

Moving instinctively, I tried to escape, but the rubble and fallen timbers barred the way. . . . A profound weakness overcame me, so I stopped to regain my strength. To my surprise I discovered that I was completely naked . . .

All over the right side of my body I was cut and bleeding. A large splinter was protruding from a mangled wound in my thigh, and something warm trickled into my mouth. . . . Embedded in my neck was a sizable fragment of glass.

Doctor Hachiya and his wife, Yaeko, who was also injured, managed to escape the house. Just as they entered the street, a house across from theirs collapsed almost at their feet.

"Our house began to sway, and in a minute it, too, collapsed in a cloud of dust," said Hachiya.

> Fires sprang up and whipped by a vicious wind began to spread. It finally dawned on us that we could not stay there in the street, so we turned our steps toward the hospital. Our home was gone; we were wounded and needed treatment; and after all, it was my duty to be with the staff. . . . I was still naked although I did not feel the least bit of shame . . .
>
> The streets were deserted except for the dead. Some looked as if they had frozen to death while in the full action of flight; others lay sprawled as though some giant had flung them to their death from a great height. Hiroshima was no longer a city, but a burnt-over prairie. To the east and to the west everything was flattened. . . . How small Hiroshima was with the houses gone.

Of Hiroshima's 76,000 buildings, 70,000 were destroyed or damaged severely.

The second bomb, dropped on Nagasaki on 9 August, killed another 60,000 people.

Late in the morning of 10 August President Truman received Japan's "conditional" acceptance of the Potsdam Declaration. Japan would surrender, but only if the Emperor retained his sovereignty.

Not a problem, Truman responded, as long as the Emperor would submit to the authority of the Supreme Allied Commander in Japan: the Emperor would stay, but the United

States would control his role and authority. As Truman wrote in his diary, if the Japanese wanted to keep the Emperor, "we'd tell 'em how."

If only the Japanese had known how many thousands of lives could have been saved.

★ ★ ★

Epilogue

IT WOULDN'T be much of a stretch to call every American who served on Saipan or Tinian a hero. Here are a few, however, who stand out in my memory.

LIEUTENANT JOHN GRAVES was not only a tough Marine who lost sight in one eye to a hand grenade at Saipan but also a writer of widespread acclaim, whose brilliant *Goodbye to a River* tells of a three-week trip down the Brazos River of Central Texas, into which is woven a history of the people who have lived along its banks—settlers, Indians, warriors, and renegades.

Originally published in 1959, fourteen years after Graves was discharged from the Marine Corps, it is one of the all-time nonfiction classics of American literature. It glances back in time for two hundred or so years as it also offers a glimpse of how life may look far into the future.

Graves was once called "the best-loved writer in Texas and one of the least known beyond the state lines." He was also called "a 20th-century Thoreau."

Two of his other books, *Hard Scrabble* and *From a Limestone Ledge*, are also "invigorating, inspiring and engrossing," to quote one reviewer. His last work, *Myself and Strangers: A Memoir of Apprenticeship*, published in 2004, is "a lovely memoir of young manhood," in the words of author Larry McMurtry.

Graves died at the age of ninety-two in what he called his "country place" outside the small town of Glen Rose, Texas, on 31 July 2013.

PRIVATE FIRST CLASS WAYNE TERWILLIGER. When it comes to running, "Twig" Terwilliger may have set some new marks during the battle for Saipan, but it was nothing compared to what he would do later on with five major league baseball clubs.

"We put together a ball team on Saipan after the battle was over," he said, "and we won twenty-five straight games without a loss before we went to Tinian. That's when I knew for sure what I wanted to do when I got out."

When Twig was discharged in late 1945 he returned to Western Michigan University, where he quickly became a star shortstop. Just one year later he was drawing attention from major league scouts. In July 1948, after finishing college, he signed a contract with the Chicago Cubs, who assigned him to the Triple-A Los Angeles Angels. He batted .275 in 115 games before being called up to the bigs in August and playing in 36 games.

Terwilliger spent the entire 1950 season with the Cubs as their starting second baseman, hitting .242 with ten home runs, thirty-two RBIs, and thirteen stolen bases. He also played with the Washington Senators for two seasons and the New York

Giants for two seasons. He spent an official nine years as a major-league ballplayer.

After his playing days were over, Twig started a career as a coach and manager. He was the third-base coach, under Ted Williams, of the Senators from 1969 to 1971, and of the Texas Rangers in their first season in 1972. He again worked for the Rangers as a major league coach from 1981–1984. In 1986 he was hired as first-base coach for the Minnesota Twins, handling the job when the team won the World Series in 1987 and 1991.

In 2003 he was named manager of the Fort Worth Cats in the independent Central Baseball League and won the 2005 Central League championship. At the age of eighty-one he accepted a job as first-base coach for the Cats and remained with the team through the 2010 season.

"I spent sixty-four years altogether in professional baseball," he said. "And I enjoyed every minute of it." In 2006 Twig's autobiography, *Terwilliger Bunts One,* was released.

LIEUTENANT DAVID BRADEN. When you've flown thirty-five bombing missions against Japan as a navigator in a B-29 Superfortress, received the Distinguished Flying Cross and an Air Medal with three Oak Leaf Clusters, and survived a ditching in the Pacific Ocean in which two of your crew members were killed in the crash, what do you do as an encore?

If you're David Braden, and you're coming in from your final mission in a B-29 when all four of your plane's engines run out of fuel at once and the plane coasts to a stop halfway down the runway, you do the only thing you can think of. "You get out and kiss the ground," he said.

Braden was born and raised in Dallas, where he graduated from North Dallas High School. He was a student at North Texas Agricultural College, now the University of Texas at Arlington, when the Japanese attacked Pearl Harbor. He enlisted in the Army Air Force on his eighteenth birthday and was among the first trainees on the B-29. "It was a superb airplane," he said, "but in the beginning it had serious trouble with overheating engines. Our results in the beginning were awful where high-altitude, strategic bombing was concerned."

After the war Braden became an architect, a popular after-dinner speaker, a humorist, and a construction arbitrator, not necessarily in that order. As someone who loved flying, he served on the board of D/FW Airport, one of the busiest in the world, for six years and was its chairman in 1994–1995.

"We didn't think of ourselves as heroes," he said. "We thought of ourselves as guys that had to get a job done and fly thirty-six missions and then you could go home. When you're nineteen or twenty years old, you don't think about stuff like that. Going on a mission was an opportunity, because it was another one you wouldn't have to do. It was like a convict marking an X on the wall."

Braden died of natural causes at his home in Dallas at age ninety on 25 April 2015.

PRIVATE FIRST CLASS CARL MATTHEWS not only suffered a most peculiar wound and recurrences for several years, but when he left the Marine Corps he weighed barely 110 pounds. He underwent treatment for a condition similar to a stroke at hospitals in New Caledonia, San Francisco, and Oakland. Even recently, more than seventy years after the fact, he couldn't recall details of his recovery period.

But Matthews never forgot the death of Lieutenant James Stanley Leary Jr., his platoon leader, constant companion, and closest friend, on the next-to-last day before the battle of Saipan ended.

"They told us to go to the bottom of the ridge, and it was very steep," he said. "The instant he gave the command, the lieutenant fell down, and I knew instantly that he was dead. We were talking, and I was his runner, and I'll never forget how I felt that day when it happened. I passed out completely after that. They said I just sat there and wouldn't respond to anything anyone said. The next eight days are still a complete blank for me."

When Carl's son was born after the war, he named him James Stanley Matthews in memory of the fallen lieutenant.

But there was also something else that set Carl apart. He was the only Marine I ever encountered who admittedly took the side of the Army troops of the 27th Infantry Division in their "feud" with General "Howlin' Mad" Smith.

"I think the Army got a bad deal," he said. "When 'Howlin' Mad' decided to use the Army to take the airport, our intelligence said most of the Japanese troops had already left, and that was wrong. And later on, most of the heavy fighting was right in the middle of our lines, and that's exactly where the Army was.

"The more I read about 'Howlin' Mad' Smith," Matthews recalled in one of his last interviews, "the less I like him!"

Matthews, who was born in Corsicana, Texas, died at the age of ninety-two on 7 January 2017. His obituary related how he returned to Saipan in 2014 for the seventieth anniversary of the battle. He and two Japanese soldiers were the only veterans of the historic island conflict to return. As Matthews requested, part of his ashes were buried in the family cemetery in Dawson, Texas, and the remainder will be taken to Saipan to be scattered from the mountainside where Lieutenant Leary was killed.

STAFF SERGEANT JOHN SIDUR. If one person could be identified as the reason I wrote this book, John Sidur of Cohoes, New York, is that person. When I first became acquainted with John, the son of two Polish-born parents, he was ninety-six years old and had lost his hearing to such an extent that he had to utilize his nephew, Bob Greene, to retell his amazing story.

In the midst of the *gyokusai* John rescued two GIs from almost certain death and carried them back to where they could receive treatment. One of them was Corporal Spike Mailloux, also from Cohoes, who served with Sidur in the 105th Infantry Regiment. A Japanese officer had stabbed Mailloux in the thigh, and he lay in a ditch for several hours before Sidur discovered him.

When they were released from the Army, Sidur and Mailloux got into a habit of meeting each other for breakfast on the first Tuesday of every month. It became a ritual that lasted for decades.

Sidur was huddled next to Sergeant Attilio Grestini when an artillery shell blew off Grestini's arm. Sidur and Sergeant John Goot managed to drape Grestini's body over a rifle and walk him away from a mass of incoming shells to find first aid.

Grestini lived through the battle and returned home to raise a family.

Colonel O'Brien appointed Sidur to conduct patrols to clean out hostile caves of enemy soldiers who often held captive civilians against their will. In one instance he heard a small child crying in a cave, but he was powerless to save the child—a situation that filled him with helpless regret.

John came home from Saipan and Okinawa with two bullet wounds, a Bronze Star, and a Purple Heart. Four weeks after he returned he married Josephine Depta, whose photo he had held onto until the night of the biggest banzai of World War II, when a wild rainstorm swept away his helmet with the photo inside. They were married for sixty-eight years.

John died at age ninety-seven on 23 January 2015.

Acknowledgments

In all likelihood this is my final book on World War II. It's not because there aren't any more stories but because only a rapidly vanishing handful of the people who lived those stories are still around. My first book on the war was published in 2003, when hundreds of thousands of veterans were still alive. Today the vast majority of them are gone.

This book featured "live" interviews with seven veterans of Saipan, and several of them passed away before the book was completed. If I hadn't had the wholehearted cooperation of people like Reagan Grau, archivist for the National Museum of the Pacific War in Fredricksburg, Texas; Jim Gandy, research librarian for the New York State Military Museum in Saratoga Springs, New York; and Floyd Cox and Chuck Hodge, conductors of scads of interviews for the National Museum of the Pacific War and other sources, the book most likely would never have happened.

I owe a lasting debt of gratitude to a host of different people who helped make the book come alive: Paul Haberman of Denver, Colorado, who supplied pictures of and information about his father, Sergeant Harold Haberman of the 2nd Marine Division, who was kind enough to conduct a phone interview with me from his sick bed; Bob Talbot, a member of the 2nd Marines, who shared his story with me on a long and enjoyable afternoon at his home in Cibolo, Texas; Canara Caruth, who commanded a tank in the 2nd Armored Amphibious Battalion and relived some of his more memorable episodes for me; Wayne Terwilliger, who served aboard Caruth's tank; James Reed, who told me of the real-life nightmare when a series of LVTs blew up at Pearl Harbor; and Carl Matthews of the 2nd Marines, who told me of the death of his platoon leader and his own collapse to a mystery disease that affected him for many months.

I also owe a tremendous thank you to Bob Greene of Loudonville, New York, who helped bridge the gap between his uncle, Sergeant John Sidur of the 27th Infantry Division, and me. John died in January 2015, but while he lived—to the ripe old age of ninety-seven—he was an absolute inspiration to me.

My wife, Lana Henderson Sloan, also deserves a round of thanks for putting up with me when the going got tough. She came to my rescue many times.

I also want to thank my longtime friend and literary agent, Jim Donovan, for all the encouragement he provided along the way.

To my editor, Bob Pigeon, and everyone else at DaCapo: thank you.

Finally, to all the Americans who fought at Saipan and Tinian—both the living and the dead—you are the heroes of this book. Godspeed.

Bill Sloan
Dallas, Texas

Sources

BOOKS

Alexander, Joseph H. *Storm Landings: Epic Amphibious Battles in the Central Pacific*. Annapolis, MD: Naval Institute Press, 1997.

Beevor, Antony. *D-Day: The Battle for Normandy*. New York: Viking, 2009.

Blair, Clay, Jr. *Silent Victory: The U.S. Submarine War Against Japan*. Vol 2. New York: J. B. Lippincott Co., 1975.

Bryan, J. III, and Philip Reed. *Mission Beyond Darkness*. New York: Duell, Sloan and Pearce, 1945.

Campbell, James. *The Color of War: How One Battle Broke Japan and Another Changed America*. New York: Crown Publishers, 2012.

Cant, Gilbert. *The Great Pacific Victory*. New York: John Day, 1946.

Crowl, Philip A. *Campaign in the Marianas: The War in the Pacific*. Washington, DC: Historical Division, U.S. Army, 1960.

Eggers, John H. *The 27th Division: The Story of Its Sacrifices and Achievements*: New York: John H. Eggers Company, 1919.

Frank, Richard B. *Downfall: The End of the Imperial Japanese Empire*. New York: Random House, 1999.

Gabaldon, Guy. *Saipan: Suicide Island*. Saipan Island: Self-published, 1990.

Gailey, Harry A. *Howlin' Mad vs. the Army: Conflict in Command, Saipan 1944*. Navato, CA: Presidio Press, 1986.

Goette, John. *Japan Fights for Asia*. New York: Harcourt, Brace and Company, 1943.

Goldberg, Harold J. D-*Day in the Pacific: The Battle of Saipan*. Bloomington: Indiana University Press, 2007.

Graves, John. *Goodbye to a River*. New York: Alfred A. Knopf, 1960.

———. *Myself and Strangers: A Memoir of Apprenticeship*. Austin: University of Texas Press, 2004.

Hoffman, Carl W. *Saipan: The Beginning of the End*. Washington, DC: Historical Division, U.S. Marine Corps, 1950.

Hornfischer, James D. *The Fleet at Flood Tide: America at Total War in the Pacific 1944–1945*. New York: Bantam Books, 2016.

Hoyt, Edwin P. *Japan's War: The Great Pacific Conflict, 1853 to 1952*. New York: McGraw-Hill, 1986.

———. *To the Marianas: War in the Central Pacific: 1944*. New York: Van Nostrand Reinhold, 1980.

Love, Edmund. *The 27th Infantry Division in World War II*. Nashville, TN: Battery Press, 1949.

Miller, Donald L. *D-Days in the Pacific*. New York: Simon & Schuster, 2005.

Morison, Samuel Eliot. *History of United States Naval Operation in World War II: New Guinea and the Marianas, March 1944–August 1944*. Boston: Little, Brown, 1953.

O'Brien, Francis A. *Battling for Saipan*. New York: Ballantine Books, 2003.

Prefer, Nathan M. *The Battle for Tinian: Stepping Stone in America's War Against Japan*. Havertown, PA: Casemate, 2012.

Reader's Digest. *Illustrated Story of World War II*. Pleasantville, NY: Reader's Digest Association, 1969.

Rottman, Gordon L. *Saipan and Tinian 1944: Piercing the Japanese Empire*. Westminster, MD: Osprey Publishing, 2004.

Smith, Holland M., and Percy Finch. *Coral and Brass*. New York: Charles Scribner's Sons, 1948.

Williams, Kathleen Broom. *The Measure of a Man: My Father, the Marine Corps, and Saipan*. Annapolis, MD: Naval Institute Press, 2013.

INTERVIEWS

Personal interviews with Canara Caruth, Harold Haberman, Carl Matthews, James Reed, John Sidur, Bob Talbot, and Wayne Terwilliger.

National Museum of the Pacific War interviews with Warren Adams, Edward Bale, James Donovan, James Fulbright, Anthony Ganarelli, Jack Gilbreath, John Graves, George Gray, Robert Groves, Ed Harrell, Ray Harrison, Jack Lent, Arthur Liberty, Henry Michalak, Floyd Mumme, H. L. Obermiller, Jim O'Donnell, Charles Pase, Carl Peltier, Olian Perry, Raymond Renfro, Rod Rohling, James Rothermel, William Roush, James Saunders, James Sigrist, Samuel Spencer, Bill Steele, Tommy Thompson, Tom Tinsley, Chris Walker, Lew Weber, and B. R. Whitehead.

New York State Military Museum interviews with Myron Bazar, William Corcoran, Nick Grinaldo, Edwin Luck, Mark Marquandt, Joseph Meighan, and Arthur Robinson.

Index